NEW PERSPECTIVES ON GLOBALIZATION
AND ANTIGLOBALIZATION

The International Political Economy of New Regionalisms Series

The International Political Economy of New Regionalisms series presents innovative analyses of a range of novel regional relations and institutions. Going beyond established, formal, interstate economic organizations, this essential series provides informed interdisciplinary and international research and debate about myriad heterogeneous intermediate level interactions.

Reflective of its cosmopolitan and creative orientation, this series is developed by an international editorial team of established and emerging scholars in both the South and North. It reinforces ongoing networks of analysts in both academia and think-tanks as well as international agencies concerned with micro-, meso- and macro-level regionalisms.

New Perspectives on Globalization and Antiglobalization
Prospects for a New World Order?

Edited by

HENRY VELTMEYER
St. Mary's University, Canada
and
Universidad Autónoma de Zacatecas, Mexico

Routledge
Taylor & Francis Group

LONDON AND NEW YORK

First published 2008 by Ashgate Publishing

2 Park Square, Milton Park, Abingdon, Oxon OX14 4RN
711 Third Avenue, New York, NY 10017, USA

Routledge is an imprint of the Taylor & Francis Group, an informa business

First issued in paperback 2016

British Library Cataloguing in Publication Data
New perspectives on globalization and antiglobalization :
    prospects for a new world order? - (The international
    political economy of new regionalisms series)
    1. Globalization 2. Anti-globalization movement
    I. Veltmeyer, Henry
    303.4'82

Library of Congress Cataloging in Publication Data
Veltmeyer, Henry.
    New perspectives on globalization and antiglobalization : prospects for a new world
order? / by Henry Veltmeyer.
        p. cm. -- (The international political economy of new regionalisms
series)
    Includes bibliographical references and index.
    ISBN 978-0-7546-7411-5
    1. Globalization. 2. Anti-globalization movement. I. Title.

    JZ1318.V45 2008
    303.48'2--dc22

                                                                    2008003564

ISBN 13: 978-0-7546-7411-5 (hbk)
ISBN 13: 978-1-138-26770-1 (pbk)

Contents

PART 3   THE MACRODYNAMICS OF ANTIGLOBALIZATION

List of Contributors

Walden Bello, Professor of Sociology and Public Administration at the University of the Philippines, and founder of the Bangkok-based Global South is a distinguished scholar and activist; winner of the Right Livelihood Award (also known as the Alternative Nobel Prize), cited for "playing a crucial role in developing the theoretical and practical bases for a world order that benefits all people." He has published extensively on the dynamics of both globalization and antiglobalization. Examples include *Development Debacle, Dragons in Distress, Global Finance, Deglobalisation.*

Paul Bowles is Professor of Development Economics at the University of Northern British Colombia. He has published widely on the political economy of reform in China and on various aspects of globalization. He also coedited *Globalization: Regional and National Perspectives* (2007).

Noam Chomsky is Professor of Linguistics at the Massachesetts Institute of Technology (MIT) and author of innumerable studies and publications in diverse fields with momentous theoretical and political significance, including *9/11* (2001) and *Hegemony or Survival: America's Quest for Global Dominance* (2003). He is widely regarded as one of the most distinguished and important intellectuals of the twentieth century.

Gian Carlo Delgado-Ramos is a Mexican political economist of global and Latin American development and author of the celebrated *La Amenaza Biológica.*

Terry Gibbs is Assistant Professor of Political Science and Director of the Centre for International Studies at Cape Breton University. She specializes in issues related to democracy and globalization and her work has been published in various journals.

Norman Girvan is Professorial Fellow at the Institute of International Relations at the University of the West Indies in Trinidad. He was formerly Director of the UN Centre for Transnational Corporations (UNCTC), Chief Technical Director of the National Planning Agency of the Government of Jamaica and Secretary-General of the Association of Caribbean States (2001–2004). He is widely published in the area of globalization and development, particularly in the Caribbean context.

James Petras is Professor Emeritus in Sociology at Binghamton University in New York and Adjunct Professor in International Development Studies at Saint Mary's University (Halifax, Canada). He is the author of over 60 books and numerous other writings on the dynamics of world and Latin American developments, including *Globalization Unmasked: Imperialism in the 21st Century* (2001) and *Empire with Imperialism* (2005). A file of his writings is maintained and can be accessed at Rebelión.com.

John Saxe-Fernández is Professor of Political Studies at the Universidad Nacional Autónoma de México (UNAM). He coordinates "El Mundo Actual", a research program of the Interdisciplinary Research Centre (CEIICH) of the university and is author of numerous studies on the political economy of Mexico, Latin America, and international relations, including *La Compra-Venta de Mexico* (2002).

Teivo Teivainen is Professor of World Politics at the University of Helsinki and Director of the Program on Democracy and Global Transformation at the San Marcos University in Lima, Peru. In 2005–06 he chaired Network Institute for Global Democratization (www.nigd.org) and on behalf of NIGD he is a founding member of the International Council of the World Social Forum. Recent publications include *Enter Economism, Exit Politics: Experts, Economic Policy and the Damage to Democracy* (2002); *A Possible World: Democratic Transformation of Global Institutions* (2004).

Lisa Thompson is Professor in the School of Government and Director of the Centre for Southern African Studies at the University of the Western Cape. She conducts research and has published findings on the linkages between grassroots development and poverty alleviation, the state and the global political economy. She also contributed to Paul Bowles and Henry Veltmeyer's coedited volume on *Globalization: Regional Perspectives* (2007).

Henry Veltmeyer is Professor of Development Studies and Sociology at Saint Mary's University (Halifax, Canada) and the Universidad Autónoma de Zacatecas (UAZ) in Mexico. He is author of, among others, *Illusion or Opportunity: Civil Society and the Quest for Social Change* (2007) and, with James Petras, *Globalization Unmasked: Imperialism in the 21st Century* (2001); *System in Crisis* (2003); *Social Movements and the State: Argentina, Bolivia, Brazil, Ecuador* (2005) and *Empire with Imperialism* (2005).

Acknowledgements

The editor and authors gratefully acknowledge the financial aid provided by the International Development Research Centre (IDRC) of Canada and the Social Science Humanities and Research Council (SSHRC) of Canada. This support allowed a number of the contributors to this volume to complete their research as well as come together at several workshops and international conferences to discuss their findings and ideas.

The editor also acknowledges the encouragement and support given to this project by his life partner, Annette Wright.

List of Abbreviations and Acronyms

AGM	Anti-Globalization Movement
APEC	Asia-Pacific Economic Cooperation
CFR	Council on Foreign Relations
CMEA	Council for Mutual Economic Assistance
CONAIE	Confederation of Indigenous Nations of Ecuador
DRC	Democratic Republic of Congo
ECCB	Eastern Caribbean Central Bank
ECLAC	Economic Commission for Latin American and the Caribbean
EZLN	Ejército Zapatista de Liberación Nacional
FDI	Foreign Direct Investment
FTAA	Free Trade Area of the Americas
GEF	Global Environmental Facility
IFI	International Financial Institution
ILO	International Labour Organization
IMF	International Monetary Fund
IVSS	Venezuelan Institute for Social Security
LAFTA	Latin American Free Trade Agreement
LDCs	Least Developed Countries
MAI	Multilateral Agreement on Investment
MNCs	Multinational Corporations
MST	Rural Landless Workers Movement (*Movimento dos Trabalhadores Rurais Sem Terra*)
MVR	Fifth Republic Movement (*Movimiento Quinta República*)
NAFTA	North American Free Trade Agreement
NEPAD	New Economic Parrtnership for Africa's Development
NGOs	Nongovernmental Organizations
ODA	Overseas Development Assistance
PT	Workers' Party (*Partido dos Trabalhadores*)
REPAs	Regional Economic Partnership Arrangements
SADC	Southern Africa Development Community
SAP	Structural Adjustment Program
SICA	Central American Integration System (*Sistema de Integración Centroamericana*)
SIDC	Small Island Developing States
TC	Trilateral Commission
TNCs	Transnational Corporations
TRIPS	Trade Related Intellectual Property Rights
UNDP	United Nations Development Programme

WBG   World Bank Group
WEF   World Economic Forum
WSF   World Social Forum
WTO   World Trade Organization

Introduction

The book examines the macrodynamics of globalization and antiglobalization in the world economy. The context of this examination is provided by an epoch-defining shift in social and economic organization associated with what has become known as "globalization"—the process of integrating societies across the world, and their economies and cultures, into one system. There are serious questions as to whether the term "globalization" describes at all the major dynamics of change and development in the world. In fact, James Petras in this volume argues that the term "imperialism" provides a better shorthand description of what is going on in the world and thus a better explanation of its major dynamics. The contributors to this book generally agree with this judgement and are disposed to accept "imperialism" as a more useful framework for their analysis, a framework that is outlined in Chapter 2.

Nevertheless, there are practical reasons for continuing to make use of "globalization" and "antiglobalization" as shorthand references to the complex dynamics of world developments. For one thing, these terms dominate the theoretical discourse in the field. For another, both terms do make reference to, and allow for a description of, several important dimensions of analysis both in regard to structural change and the forces of resistance against this change—against the forces that drive the system forward. In these terms, globalization has the appearance of a process that is irresistible, inevitable and inescapable—all countries and people having to adjust to it the best way they can, to insert themselves into the process under the most favorable conditions or to make the best deal possible.

This book explores some macrodynamics of this process as well as some strategic and political responses to these dynamics. Appearances and arguments to the contrary, globalization is neither inevitable nor immutable. Diverse groups of people in an increasingly organized, albeit divided and fragmented, global civil society are coming together to mobilize the forces of resistance into an antiglobalization movement. This book deals with the political dynamics of this movement as they are played out on the world stage, particularly in Latin America, the Caribbean and Asia.

Alternative Understandings: Development, Globalization and Imperialism?

In the post World War II period it is possible to identify diverse permutations of three alternative ways of understanding the fundamental dynamics of change in the world—*development, globalization and imperialism*. Each of these terms can be constructed as a descriptive or analytical category, a tool for decoding what is happening in the world and providing a theoretical discourse for explaining it. In each case, a reference is made to a geopolitical or geoeconomic "project" that is pursued as a means of advancing the interests of a particular social class or organized grouping of people—interests with which the agent of the project tends to identify. In these terms we can speak of these projects as *ideologies*—ideas used to mobilize action in a direction desired by the agent group. However, more often than not, these "projects" (development, globalization, imperialism) have the appearance not of ideology but of a process driven forth by forces generated by the structure of the system. It is in these terms that social scientists of various disciplinary orientations enter the fray, providing alternative theoretical representations of the world—models for understanding the world and advancing change.

The "development" project

According to Wolfgang Sachs and his associates in the theory of postdevelopment (Esteva and Prakash 1998), the idea of "development" was invented in the period immediately after World War II as a means of directing the future of those societies involved in the process of liberating themselves from the yoke of European colonialism. The aim, not to put too fine appoint on it, was to prevent these societies from falling prey to the lure of communism. To this end, the capitalist powers at the time, at a summit meeting held at Bretton Woods, designed a world economic order that would promote the free movement of capital and tradable goods in a global economy; and, to facilitate participation in this system, they instituted a program of international cooperation—"foreign aid"—providing thereby both development finance and technical assistance.

Over the next five decades the development process was advanced on the basis of diverse models designed to bring about the modernization and development of societies in the capitalist world. Generally speaking, in these models the major agency for this development was the private sector, which is to say, the capitalist corporations that dominated the world economy. However, in the Third World—the "developing" countries to the south of a major (and growing) global divide in income and wealth—because of the relative weakness or absence of a capitalist class able to exercise this role, the state (or rather, the government) was assigned the role of development agent. This role was facilitated with a policy regime of nationalization (of the means of social production), protection for domestic enterprises unable to withstand the competitive pressures of the world economy, access to public credit and subsidies, regulation of private economic activity and the international movement of capital, and the promotion of domestic industry via a policy of import substitution.

This model was functional in both theory and practice for close to three decades—from the late 1940s to the early 1970s—until the world capitalist system underwent the conditions of a major crisis that exposed cracks that went to its very foundation. In the context of this crisis there emerged pressures, from the Left, for revolutionary change (directed by an alternative socialist project), and, from the Right, to abandon the development enterprise in favor of another—globalization. Reeling from these political blows on the Left and the Right, the theoreticians and practitioners of international development went in a different direction—liberal reform of the system—and they launched the search for an alternative form of capitalist development—another paradigm—initiated not from above and the outside but from below and the inside—development that is participatory, more socially inclusive and equitable, and sustainable in terms of both the environment and livelihoods. By 1990 this search for "another development" had grown into a worldwide movement that was advanced with the participation of a myriad nongovernmental organizations in partnership with those governments and international organizations that stayed with the development project.

The "globalization" project

The idea of "development" was predicated on identifiable improvements in the socioeconomic conditions in which the larger part of the world's population lived and the corresponding changes in the structure of institutionalized practices needed to bring about these improvements. However, the threat of a major economic crisis in the process of capital accumulation gave rise to an alternative project to activate the accumulation and economic growth process. The project was designed to facilitate the renovation of the Bretton Woods world economic order on the basis of a program of structural adjustments in the macroeconomic policies pursued by the governments in the world capitalist system.

The "new economic model" (neoliberal capitalist development) was designed to create a global economy in which both the major factors of production—capital, technology (not labor)—and the social product were liberated from the constraints and regulatory apparatus of the state, creating, in the process, an economy of free trade and the free movement of capital. The free market, rather than the state, was conceived of as the motor of this globalization process, and the private sector as its driving force.

Under the aegis of the new economic model government after government was encouraged or induced to adopt a program of macroeconomic policies designed to arrest and reverse the development process under way. In this program the policy of nationalizing the strategic industries and setting up strategic state enterprises was replaced with a policy of privatization—turning over or selling state enterprises to the private sector in the local or global economy. The state in this process was downsized in favor of an expanded private sector and a retreating state was replaced with a strengthened "civil society." The regulation of private enterprise and economic activity was replaced with a policy of deregulation and the movement of both investment capital and trade was liberalized, undoing the protectionist measures adopted under the old economic model. The end product of this process, in theory, was the reactivation of the global accumulation process and conditions of economic growth. Those countries able to participate in the process—to integrate into the global economy, to participate in the process of productive transformation and technological conversion—would share in the anticipated prosperity.

The economic globalization project also has a political dimension. At the structural level, the process entails a weakening of the nation-state—at least in what we might term the "periphery" of the global economy and areas outside the imperial state system—and a search for new forms of governance (and political control of the forces of resistance unleashed in the globalization process).

At a more general level, globalization in its neoliberal form is predicated on an arranged marriage (of strategic import regarding a coincidence of economic and political interests) between "capitalism" (the free market) and "democracy" (free elections) in the search for a "new world order" in which the "forces of freedom" (to use George W. Bush's terminology) are released from the constraints of the welfare-developmental-regulatory state.

"Democracy" in this context has a double meaning, with reference to both the institution of the "rule of law" (and the machinery of liberal democratic politics) and the strengthening of civil society vis-à-vis the state. What it means is that the architects of the new world order need and are concerned to strike a new balance between the market and the "public interest," the former understood not in isolation from but embedded in the institutions of civil society, and the latter (the sphere of public interests) understood not just in terms of the state but as the "meeting point of collective interests"—"collective action in pursuit of the common interest" (Ocampo, Jomo and Khan 2007: 11).

In effect, the policy of democratizing the relation between the state and civil society is designed as a means of privatizing the responsibility for political development. That is, "civil society" is called upon (see Chapter 3 for a discussion of the dynamics involved) to share with the international organizations the responsibility for maintaining or restoring political order, and to do so by means of "good governance."[1] To this end, a host of civil or nongovernmental organizations that define "civil society" (the space between the family and the state) were enlisted as strategic partners of the World Bank and other international organizations that took on the task of securing "good governance"—political order under conditions (instability, even ungovernability) generated by several rounds of "structural" reforms in macroeconomic national policy.

The nature of the problem is well understood and outlined, if not dissected, in a recent report published by the UK Ministry of Defence: *Global Strategic Trends 2007–2036* (2007). The report warns that the whole system might be brought down by the combined forces of opposition and resistance to the excessive inequalities (the widening global wealth/income divide) that characterize the global economy. These "excessive inequalities" (or the "global divide"), the report adds, could well lead to a "resurgence of not only anti-capitalist ideologies ... [and] also to populism and the revival of Marxism" (UK Ministry of Defence 2007: 3). More specifically, the report notes its concern that the widening divide will spawn a mass global justice movement, a broad antiglobalization movement, that will unite the most diverse forces of resistance and opposition to neoliberal globalization, threatening thereby

---

1   The need for "good" or "democratic" governance in the development process was theorized, or at least prescribed, by economists at the World Bank and the UNDP. As to what "good governance" entailed in practice, however, this was never clear in two decades of studies and reports. However, the World Bank Institute in a recent systematic effort to measure "good governance" on a global scale, and in comparative form (Kaufman and Kray 2007), has remedied this problem. "Good governance" in this study is measured as an index of six aggregate indicators: accountability/transparency; the absence of major violence (or terror); effective government; the "quality" of regulation; the rule of law; and control of corruption.

the entire project (and, one could add, scuttle the best-laid plans of the new world order architects for imperial rule).

The political dynamics involved in this process are explored in some detail by various authors below, particularly in Chapters 3, 7 and 10. At the root of these dynamics is a widespread and growing disaffection with the neoliberal form of globalization among different groups and classes within an emerging global civil society (on this see Chapters 9–12).

A generalization that has stood the test of time (two decades and more of neoliberal globalization) is that globalization has few beneficiaries and many victims. In effect, globalization has resulted in the growth of islands of prosperity within a growing sea of pauperization and immizeration—the sprouting of super-rich billionaires at one social pole and the ravages of poverty on the other. Under these conditions, the globalization process has given rise to an antiglobalization movement of growing proportions. This movement has been organized to mobilize the forces of resistance—forces based on a growing disenchantment with the negative social, economic impacts of globalization. Chapters 8–10 explore the political dynamics of these forces.

Neoimperialism in Theory and Practice

Globalization, as the authors of this volume see it, is a project designed to serve the economic interests of what has been termed the "transnational capitalist class" (Sklair 1997) and that we can construe as a global ruling class. The precondition for this process, for advancing these interests, is a structural adjustment of the economy— structural reforms in the macroeconomic policies pursued by governments in the so-called Third World. These reforms, as it turns out, are designed to open up these economies to the forces of the "free market" and the competitive pressures of the global economy.

To the degree that the end result of this process is the domination of these economies by the forces wielded by the global ruling class some radical political economists have written of "neoimperialism." The "old imperialism" in this context had two centers of reference—one economic, the other military and political. One was a system of international exchange or "trade" based on the exchange of raw materials and commodities, produced on the margins or periphery of the world capitalist system, for goods manufactured in the center of this system. The other is a system of direct political domination based on military occupation and direct control of the state apparatus in the dominated societies by political and military forces of the imperial state. This form of imperialism has had a long and inglorious history but after World War II it was substantially replaced by imperialism in economic form—the domination of the subjugated economies in the Third World by the agents of economic power such as the multinational corporations (MNCs), the International Monetary Fund (IMF) and other "international financial institutions" (IFIs).

With this "development" a number of analysts have turned away from a theoretical discourse on imperialism and started to write of the emergence of a "post-imperialist" period or even of an empire without imperialism (essentially the view of Hardt and Negri 2000). However, in the same context, other analysts have drawn attention to a growing trend towards the resurgence of a new form of what once was the "old imperialism"—the projection of military force and political power by the imperial state. Chapter 2 elaborates on various dynamics of this projection of power with reference to what could well be termed "the new imperialism." Chapter 3 explores another dimension of imperial power, via the agency not of military power and war but of "development," the soft glove over the hard fist of US imperialism. This project, as noted, has both an economic and a political face. The chapter exposes the latter.

The Dynamics of Globalization and Antiglobalization

Chapter 1 provides an introduction to the theoretical *discourse* on "globalization"—alternative ways of theorizing about and analysing the dynamics of globalization. *Paul Bowles* in this chapter provides a taxonomy of the literature in terms of four basic theoretical approaches. This taxonomy is a useful tool for making sense of the voluminous and growing scholarly literature and associated discourse.

The next chapter elaborates on one of the theoretical perspectives identified by Bowles. From this perspective, the doctrine of "globalization" essentially emerges as an ideology that serves not as a useful description of the actual dynamics of change and transformation but as a means of advancing the agenda and interests of what John Pilger (2003), the Australian broadcaster, filmmaker and critic, terms "the new rulers of the world." From these optics, and the formation of a global ruling class, the chapter brings into focus several critical issues.

One of these has to do with the claim that "globalization" is a new phenomenon; another is that the state has become an anachronism; and a third that the technological revolution is the main impetus behind globalization. *James Petras*, in this connection, argues that the concept of globalization obscures more than it reveals; that the macrodynamics of the world economy can best be understood through an analysis of the active role of the imperial state and the opening up of overseas opportunities via the projection of power, economic, political, and military; and that developments associated with the new information technology are subordinate to more important developments. These developments, he argues, are better understood by reference and use of a concept (imperialism) that until recently had been largely abandoned by social scientists, viewed as it was as an ideology rather than as a scientific theory. In any case, Petras observes, world developments over the past decade have led to a resurrection of the theory of imperialism as a way of explaining the dynamics of world events and developments. Indeed it provides the best, if not only, such explanation.

Chapter 3 deconstructs the academic and official discourse that surrounded the initial call for a new world order and subsequent efforts to "sell" the idea of "globalization" as both an irresistible force and the only way for a country to progress. The main argument of this chapter is that the nongovernmental organizations formed in what was once termed the "third sector" (not motivated by profit-making) have been used by the agents of the new world order to advance the strategic interests of corporate capital and the global ruling class. The argument is that the official and academic discourse on "globalization," "civil society," "democratic governance," and "development" serves to mask the actual workings of what might better be described as a global class war—more a war on the poor than on poverty.

Part Two of the book is organized as a series of case studies into the macrodynamics of globalization in its neoliberal form. The opening Chapter 4 by *Saxe-Fernández* and *Delgado-Ramos* brings a historical perspective to the structural adjustment program, which, it is argued, is designed to facilitate the globalization process. The authors examine in some detail the regional dynamics of this process in the case of Mexico, once a favored "model" of how to implement the structural adjustment program. Focusing on Mexico's oil industry, Saxe-Fernández and Delgado-Ramos analyze the workings of the World Bank both in regard to shaping economic policy in Mexico—constituting, in effect, a species of co-government—and the pillaging of the country's productive resources, particularly in the strategically important oil industry.

Chapter 5 turns to South East Asia, the major region of economic growth and transformative change on the world stage of capitalist development and globalization today. *Walden Bello* in this chapter explores and dissects the conjuncture of capitalist development in the region associated with the emergence of financial crisis and an upheaval, which raised serious questions about the presumed beneficence of the globalizing dynamics of corporate capital. In the context of a generalized crisis in the process of capital accumulation Bello identifies the beginnings of a retreat from neoliberal globalization. Governments in the region share a disposition to put the genie of neoliberal globalization (freewheeling and footloose capital, liberated from regulatory control) back into the bottle of regulated control, albeit not by a system of sovereign nation-states but a new system of global governance.

The chapter reviews some of the dynamics of the resulting process in the region. It argues that the key crisis that has overtaken the global economy is the classical capitalist crisis of over-accumulation. Reaganism, Thatcherism and the economics and politics of structural adjustment in the 1980s, followed by globalization in the 1990s, concerned diverse efforts to overcome this crisis. Globalization in this context emerged as the "grand strategy" pursued by the US administration with the aim of creating a new world order in which the forces of freedom could flourish, a multilateral system of global governance based on the pillars of the World Trade Organization, the International Monetary Fund and the World Bank. However, the fallout of the inevitable and widespread crises led to the retreat of the US, under the administration of George W. Bush, from the globalist project and to revert to a more nationalist strategy based on a unilateral projection of state power and more traditional methods of economic exploitation in the South.

In Chapter 6, *Norman Girvan* explores the dynamics of globalization in the Caribbean—a "backyard" of the US empire. As Girvan sees it, globalization is essentially an ideology masquerading as theory, designed to convince governments and people in the region that there is no other way to progress and that everyone benefits from it. The chapter, first of all, examines in some detail the actual dynamics of policy reform and transformative change associated with diverse efforts to advance globalization in the region—to put the globalization project into practice. The chapter concludes with an analysis of various strategic responses that governments in the Caribbean could and should make to these globalization dynamics. In this connection, Girvan argues that governments in the region in fact have a degree of maneuver; that the world financial crisis discussed by Bello in the previous chapter provides the region a "window of opportunity;" and that governments are in a position to make a strategic planned response to the globalization process, to improve or maximize some elusive benefits that might be derived from globalization in the region.

Girvan basically seeks and argues the need to come to terms with globalization, to accommodate its various forces in the collective interest of people and governments in the region. That is, Girvan assumes that the best or only strategic response is not to counter or oppose globalization but to intervene in such a way as to allow for some shared benefits, i.e. to accept globalization but not in its neoliberal form, which is undoubtedly not in the interest of the South. However, others argue that globalization in any form of capitalist development cannot deliver its presumed benefits; that the problem is not globalization as such but globalizing capitalism, which necessarily works in the interests of the rich and powerful countries and which cannot be harnessed by people and governments in the South. That is, the best strategic response is antiglobalization, anticapitalism, anti-imperialism.

The dynamics of antiglobalization are generally associated not with governments or the strategic responses of nation-states but with social movements—with what has been termed "the antiglobalization movement (see Part Three). Nevertheless, a number of governments or nation-state regimes have attempted, or are attempting, to resist the pressures to globalize—to integrate into the new world order of capitalism and democracy. One such regime is led by Hugo Chávez, who is seeking to navigate the ship of the Venezuelan state towards socialism in the turbulent waters of neoliberal globalization. *Terry Gibbs* in Chapter 7 explores what this means, with particular reference to for liberal (or neoliberal) "democracy," one of the two pillars and gateposts of the new world order.

In the context of struggling neoliberal "democracies," many analysts today—even the guardians of the new world order (see Chapter 3)—have discovered a concern for poverty alleviation and the reduction of social inequality through a carefully managed redistribution of wealth, access to society's productive resources, and income. The reason for this concern is that globalization in its neoliberal form is recognized to be economically (and environmentally) dysfunctional, socially exclusive and politically unsustainable. Indeed it is recognized that the deep and extensive social inequalities spawned by the process of neoliberal globalization threaten the viability of the global economy and the very survival of the world capitalist system. However, in the efforts of policy-makers and analysts to manage national development and globalization they generally fail to question the overall logic of macroeconomic market-based reforms. Thus, these "post-neoliberal" policies should not be seen as a paradigmatic shift but as an attempt to rescue the system from itself—to make some improvements, belated and minimal as they might be, and bring about those changes that will allow the capitalist system to survive.

Most nation-states at the level of government are engaged in this process: to adapt their national policies to the neoliberal requirements of the capitalist world order while, at the same time, demanding an adjustment in the institutional framework ("architecture") of the system. But not all heads of states and government regimes are taking this route. Cuba, for one, thus far has managed to retain the institutionality of a socialist state within a raging capitalist sea. And the government of Venezuela, headed by Hugo Chávez, surprisingly enough considering the obstacles and pressures of globalization, has turned the economy, if not the state, in a socialist direction. In fact, the Bolivarian Revolution underway in Venezuela represents an all-out assault on neoliberal doctrine and practice. In theory, neoliberalism is a marriage of convenience, if not principle, between capitalism and democracy; and, to secure this marriage, it entails a commitment to the forces of economic and political freedom. However, in practice neoliberal regimes are dominated by the capitalist class and, more often than not, take an authoritarian form—elite rule and control of the economy.

A key aspect of the Bolivarian Revolution, according to Gibbs, is the effort to revitalize citizenship through the construction of mechanisms for public participation in decision-making, particularly in regard to the poor majority. In this connection, the dramatic transformations taking place in health and education policy in Venezuela are indicative of what can happen when poor communities are invited to participate in decision-making. For one thing, it means true "democracy" as opposed to the de facto authoritarianism of many neoliberal regimes that are nominally "democratic."

In Chapter 8, *Lisa Thompson* explores the meaning of globalization in the context of Southern Africa, a regional grouping of countries comprised of Angola, Botswana, the Democratic Republic of the Congo (DRC), Lesotho, Madagascar, Malawi, Mauritius, Mozambique, Namibia, South Africa, Swaziland, Tanzania, Zambia, and Zimbabwe. She examines the argument that Africa's continued poverty and degradation ("marginalization") are a direct outcome of globalization, not of a lack of it. The author explores the issue by expanding on and critically confronting diverse understandings about globalization against the evidence of recent developments in Southern Africa.

In Part Three the analytic focus of the book shifts away from the dynamics of national development to the politics of antiglobalization—forces of opposition and resistance mobilized by diverse forms of civil society organizations. The central issue here is "antiglobalization"—to be precise, a new, more humane, form of globalization? There are a number of unresolved theoretical and political issues at play. What is the character and strength of the social forces of opposition and resistance to globalization? What is the social base of the movement involved? In what direction are the available forces of resistance and opposition mobilized? And by what type of organization and with what consequences and outcomes? What is the scope of changes involved—reform of the existing worldwide system (and the associated process of capital accumulation) or social transformation—a radical overhaul of this system? What are the political dynamics of this process?

Noam Chomsky, in Chapter 9, reflects on the political dynamics of power and ideology associated with the globalization project. He examines these dynamics in the context of events that have unfolded over the past year since 9/11, with particular reference to the concentration and projection of power in the United States, both state and private. In these reflections he also discusses the implications of this projected power for both the prospect of a new general world war and the possibilities for opposition and dissent.

Teivo Teivainen, in Chapter 10, explores the expanding boundaries of the "political" in terms of the global antiglobalization movements in relation to he nation-state. As he constructs it, social movements politicize the economic and redefining the boundaries of the political is a "necessary condition for any radical democratic transformation of the world." He expands on this with reference to the political dynamics involved in the, formation of diverse "transnational networks of democratic participation" and the World Social Forum, "perhaps the world's most important space in which social movements and other non-state actors gather."

The concluding chapter by *Henry Veltmeyer* provides a somewhat different perspective on the essentially middle-class-based antiglobalization movement in the North.. For one thing this movement is by no means monolithic. Indeed it is divided at the fundamental level of an envisioned alternative and in terms of the strategy and tactics of struggle. The prospects for unifying the highly diverse social forces of opposition and resistance are not clear but they do not appear to be good. For one thing, the agents of globalization operate in different ways in diverse contexts. The international financial (and Bretton Woods) institutions, such as the World Bank and the World Trade Organization (WTO), may share a strategic interest with both the multinational or transnational corporations that dominate the world economy and the organizations that represent the club of rich and powerful nation-states, but the dynamic effects of their "operations" are different and should not be lumped together. Likewise, the social base of the antiglobalization movement is composed of diverse groups and classes, whose strategic interests intersect on some issues but diverge on others. The antiglobalization movement is also divided as to strategic direction, ultimate goal and the appropriate forms of struggle. In this connection, the actions associated with the urban-centered, middle-class-based antiglobalization protest movement in the North cannot be equated with the struggles of the indigenous communities and peasant producers in the South, nor even with the anti-IMF/structural adjustment/globalization protest movements in the urban centers of Latin America and elsewhere in the South. The large and growing global divide in incomes and productive resources is not easily overcome with the formation of a global antiglobalization movement. Many issues arise and need to be resolved but, first of all, the dynamics of both globalization and antiglobalization need to be more clearly understood. It is to this purpose that this book is written and put together. Although no definitive conclusions are reached, the critical issues involved are brought into analytical focus and theoretical perspective.

In short, the essays that make up the book provides critical reflections on the epoch-defining changes that are sweeping the world today—the dynamics of globalization and antiglobalization. It is hoped that these essays will help dispel the fog of confusion brought in by the sweeping winds of "globalization." What is in a word—globalization? In this book, it is argued, it is both nothing and everything.

PART 1
The Theory and Practice
of Globalization

Chapter 1

Globalization:
A Taxonomy of Theoretical Approaches

Paul Bowles

The term "neoliberal globalization" has become a common one in both academic discourse and in the nongovernmental organizations (NGOs) and social movements which are lumped together as the "antiglobalization" movement. Despite the popularity and frequent use of the term, however, the concept of "neoliberal globalization"—and the relationship between neoliberalism and globalization—is not as straightforward to understand as this frequent use would imply. The reason for this is that the term "globalization" has been interpreted in a variety of ways each of which has its own implications for the relationship to neoliberalism. The purpose of this essay is to provide a taxonomy of approaches to globalization and to draw out what each of these approaches implies about the relationship with neoliberalism. I conclude with a sketch of what this implies for our understanding of the "antiglobalization" movement.

To begin, let us start with a definition of "neoliberalism." This shares with classical liberalism the belief in the efficacy of market mechanisms for the allocation of resources and the reward of factors of production. It is based on the belief that markets are competitive, or can be made competitive by deregulation, and that competitive markets, based on private ownership, produce the most efficient economies and highest levels of welfare. Thus, a menu of neoliberal policies can be readily identified. A strong preference for privatization and deregulation underpins this menu and is applicable to the vast majority of areas of production including the markets for labor, capital, land, and natural resources.

There are, however, some areas of ambiguity. Two of the most important examples of these are the topics of money and regionalism. There is no neoliberal position on money with some writers (such as Hayek) advocating private money issuing banks, others (such as Friedman) preferring national monies but with flexible exchange rates, while others still (such as Mundell) prefer a world currency. Similarly, some neoliberals see regional trading areas as stepping stones to global free trade; others (such as Bhagwati) see them as undesirable distractions from the multilateral cause. There are also disagreements about the sequencing of market liberalization; with respect to capital account liberalization, for example. Thus, neoliberalism should not be seen as a monolithic body of thought and there areas of considerable dispute between its followers. Nevertheless, there is still an identifiable core set of policies, based on privatization and deregulation, which gives this school of thought its coherence.

As noted, neoliberalism shares this coherence with classical liberalism. The prefix "neo" often serves little purpose other than denote the new time period, since about 1980, that liberal ideas have returned to the ascendancy. "Neo" therefore indicates that we are talking about the late twentieth and early twenty-first centuries rather than the mid-nineteenth century. There is one other reason for using "neo" which I think is worth discussing. This relates to governance. Put simply, classical liberal thought is typically associated with democracy as a system of governance. This, despite the fact that there was very little democracy about in the mid-nineteenth century and this was the era of antidemocratic colonialism. Neoliberalism, in contrast, has no such *necessary* association with liberal democracy. Neoliberalism is *primarily* an economic concept dedicated to "free markets" but this can be, and has been, implemented in a variety of polities, from representative democracy to authoritarian. The governance structures of neoliberalism are, therefore, "underdetermined."[1]

While there are some complications, therefore, the core body of neoliberalism can be readily identified. The task of understanding globalization is not so easy. Globalization, according to Tony McGrew, "is in many respects an idea in search of a theory." He continues that "despite the fact that, in a little over a decade, it has colonised the intellectual imagination of the social sciences, it remains for the most part largely under- (if not un-)theorised" (2001: 293).

McGrew has a point: there is no agreed theory of globalization. My purpose here is not to provide one. Rather it is provide a taxonomy of the various approaches that have been taken to analyzing what globalization might be. There are already a number of taxonomies—ways of classifying and summarizing a vast literature—available. Held *et al.* (1999: 10), for example, distinguish between hyperglobalists, skeptics, and transformationalists as a device for distinguishing between theories analyzing the politics, economics, and culture of globalization. Hobson and Ramesh (2002: 5) write that "much, although certainly not all, of the literature on globalization is cast in terms of two main propositions: either a strong globalization/decline of the state or weak globalization/strong state thesis."

---

1 In defining "neoliberalism" in this way, I differ from authors such as Harvey (2004: 1) who argues that "neoliberalism is in the first instance a theory of political economic practices that proposes that human well-being can best be advanced by the maximization of entrepreneurial freedoms within an institutional framework characterized by private property rights, individual liberty, free markets and free trade. The role of the state is to create and preserve an institutional framework appropriate to such practices. The state has to be concerned, for example, with the quality and integrity of money." As discussed above, I do not think that neoliberals' "concern" for the "integrity of money" necessarily implies state ownership of money, and nor does "individual liberty" necessarily extend to the political sphere although it certainly does to the market sphere. Neoliberals assert that individual liberty in the market sphere is likely to lead to political democracy but I do not regard the latter as necessary to the definition of neoliberalism as a concept. Of course, Harvey does not suggest that the neoliberal conditions which he provides above are typically realized and argues that "the principles of neoliberalism are quickly abandoned whenever they conflict with this class project [of restoring capitalist class power]" (2004: 8).

In this chaper, I propose a four-fold taxonomy extending the propositions relating to state and market suggested by Hobson and Ramesh.[2] The four main interpretations of globalization identified here are:

1. Globalizatio:1 as a primarily technologically driven process which strengthens markets and market actors while weakening and requiring adaptation by nation-states.

2. Globalization as a "myth" that has not significantly weakened the national basis of economic activity and the dominance of nation states. The popularity of "globalization" has more to do with its neoliberal ideological agenda than as an objective description of contemporary capitalism.

3. Globalization as imperialism. Some states are weakened by globalization while other states and their market actors (corporations) are strengthened. The process of globalization is a strategy designed to enhance to interests of imperial powers by opening up the markets of weaker countries.

4. Globalizatior is inadequate as a descriptor of the processes under way in which contemporary period and is better described as regionalization and/or regionalism. Nation-states may be weakened but emerging production and governance structures are regional in nature (at both the macro and micro-regional levels) rather than global.

In the sections which follow, I will outline each of these interpretations of globalization and explore what they imply about the relationship between globalization and neoliberalism.

The "Globalization Weakens the Nation-State" View

This is probably the most well known of the four views and finds support across the political spectrum. According to this view, the beginning of the twenty-first century is marked by an inexorable and inevitable process of globalization driven by technological change. The basis of this is the information, computing and telecommunications (ICT) revolution which allows the possession, processing, and transmission of huge quantities of information at very low cost and at very high speed. In general, this view therefore sees globalization as a technologically

---

2 Taking this approach (deliberately) simplifies my task in discussing the meanings of globalization to works which fall under the general heading of "political economy." Of course, there are other meanings of globalization which fall outside of this general category but they lie beyond the scope of this paper. Even with this simplification, providing a taxonomy is a problematic exercise for the globalization literature. It is a literature which changes quickly and the dividing lines between categories are often blurred. Authors do not always fit neatly into one box either in single works or in works over time. Despite these limitations, taxonomies can be useful in provid:ng greater clarity in contentious debates.

driven process where the current period is characterized by the scope and intensity of technological change, a factor which differentiates the contemporary era both from the period immediately prior to it and from other episodes of "globalization" that have occurred in the past.

Technology is identified as a critical (although not necessarily the only) causal factor. For example, the World Bank (2002: 325) answers its rhetorical question "What is globalization?" as follows: "In broad terms it reflects the growing links between people, communities, and economies around the world. These links are complex—the result of lower communications and transport costs and greater flows of ideas and capital between high- and low-income countries."

On the basis of this definition, the bank then continues by distinguishing between three waves of globalization each of which is defined in technological terms.

> The first wave of global integration, between 1870 and 1914, was led by improvements in transport technology (from sailing ships to steamships) and by lower tariff barriers. Exports nearly doubled to about 8 percent of world trade. The second wave from 1945 to 1980, was also characterized by lower trade barriers and transport costs. Sea freight charges fell by a third between 1950 and 1970. And trade regained the ground it lost during the Great Depression. Spurring the third wave of integration has been further progress in transport (containerization and airfreight) and communications technology (falling telecommunications costs associated with satellites, fiber-optic cable, cell phones, and the Internet). And along with declining tariffs on manufactured goods in high-income countries, many developing countries lowered barriers to foreign investment and improved their investment climates (World Bank 2004b: 326).

Globalization in this, and other periods, is therefore seen as being driven by scientific advance coupled with policy responses which lower barriers to economic flows. As just one example of the lower of costs as a result of the ICT revolution, the UNDP (1999: 28) provides the following example: in 1960, the average cost of processing information was US $75 per million operations; in 1990 it was less than one hundredth of a cent.

The Global Policy Forum (GFP), an NGO with consultative status at the UN, also appeals to the technological basis of globalization:

> Human societies across the globe have established progressively closer contacts over many centuries, but recently the pace has dramatically increased. Jet airplanes, cheap telephone service, email, computers, huge oceangoing vessels, instant capital flows, all these have made the world more interdependent than ever. Multinational corporations manufacture products in many countries and sell to consumers around the world. Money, technology and raw materials move ever more swiftly across national borders (www. globalpolicy.org, accessed 2 November, 2004).

The GFP collates various measures of this global "connectivity" arising from technological and other trends. For example, the percentage of the world's population that is internet users has risen from 0.73 percent in 1996 to 9.57 percent in 2002. The radio took 38 years from invention to gain 50 million users, the worldwide web took only four years.[3]

Other analyses posit a key role to technology although also rely on other inter-related and codependent causal factors to explain the onset of globalization. Scholte (2000: 99), for example, argues that "globalization patently could not have occurred in the absence of extensive innovations in respect of transport, communications and data processing" although he adds rationalism, capitalism, and political regulation as other causes.[4]

The argument is that these technological changes are leading to (or have led to) a global economy as evidenced by the trends in production, trade and finance. With respect to production, it is argued that there has been a dramatic change in the way in which businesses operate and that they have "gone global." The period prior to 1980 looked more like the linking of national economies whereas now we see genuine global production and markets.

Scholte (2000) uses the term "supraterritorial" to describe the way in which firms have had their relationship with territorial space changed by globalization. He argues (2000: 125) that, "thousands of firms have in the context of globalization given their organization a substantial supraterritorial dimension, either by establishing affiliates in two or more countries or by forging strategic alliances with enterprises based in other countries." Some of these global company networks are huge. For example, as of the mid-1990s the Unilever corporation encompassed more than 500 subsidiaries in over 90 countries. Global companies have acquired a very prominent place in contemporary capitalism. For example, "the collective annual sales of the 50 largest unitary global enterprises rose from $540 billion in 1975 to $2,100 billion in 1990, equivalent to around 10 percent of recorded world product." For this reason Scholte prefers the term "transborder companies" to *multinational* corporation (MNC). The annual sales of some of these companies surpass the gross national products of even medium-sized national economies.[5]

An integrating world economy can be seen from the data that between 1990 and 2002, the percentage of trade in goods to world GDP increased from 32.5 percent to 40.3 percent, gross private capital flows increased from 10.1 percent of world GDP to 20.8 percent, and gross direct foreign investment from 2.7 percent to 6.0 percent of world GDP (see World Bank, 2004b: 308). The turnover in foreign exchange markets is now well in excess of US $1 trillion a day, over 40 times the daily volume of world trade.

---

3   The importance of technological factors also finds expression in the A.T. Kearney/ Foreign Policy Globalization Index which tracks and assesses changes in four key components of global integration and incorporates such measures as trade and financial flows, the movement of people across borders, international telephone traffic, internet usage, and participation in international treaties and peacekeeping operations. See the Foreign Policy website, www. foreignpolicy.com.

4   Still other analyses, such as Rycroft (2002), stress the importance of technological change but argue that technology has "coevolved" with globalization rather than positing a direct causal relationship.

5   For example, on the basis of this type of comparison, General Motors is larger than Thailand and Norway; Ford is larger than Poland; Toyota, Wal-Mart, and Exxon are all larger than Malaysia, Venezuela, and the Philippines. See UNDP (1999: 32).

All of this has led to what Kenichi Ohmae (1990) calls in a provocative but brilliantly encapsulating phrase "the borderless world." It should be noted, however, that while this view of the world can readily be found in business-oriented publications, in the documents of the Bretton Woods institutions as well as in the NGO movement, it can also be found in the work of those who adopt a Marxist approach. For example, Teeple (2000) argues that the 1970s witnessed the start of a "revolution in the means of production" with this revolution being "grounded in the development of computers" (2000: 13). Furthermore, "these changes were revolutionary because of the qualitative turn they brought to the pursuit of knowledge, the objectification of science, the transmission of information and the production process" (2000: 13). The result of this revolution was that "national structures of accumulation" were no longer compatible with the new technologically driven global accumulation strategies of firms. As a result, Teeple argues that the role of nation-state has changed and been weakened. As he colorfully puts it, "if the 'first' bourgeois revolutions represented the political consolidation of capitalism by creating the nation state, then this 'second' bourgeois revolution is the globalization of national regimes of accumulation. It represents a shift from the mitigated framework for capital, the Keynesian Welfare State, liberal democracy, and so on, into a more or less unmitigated framework, supranational agencies for capital alone" (2000: 14). These supranational agencies (such as the IMF, World Bank, the World Trade Organization or WTO, and the BIS – Bank of International Settlements) oversee a corporate dominated globalization in which there is a "decline of national political powers" (2000: 17). Indeed, Teeple argues that globalization represents "the end of national history" (2000: 22).

Bryan (1995) provides a novel approach in analyzing capital's "chase across the globe" for profit. He argues (1995: 8), using a Marxist framework, that there is a "contradiction between the internationality of capital accumulation and the nationality of the state." National categories, used in balance of payments calculations for example, are flawed accounting measures: they ascribe a nationality to international capital flows where there is none.

Bryan's (1995: 6) purpose is to "explore the historical logic of the chase [across the globe], and in particular to address the wishful view that nation states can confront the chase, and avert its damning consequences. The analysis is by no means dismissive of the role of nation states, but confronting the consequences of the chase of capital requires a broader politics than can be achieved by the re-direction of national policy."

For Desai (2004), globalization represents "Marx's revenge." Revenge, that is, against twentieth-century attempts to construct state socialism under his name. Desai invokes Marx's belief that capitalism would only come to an end after it had become global and had played fully its historic role of developing the productive forces. Capitalism was playing this role until it was sidetracked by the First World War. For the next seventy years, state socialist and capitalist countries, in their different ways, deglobalized the world as the state took center stage in economic management. However, it is "the underdevelopment of capitalism that allows and supports substantial market intervention. As capitalism develops, it sheds rather than strengthens such restrictions" (Desai 2004: 214).

When capitalism underwent a process of reglobalization in the 1980s, therefore, the state as economic manager was weakened. Capitalism became more like Marx's vision of a "self-organizing organic process" (Desai 2004: 222) with a more limited role for the state. The reglobalized economy has placed severe restrictions on the ability of states to manage their economic affairs. As Desai argues, "the state has to adapt and adjust to forces which it cannot control but must respond to" (2004: 300). And it is applicable to all states: "For the first time in two hundred years, the cradle of capitalism—the metropolis, the core—has as much to fear from the rapidity of change as does the periphery" (2004: 305).

This is a conclusion which finds wide agreement. Scholte (2000: 102) for example argues that globalization has "put even regulators from the most powerful states under great pressure to facilitate the rise of supraterritoriality." For Susan Strange (1995), globalization has marked the "retreat the state" as a result of the "diffusion of power" in the world economy among non-state actors.

The conclusion that a primarily technologically driven globalization has weakened the nation-state is a common proposition. The point is that in all these accounts the integration of markets, the increased mobility of capital, and increases in connectedness have reduced the efficacy of state regulatory regimes. However, while both the contours of globalization and its general implications for a strengthening of "markets" at the expense of states would find much common ground amongst many contributors, there is nevertheless a sharp divide on the desirability of this dynamic and the appropriate policy responses to it.

For the proponents of globalization, the reduced role for the state is a desirable outcome. Or, put in a different way, neoliberalism is the rational policy response to globalization. It is not so much the cause of globalization as the policy response necessary to ensure that globalization achieves its potential. For advocates, the new global economy offers the prospect of rising living standards for all, through increased trade and the international diffusion of technology, and of the consolidation of democratic institutions. An open global economy offers the developing countries, for example, the opportunity to "catch up" with the core countries. The vehicle for this "catch up" is the access to technology embodied in traded goods and from the technology that open borders can bring with the global corporation. The policy implications of this are that national governments should maximize the flow of technology, the basis for the new global economy, into their countries through a package of trade and investment liberalization measures, security of property rights including intellectual property rights, low taxes on profits in order to encourage firms to operate in one particular jurisdiction rather than another, and a ready, disciplined, and low-taxed supply of highly trained workers. Any state able to refashion itself in this way would be well placed in the new global economy.

The implication of this is that it is firms, mobile capital, which have new power as the much sought-after providers of success in the global economy. International agreements, such as free trade agreements, world trade liberalization, and multinational investment agreements are seen as providing the international architecture necessary to encourage the greatest spread of the benefits of global firms. These types of agreements tie the hands of national governments in many ways, ways which are viewed as beneficial by the supporters of globalization because they prevent interventionist politicians from interfering with the course of market progress. Thus, with capital-friendly national governments and capital-friendly international agreements, globalization is seen as delivering greater economic efficiency and higher levels of material well-being to all who participate.

It is important to note that supporters of globalization not only claim that all can prosper by participation in the global economy but that poor countries will benefit more than others; as a result global income inequality can be expected to decline and economic convergence will occur. In the language of economists, this is referred to as "conditional convergence," that is, convergence is conditional on the right—read neoliberal—policies being adopted.

If the conditions are right, a utopia is possible. Consider, for example, the views of prominent Chicago economist Robert Lucas (2000: 160):

> Ideas can be imitated and resources can and do flow to places where they earn the highest returns. Until perhaps 200 years ago, these forces sufficed to maintain a rough equality of incomes across societies (not, of course, within societies) around the world. The industrial revolution overrode these forces for equality for an amazing two centuries: That is why we call it a 'revolution'. But they [the forces of equality] have reasserted themselves in last half of the twentieth century, and I think the restoration of intersociety income equality will be one of the major economic events of the century to come.

Globalization, by facilitating the flow of ideas and resources, leads Lucas to predict that by 2100 all states could be "equally rich and growing."

The same contours of globalization are analyzed very differently by the opponents of globalization. For them, globalization, applied within a neoliberal framework, presents us with a new catastrophe, economically, socially, politically, culturally, and environmentally. The rise of corporate power, and the increasing inability of nation-states to control their activities as corporations become "stateless," presents opponents with a scenario of an undemocratic, intensified capitalism. States are forced to comply with the demands of global corporations in the latter's pursuit of profits. The drive for profits by global corporations opens up more and more areas of life to corporate or market control; new areas are commodified and others, such as health and education, re-commodified. States themselves are commodified and seek to "brand" themselves, as van Ham (2001) puts it.

According to this interpretation, the desirable policy response is to develop new forms of (non-neoliberal) governance that enable the benefits of globalization to be realized. As an example, consider the World Commission on the Social Dimensions of Globalization (2004) which reports that: "the potentials of globalization, in terms of growing connectivity and productive capacity, are immense. However, current systems of governance of globalization at national and international levels have not realized such potentials for most of the world's people-and in many instances have made matters worse." They continue, "we judge that the problems that we have identified are not due to globalization as such but to deficiencies in its governance" (2004: xi).

Globalization and neoliberalism are seen therefore as conceptually different processes. Neoliberalism is seen as a rational policy response by some, enabling the benefits of globalization to be spread far and wide. Others view neoliberalism as an undesirable response, to be rejected and replaced by new forms of governance so that the potentials of globalization can be realized by those who are currently excluded by the neoliberal architecture.[6]

The "Globaloney" or "States are Still Powerful" View

A second interpretation starts from the premise that the argument set out above about the relative decline of nation-states greatly exaggerates the extent of "globalization." As an empirical matter, it is argued that the vast majority of production and investment—around 90 percent—remains national in character. For example, Lipsey, Blomstrom and Ramstetter (1995: 60–1) write that "given all the attention that 'globalization' has received from scholars, international organizations, and the press, [our data] are a reminder of how large a proportion of economic activity is confined to single geographical locations and home country ownership. Internationalization of production is clearly growing in importance, but the vast majority of production is still carried out by national producers within their own borders."

This "home country bias," meaning that firms and consumers are much more likely to trade with and purchase from fellow nationals than across borders with foreigners, has been supported by numerous studies. For example, Helliwell (1998: 118), after reviewing the data on flows of goods, capital and people, concludes that "the striking size and pervasiveness of border effects reveal that the global economy of the 1990s is really a patchwork of national economies, stitched together by threads of trade and investment that are much weaker than the economic fabric of nations."

The longstanding Feldstein-Horioka (1980) result that domestic savings and investment rates are highly correlated suggest that international capital markets remain limited as devices for redistributing the world"s capital.[7] Zevin (1992) also argues that international financial markets are now only reaching the levels of integration which they attained in the late nineteenth century. In fact, he argues that "while financial markets have certainly tended toward greater openness since the end of the Second World War, they have reached a degree of integration that is neither dramatic nor unprecedented in the larger historical context of several centuries" (1992: 43). As Bairoch (1996: 173) has written, "what many regard as a new phenomenon is not necessarily so." What globalization there is, therefore, is hardly new.

The rise of the "global firm" is also cast into doubt. Veseth (1998: 49–50), for example, argues that a global firm signifies:

a business form that both produces and sells in global pools—that it exhibits both demand-side and supply-side globalization. There is a qualitative difference between a global firm, as defined here, and a firm that produces in one place and sells everywhere or has international production processes but essentially sells in distinct local markets (with distinct local character and competition). The former type of firm is multilocal and the

---

6   This opposition is discussed further below.

7   See, however, Greenspan (2004) who states that "the correlation coefficient between paired domestic saving and domestic investment, a conventional measure of the propensity to invest at home for OECD countries constituting four-fifths of world GDP, fell from 0.96 in 1992 to less than 0.8 in 2002."

latter is transnational. These are important and growing types of business arrangements, but they are not *global* in a meaningful sense. ... The definition of a globalized business is not easy to satisfy. There are not many truly global firms, but some do exist.[8]

Furthermore, the share of government spending in the national incomes of the core capitalist economies shows no sign of being reduced (despite the best efforts of neoliberal governments such as those of Thatcher and Reagan to achieve this outcome). For example, Navarro, Schmitt and Astudillo (2004: 133), argue that:

> the welfare states of most developed capitalist countries have not converged during the globalization period towards a reduced welfare state. On the contrary, over the globalization period, whether measured as a share of GDP or by public employment, welfare states have grown across the large majority of the world's richest economies. Also, during this period, welfare states have continued to be different, retaining their individual characteristics, shaped primarily by the dominant political tradition that governed each country during the pre-globalization period.

This line of reasoning is supported by a plethora of studies pointing to the continued importance of national systems. Summarizing this literature, Radice (2000: 721) writes that:

> many writers argue that both the extent and the consequences of globalization have been greatly exaggerated: recent monograph contributions along these lines ... as well as a raft of shorter contributions ... indicate the wide support for this "sceptical" view of globalization. Equally, although some *comparativists* have charted the erosion of *Rhenish* and/or East Asian models by both external and internal pressures for change ... many have maintained that national differences are not being significantly eroded, and this is probably the majority view among students of comparative political economy.

To draw upon just one example from this literature, consider the conclusion of Fligstein (2001: 189) who argues that:

> there is no evidence that the world is converging on a single form of state-finance sector-industrial corporation relations. Families, managers, and states alternate in their domination of ownership in various societies. There is also little evidence that relations between firms are converging toward markets, hierarchies, networks, or strategic alliances as the dominant form of governance, and stable situations with different configurations abound across various societies. Large firms in different societies also differ in their product mix and integration. Finally, the types and degree of state involvement in markets vary widely within and across regions. The total effect is still one of national capitalisms.

According to this interpretation, therefore, national economies are still the basic economic units of the global economy, economic activity remains deeply embedded in national structures and states remain powerful economic actors. As *The Economist* (1995: 15) and Weiss (1998) popularly put it, the powerless state is a "myth." Or in Robert Wade's (1996: 60) words, "reports of the death of the national economy are

---

8   According to Veseth, Nike would satisfy the global firm definition but even large firms as Boeing and Microsoft would not.

greatly exaggerated." Martin Jacques (2004) has gone even further and argued that "the era we have now entered would be more appropriately described as the moment of the nation state."

However, if "globalization" is in fact "globaloney," how can the widespread presence of arguments for its existence and inevitability be explained? One explanation is that it is simply an intellectual fad, a catchphrase that has caught the popular and academic imagination but which is likely to become redundant when the next fad comes along. Other fads—the leisure society, the peace dividend—can be given as other examples which have failed to stand the test of time. A more sophisticated explanation suggests that while the case for globalization may not be compelling empirically, its real purpose is to serve as an ideological weapon of the neoliberal agenda. That is, what is occurring is not so much globalization but globalism, an ideology.

This ideology, "a set of ideas that reflect a point of view" (Fligstein 2001: 221), is based on the neoliberal view that markets and firms *should* play the dominant role in the organization of capitalist economies and that states *should* play limited roles. The purpose of this ideology has been to get citizens to accept that "there is no alternative" (TINA) and to promote what McQuaig (1998) has called a "cult of impotence." Governments could be more powerful if they wished but the ideological onslaught of neoliberalism has found in globalization a powerful and convenient argument which posits that capital must be allowed to have more power and that states must adjust to the imperatives of the global economy. It is for this reason, as an ideological tool to make citizens accept a restructuring of their working lives and a restructuring of public services that globalization has found such resonance amongst global elites. In other words, as Veseth (1998: 133) argues, "globalization is a lever that special interests can use to pry open certain public policy doors that would otherwise be tightly shut." He therefore concludes that (1998: 2) "globalization is really a delivery system, not a final product." What is being delivered is neoliberalism in the form of the "inevitability" of globalization.

And while state elites, especially of the neoliberal persuasion, and corporations have been successful in persuading the doubters of the "inevitability" of globalization, they have also been actively dismantling the power of the state by liberalizing markets in order to give credence to that very "inevitability." That is, much of the impetus for the globalization of trade, finance, and production has come from states themselves. Globalization has, to a significant extent, been state-led rather the state being the passive adaptor to an exogenously determined technologically driven globalization. Thus, Bienefeld (1996: 420) argues that "the claim that the nation-state's decline is an irreversible result of exogenous, technological changes is as ubiquitous as it is implausible ... The primary driving force behind the liberalization of the world's financial markets is political, not technological." The "big bang" of the 1980s in world financial markets can be read as an attempt by a number of core states, the UK and US especially, to secure a larger portion of the financial services industry for themselves (see Helleiner 1994). Free trade agreements, such as the NAFTA, were similarly not driven by technological necessity but by an ideological preference for free trade and greater power for capital over labor. The purpose was to deliberately limit state capacity.

Thus, globalization is really a myth, an over-hyped idea designed to support the neoliberal agenda with its political redistribution of power to corporate and financial elites.

The "Some States are Still Powerful" or the "New Imperialism" View

A third view of globalization is that while it has weakened some states, it has enhanced the power of others and deliberately so. It is argued that the most powerful core capitalist countries, particularly the US, have used globalization as way of expanding their global power and the profitability of their corporations. Globalization—or the global spread of capitalism—is a project being carried out by core capitalist states in support of the expansion of the capitalist system as a whole and their multinational corporations in particular.

There is no dispute that globalization is occurring; what is disputed is how it should be understood and interpreted. As McQueen (2001: 210) argues, "one of the few certainties about globalization is that it is most often Americanisation. Its logic does not require the US to be borderless, only everybody else." This is the key point in this interpretation of globalization. It is a process which weakens only some states—the weakest—by either forcing on them or by having their comprador leaders willingly embrace, market liberalization measures and privatization which give greater reign to foreign capital.

Meanwhile, the core states' positions are enhanced by the continued opening of more areas of economic activity in other countries to their firms. Globalization is therefore characterized by advanced capitalist states, finance capital, and multinational corporations acting in concert to open up foreign markets. These characteristics recall late nineteenth-century imperialism. "Free trade" is again the banner under which imperial powers seek to open up the economies of others. Just as imperialism in the late nineteenth century encompassed not only the economic and political spheres but also the domination of the colonies' cultures and values by those of the imperial powers, so too does imperialism at the beginning of the twenty-first century. And, of course, the willingness of imperial powers to use military force to ensure this domination is also common to both periods.

Thus, globalization appears, not as an objective description of what must "inevitably" happen but as the ideology of imperialism. For McQueen (2001: 197) the term "globalization" is seen as a "public-relations gloss." The purpose of this gloss is to present "monopolising capitals as the outcomes of ineluctable forces of nature, rather than of contestable social practices, [which] helps corporations to elude the hostility sparked by the word *imperialism*" (2000: 197).

A similar conclusion is reached by Petras and Veltmeyer (2001: 62), who argue that "to the extent that globalization rhetoric persists, it has become an ideological mask disguising the emerging power of US corporations to exploit and enrich themselves and their chief executive officers to an unprecedented degree. Globalization can be seen as a code word for the ascendancy of US imperialism."

For Petras and Veltmeyer (2001), the argument that globalization is "inevitable" and the result of the types of technological developments discussed in the "globalization weakens the nation-state" view outlined above, is fundamentally misleading. While accepting that technological change has taken place, they reject the claims that it is of such a large nature that is has of necessity revolutionized production methods. Indeed, the empirical evidence which they present points to the absence of any great technological breakthrough in productivity over the past few decades. In short, if globalization is being driven by a qualitative, indeed a revolutionary, leap in technology, why is productivity growth on a global scale still lower than that achieved in the "pre-global" period of the 1950s and 1960s?

They argue that "globalization" is a ruling class and imperial project aimed at restoring profitability in response to the "crisis of capitalism" from the 1970s onwards. They argue that "globalization" exhibits a cyclical pattern under capitalism, with its latest manifestation being structurally similar to other previous phases. Capitalism has had periods when accumulation has been focused on the national market and others when international market expansion has been in the ascendancy. The determinants of these phases include the strength of the export class, the strength of labor, and the political composition of the state. In the period 1930–70, they argue that national economies were the basis of capitalist expansion as a result first of the international crisis of the 1930s and then of the post-war power of labor and its influence over the state. However, the crisis of profitability which arose from these constraints led to a capitalist class counter-revolution which launched the "globalization" project aimed at weakening labor, re-orientating the state and forcing the creation of a world market open for capitalist exploitation. "The origins of globalization as an economic strategy were thus the consequences of an ideological project backed by state power and not the "natural unfolding" of the market" (Petras and Veltmeyer, 2001: 43), a project which was first piloted in Chile and then adopted elsewhere in the Reagan/ Thatcher era. For the imperial powers, globalization is therefore a project aimed at weakening the power of labor domestically and advocating and requiring the opening up of markets abroad. Neoliberalism has been used as the policy thrust to achieve these objectives.

This latest phase therefore, represents a "cyclical process which is still deeply implicated in national economies and highly dependent on the nation-state for its projections abroad" (Petras and Veltmeyer, 2001: 36). Thus, they argue that contemporary globalization differs from previous cycles in quantitative terms but not in terms of the "structures and units of analysis that define the process" (Petras and Veltmeyer 2001: 41); i.e. the imperial states and large capitalist firms. To suggest that this process, as globalization theorists do, represents a weakening of the core states is to miss the point. In fact, "never has the nation-state played a more decisive role or intervened with more vigour and consequence in shaping economic exchanges and investment at the local, national and international levels. It is impossible to conceive of the expansion and deepening involvement of multinational banks and corporations without the prior political, military and economic intervention of the nation-state" (Petras and Veltmeyer, 2001: 54).

In this process, the main actors are the capitalist class through its control of the world's some 37,000 multinational corporations, imperial states' governments which have become a servant to the interests of the capitalist class and which promoted the latest incarnation of a "world market" through domestic deregulation (particularly of finance) and, through their influence in the IMF and the World Bank, the rest of the world through structural adjustment, "market-friendly" policies, and privatization. The Trilateral Commission and the Word Economic Forum are added to the international financial institutions as agents representing and serving the interests of the new international capitalist class.

They prefer the term "imperialism" to "globalization" as the descriptor of the current phase of capitalism on a number of grounds. First, it clearly identifies the main actors and agents in the creation of the world market rather than relying on the fetish of attributing to abstract "market forces" human qualities, needs, and "imperatives." Second, it highlights the power relationships operating in the world political economy rather than implying an interdependent, mutually reliant "global economy." Third, it highlights the key role played by imperial states and the country-based nature of multinational corporations operations rather than globalization's characterization of the world as one inhabited by stateless global corporations and weakened states. Fourth, the term "imperialism" indicates that the methods of enforcement in the "global economy" are not simply "markets." Instead, "Washington is prepared to defend its newly regained economic ascendancy by all means necessary: by free trade if possible, by military force if necessary" (Petras and Veltmeyer 2001: 65). And for the latter to be realized, "the political-economic role of the state is accompanied by the deep penetration of the police, military and intelligence agencies of dominated nations by the US" (Petras and Veltmeyer 2001: 54–5). Imperialism is not simply an economic system. Fifth, in terms of distributional outcomes, the dynamics of increasing world income and wealth inequalities, the enrichment of the few and the impoverishment of the many, are better captured by the concept of imperialism with its structures of dominance, than globalization which suggests a mutual interdependence and offers, at least to its proponents, the prospects of a generalized rise in living standards.

Petras and Veltmeyer argue that the imperial powers are the US and "Europe" although it is unclear whether this means imperial nations within Europe or an "imperial Europe" as a whole. Panitch and Gindin (2004), however, argue that because of the pattern of corporate alliances and US investment in Europe, European capital is in fact tied to, and dependent upon, US capital, with the result that the site of imperialism shrinks more unambiguously to that of the US. For them, inter-imperialist rivalries are not as prevalent as in previous imperial eras.

While these writings are derived from Marxist analysis, historians who do not subscribe to this framework, have nevertheless agreed that globalization cannot be understood without reference to empire. Niall Ferguson (2001: 6–7), for example, argues that:

> that empires did not (and do not) matter in globalization seems implausible ... The history of the integration of international commodity markets in the seventeenth and eighteenth centuries is inseparable from the process of imperial competition between Portugal, Spain, Holland, France and Britain. The spread of free trade and the internationalization of capital markets in the nineteenth century are both inseparable from the expansion of British imperial, and especially naval, power.

For Ferguson, therefore, "globalization" must be seen as an historical process "inseparable" from imperialism, a conclusion in keeping with the analysis of Petras and Veltmeyer. However, while Petras and Veltmeyer view imperialism as a force for inequality and oppression, Ferguson (2001: 7) prefers to argue that "the British Empire in the nineteenth century, for example, can be understood in part as an agency for imposing free trade and the rule of law directly on a quarter of the world's land surface and indirectly on a great many other places, to say nothing of the world's oceans. If we believe that economic openness is good then, by extension, one might have expected some global benefit to result from this immense undertaking."

The "globalization as imperialism" interpretation shares some similarities with the "globaloney" interpretation in that it points to the continued importance of nation states and stresses the importance of neoliberalism as the ideological underpinnings of globalization. However, the two interpretations differ in the extent to which they believe states have maintained autonomy. The "globaloney" position argues that nation states are still viable decision-making structures, especially the core states, and that national projects are still possible. The imperialism view, in contrast, stresses the power relations that condition and constrain national possibilities for all but the imperial states. While the globaloney position is likely to ascribe some autonomy to national elites, the imperialism interpretation, especially in its Marxist variant, is more likely to stress the role of those elites as compradors with imperialism.

The "Regionalism is More Important" View

The final interpretation presented here argues that state and corporate structures and activities are changing but that regionalism is a more accurate description of the changes underway than globalization. This interpretation comes in various forms with one difference between them being the extent to which they view regionalism and globalization as competing or complementary processes.

The major regional blocs are, of course, Europe, the Americas, and East Asia. The view that contemporary capitalism is best described as regional rather than global rests on the strong regional biases to trade and investment flows as well as on the regional supranational political structures which have been put in place. In terms of the former, while world trade and investment has expanded rapidly over the past two decades, there is a strong regional bias in these flows. In trade terms, gravity models have been used to examine the extent to which trade flows are determined by "distance" (a negative relationship) and a common border (a positive relationship) in addition to other economic determinants such as size of the economy and gross national product per capita. Regional biases in trade are typically measured by the size and statistical significance of the coefficients on the "distance" and "common border" variables. An examination of the data lead Chortareas and Pelagides (2004: 253), for example, to conclude that "trade integration is more of a regional phenomenon than a global one."

Added to this are regional biases in foreign direct investment (FDI). Investment "clusters" with each member of the dominant "Triad" in the world economy—the US, Japan and the EU—having its own set of countries with which it is tied in terms of

FDI flows.[9] The *World Investment Report* in 1999 concluded that "the overwhelming focus of TNCs is on the Triad countries of North America, Western Europe and Japan. The concentration of FDI assets in the Triad has risen from 61 percent in 1988 to 63 percent in 1997" (UNCTAD, Division of Transnational Corporations 1994).[10]

On the basis of reviewing the evidence in the late 1980s and early 1990s, Hirst and Thompson (1996: 95) conclude that MNCs still rely on their "home base" as the center for their economic activities, despite all the speculation about globalization. "From these results we are confident that, in the aggregate, international companies are still predominantly MNCs and not TNCs ... There are two aspects of the home centredness. One is the role of the home country and the other that of the home region."

Both of these regional trends have been reflected in, and furthered by, regional economic integration agreements. Almost all countries are signatories to at least one such agreement with the number of agreements worldwide increasing dramatically over the past couple of decades: 87 were signed in the 1990s alone (see Schiff and Winters 2003: 1).

To this evidence of regional economic integration must be added the political dimensions most evident in Europe with the European Union and the European Parliament. There are no comparable bodies in other regions. The North American Free Trade Agreement (NAFTA) of 1994 between the US, Canada, and Mexico and the proposed Free Trade Agreement of the Americas do point to the existence of a regional project but its supranational political structure is currently very limited. In Asia, the ten members of the Association of South East Asian Nations (ASEAN), which was formed in 1967, created a free trade area in 1992 and have now negotiated an agreement with China. In the wake of the 1997 financial crisis, the ASEAN countries have also joined with China, Japan, and South Korea, in an ASEAN + 3 framework, to put in place mechanisms for financial cooperation.

Thus, macro-regional economic and political integration is taking place although one aspects on which all commentators agree is the degree to which regionalism, especially the political dimension, differs around the world. For some this indicates that regions are at different stages of integration in a linear path that all might be expected to follow. For others it represents fundamental differences in the nature of the regional projects. This opens up the possibility for some regional projects to be neoliberal in orientation (such as that in the Americas) whereas as others might be less so or not so at all (as, for example, in the claims for a "Social Europe"). The key is that regionalism is not a homogenous process and regional differences are evident.

Mittelman (2000: 41), for example, argues that "it would be fruitless to seek to define a single pattern of regional integration, especially a Eurocentric model emphasizing legal principles, formal declarations, routinized bureaucracies, and institutionalized exchange." The distinctiveness of regionalism in Asia has also been

---

9   For an early view on this see UNCTC (1991). See Poon, Thompson and Kelly (2000) for a critique of the Triad notion as it applies to FDI.

10   See UNCTAD website http://www.unctad.org/Templates/Webflyer.asp?docID=3064 &intItemID=2068&lang=1 (accessed November 12, 2004).

emphasized by writers such as Stubbs (1995), who has argued for a distinctive form of Asian capitalism based on the networking activities of Japanese multinationals and the Chinese diaspora.

Regionalism, therefore, may or may not be accompanied by neoliberalism. Each region has its own political dynamic and regionalism can be used for a variety of political purposes. Neither is there agreement on the relationship between regionalism and globalization, that is, whether they are competing or complementary processes. This has more popularly been expressed by economists as a view of regional blocs as either "stumbling blocs" or "building blocs" for the global economy. The fear of those who interpret regional arrangements as stumbling blocs is that we will witness a return to the insularity of the 1930s where imperial trading blocs were formed in attempt to avoid the transmission of volatility from other regions. This fear finds expression in the description of the EU or the NAFTA as creating "Fortress Europe" or "Fortress America." For others, however, the "new regionalism" of the 1990s is characterized by its "openness" and its potential to spur greater global integration.

Political scientists have focused more on regionalism as a process in which the policies of states must be explicitly analysed. To quote again from Mittelman (2000: 4), "globalization proceeds through macroregionalism sponsored by states and economic forces seeking to open larger markets as a means toward greater competitiveness." Others have referred to the process of "continental globalization" in the context of North America indicating that regionalism is the vehicle through which globalization is delivered. Similarly, Mittelman's analysis points to the emergence of "global regions."

Thus, not only are regions therefore central to the dynamics of globalization, being the units through which globalization's effects and impacts are felt, but these regions themselves are distinctive in character; they may to greater or lesser extents be characterized as "neoliberal."

Some Implications for the Understanding of "Antiglobalization"

The above review has outlined some of the critical differences in approaches to theorizing globalization and how the relationship with neoliberalism is conceived. While this review has been important for clarity of theory, I now want to turn my attention in conclusion for the implications for clarity of action. In short, given the differences in the understandings of globalization that I have outlined, and given the differences in the way that neoliberalism is linked, or not linked, with globalization, what is it that the "antiglobalizers" are against? And where are the sites for resistance?

The answers given to these questions depends on which of the four approaches surveyed above are adopted. The analysis here can only be given in sketch form but should be readily understandable given the context of the taxonomy provided in the previous sections.[11] To start, the first approach to globalization views globalization

---

11 The limitations of taxonomies outlined in footnote 3 apply even more in this final section which is no more than a sketch of a vast literature.

as a primarily technologically driven process which is weakening nation-states and promoting markets. The problem for opponents of globalization is not so much its technological basis—this is more or less presumed to be a given—but the neoliberal policies which have accompanied it. In this view, "antiglobalization" is really better understood as "anti-neoliberalism." The problem is that technological change has occurred within a governance framework which has exposed most to greater economic and social insecurity, has privileged the interests of large corporations over those of citizens, and has led to increasing inequality within and between countries. The solution is to develop new forms of governance which replace the present neoliberal framework with one more amenable to social progress. These new governance forms are not simply or even primarily to be found at the level of the nation-state—this has already been weakened by the technological force of globalization—but at the global and the local levels. That is, both above and below the nation-state level. At the global level, new global institutions are required to protect the global commons and give voice to global civil society. It this latter social force—a global civil society itself exploiting the new technologies associated with globalization—that provides the opposition to corporate globalization.

Thus, Castells (2001: 143) writes that "reversing the popular motto of twenty-five years ago, social movements must think local (relating to their own concerns and identity) and act global—at the level where it really matters today." They are able to do act at this level because of the Internet, the "essential medium" for "loose coalitions," for "movements [that] seize the power of the mind, not state power" (Castells 2001: 141). The technology of globalization is used to oppose the ideas of neoliberalism.

At the global level, some support creating new global institutions while other seek to reform existing institutions.[12] Held (1995) argues for "cosmopolitan governance," while other writers see global social movements "leapfrogging" the nation state to directly confront the multilateral economic institutions.[13] All of these are designed to provide an alternative to globalization in its neoliberal form. At the local level, forms of participatory development and community-based organizations and institutions are seen as the governance structures necessary to empower the losers in the neoliberal globalization process and to democratize local processes.

Interestingly, and parenthetically, the response by the bastions of neoliberal orthodoxy (such as the World Bank) has not been unfavourable to many of these initiatives particularly those at the local level. As indicated earlier, neoliberalism is consistent with a variety of forms of governance and can coexist with democractic and authoritarian structures alike. A concept like "global civil society" is quite capable of being incorporated into the mainstream by expanding the definition, and hence consultative processes, to include all non-state actors (including firms), and hence deradicalize it in the process.[14] In this sense, civil society is following

---

12	For disputes between the ICFTU and the Third World Network on which strategy to use to support international labor standards see O'Brien *et al.* (2000), Chapter 3.

13	The phrase is from O'Brien *et al.* (2000: 61).

14	An example is provided by the World Bank's use of the term "voices" in its publications. In 2002 a three-volume series on "Voices of the Poor" was published (comprising *Can Anyone*

in the well-worn footsteps of other concepts such as "gender" and "sustainable development." To avoid this deradicalization of "global civil society," others prefer to refer to antiglobalization as the "global social justice" movement.

To return to the main argument, the position of "antiglobalizers" adopting this interpretation of globalization can be illustrated by the ideas of Walden Bello.[15] He argues that in the short term the WTO is the critical institution of globalization that must be opposed. Thus, he states (2002: 109) that "for the movement against corporate-driven globalization, it seems fairly clear that the strategic goal must be halting or reversing WTO-mandated liberalization in trade and trade-related areas." In the longer term, the aim is "deglobalization," understood to be a new governance structure which decentralizes decision-making to the local and national levels and pluralizes it at the global level. The aim of this new global-level pluralism is to provide more space for local and national paths to development to be realized. In Bello's view, the aim is not to reform or replace the World Bank and the IMF with another global institution but rather to "drastically reduce [their] power and jurisdiction" (2002: 109).

Other parts of the global social justice movement, especially the NGO movement and the church-based elements within it, have tended to focus more on the need for community-based development at the local level and with promoting fair trade at the international level. But while differences of emphasis and strategy are clearly evident, a central point of the global social justice movement is that local spaces needed to be opened up in order to resist corporate driven, or neoliberal, globalization. To use a favorite slogan from the antiglobalization movement, "Another Way is Possible." It is a non-neoliberal way.

The second approach to globalization presented above would agree with the need to counter neoliberal or corporate-driven globalization. However, adherents to this view see the nation-state as the appropriate level at which to do this. Since globalism, the ideology of neoliberalism, asserts rather than reflects the weakening of the nation-state, resistance should primarily be focused not on global institutions such as the WTO but on the nation-states which constitute the membership of these institutions. This is the way, for example, that the MAI was defeated according to Laxer (2003), who argues that while NGOs did link together they did not become "de-nationalized" in the process, becoming some kind of supraterritorial "global civil society," but rather are best described as coordinating their efforts to pressure their own national governments. It was a case of "national movements" confronting—and defeating—globalism.

Hear Us?, *Crying Out for Change*, and *From Many Lands*). In 2003, "Investment Climate Around the World: Voices of the Firms from the World Business Environment Survey" appeared.

15 I interpret Bello's arguments here as falling within the "globalization weakens the nation state" approach. However, his more recent writings have more explicitly become concerned with imperialism. His advocacy for "deglobalization" also places him at the radical end of the antiglobalizers included in "globalization weakens the nation state" approach; others are more reformist in orientation.

Most commentators within this category argue that not only does the nation-state remain viable, it is also desirable. Nation-states remain the political units most capable enabling democratic control and income redistribution. As such, as Bienefeld (1996: 434) puts it, "a return to stronger nation-states is not Utopian, but inevitable." The ravages of neoliberalism, hiding behind the cloak of globalization, will require citizens to regain control over the nation-state to make it a progressive force.

The third interpretation, of globalization as imperialism, implies a different dynamic for resistance. Here, to focus on the WTO, or to speak of corporate-driven globalization, misses the power behind global institutions and the partner of the corporations, namely, the imperial state (see Petras and Veltmeyer 2005). It must be realized that state power in the imperial countries is the driving force of globalization and that this power is being used to force a solution to the capitalist profit crisis. And that this solution is a class solution. Thus, resistance must be anti-imperial and socialist.[16]

This interpretation of globalization has different implications for resistance to neoliberalism. As we have seen, the first two interpretations of globalization focus strongly on the need to oppose the neoliberal agenda. This is supported in this third interpretation but it should be understood that neoliberalism can be defeated, or retreated from, but imperialism can remain. That is, imperialism in the late twentieth century has (selectively) utilized free trade and neoliberal policies to open up markets and advance the imperial interests of political control and economic exploitation. However, "free trade imperialism" is not the only model on offer. Ditching the "free trade" part does not necessarily mean ditching the "imperialism" part; defeating neoliberalism may be desirable but it is not sufficient. Or, to restate the issue in a different way, defeating the WTO is not necessarily the same as defeating US imperialism. According to this interpretation, therefore, imperialism can be, and throughout history has been, supported in numerous ways and not simply by the (selectively implemented) neoliberalism which accompanies it now. To focus exclusively on the latter, is to mis-specify the problem.

The final interpretation reviewed here, that regionalism is the more important force in restructuring the world economy, suggests its own paths of resistance. And they may not, indeed are unlikely, to be the same in all regions. While there

---

16 Laxer (2004: 1) has more recently extended his "left nationalist" critique of global civil society by addressing opposition to US imperialism and in so doing he also refines the concept of nation. His purpose is to challenge "the idea that working towards a global civil society, in present circumstances, is a laudable goal. We live in the age of the US capitalist empire, which aggressively asserts its right to unilateral action and demands that the sovereignty of every other political community be breached. To the extent that proponents of global society forecast and approve the 'inevitable' weakening of popular and national sovereignties of rooted political communities, they support the power of the US empire. Instead of global society, I argue that the goal should be support for deep democracy everywhere and *inter-national solidarity from below*. By inter-national solidarity, I mean supporting struggles for the sovereignty of democratic political communities and regions wherever they are found. Nations are understood in the French Revolution sense as 'citizen-peoples rather than states, but not in the French Revolution sense of a nation one and indivisible,' in which the rights of minority nations within countries are crushed."

are many commonalities among peoples across the world in terms of the forces of neoliberalism, and hence links between them, in other respects their ability to resist depends critically on the nature of regional institutions. Thus, in Europe, for example, the European Court for Human Rights, the idea of a "Social Europe," the idea of a federalist post-national Europe, have all been readily embraced by many European social democrats. In these they see the possibility of a progressive, non-neoliberal regional system of governance in which the freeing of the markets for goods, capital, and labor takes place within the context of a progressive social system. This is still a work in the making, and opposed by European neoliberals, but is illustrative of the regional dynamics at play. In the Americas, however, a different dynamic is in play and a more neoliberal version of regionalism is being followed. The oppositional focus, originally for a rejection of NAFTA, has now changed to finding "alternative futures" for the Americas and in many ways parallels the debates taking place within the antiglobalization movement discussed above under the first interpretation. This is not surprising given that in the Americas, the regional project is often referred to as one of "continental" or "hemispheric" globalization.[17] However, there are also reformers, perhaps found most prominently in academic circles but also evident in the Quebec sovereignty movement, who see prospects for shifting American integration onto a track closer to the European model, to see what "lessons" can be learned from the latter. In East Asia, regionalism is much less well developed at the governance level with complex interactions of developmental (nation) states and regional trade liberalization initiatives. Civil society organizations have more complex relations with the state in many countries and soft authoritarianism is a more enduring political system. This too has created its own regional dynamic for resistance.

This has been no more than a brief sketch of the implications of considering the links between globalization and neoliberalism for resistance. The purpose of the paper has been to lay out some of the terrain for further analysis in this respect.

The argument of the paper has been that the oft-used term "neoliberal globalization" may be common but it is not unproblematic. The relationships between globalization and neoliberalism are in fact complex and their specifications differ between the four approaches surveyed in this paper. Understanding these differences and subjecting them to critical analysis is an important theoretical exercise. But its importance does not end here; this understanding is also necessary to define the aims of the "antiglobalization" movement.

---

17 The opposition to "hemispheric globalization" has therefore termed itself the Hemispheric Social Alliance.

Chapter 2

World Development: Globalization or Imperialism?

James Petras

Many writers have argued that we have entered a new era characterized by globalization, the driving force of epoch-defining changes in the nature of societies and economies across the world, resulting in the creation of an interdependent system. This notion of globalization has become a part of the everyday discourse in academia and among policy-makers. It serves as a point of reference and a framework of ideas for the analysis of macro and micro socioeconomic developments and of the process that gave rise to them. The notion of "globalization" spans the ideological spectrum and crosses academic disciplines. Even trenchant critics of the dominant discourse have been constrained to adopt the term and, in the process, tacitly accept its presuppositions.

The very pervasiveness of the notion of globalization points towards a problem. Not only does it reflect the presence of a fundamental paradigm, a world view that structures the thinking and practice of most scholars in the field, it also suggests the working of an ideology that obfuscates reality. Although globalization is presented as an economic process, a paradigm for describing and explaining worldwide trends, it is better viewed as a political project, a desired outcome that reflects the interplay of specific socioeconomic interests. We argue that "globalization" provides an inadequate description and understanding of worldwide trends and developments. More useful in this regard is the concept of imperialism, a notion that is currently a minority view, but one that is beginning to gain attention from scholars, including some former supporters of the Vietnam War (Chalmers 2000).

In the process of critically analyzing the notion of globalization, and supporting the greater intellectual relevance of the concept of imperialism, we proceed first by critically discussing the presuppositions and claims of globalization theorists. Then we will proceed towards a systematic critique of globalization theory. This is followed by an argument in support of an alternative way of understanding worldwide trends and developments based on the concept of "imperialism."

The Origin and Rise of Globalization Theory

What is globalization? The term has been used in a multiplicity of senses. For some writers it refers to an increasing number of events and developments taking place simultaneously in more than one country—in an increasing number and range of countries worldwide (Stalker 2000). For others globalization implies something beyond similarity. They argue that these trends and developments are connected and that there is a steady multiplication and intensification of links and flows among discrete national entities—a higher level of organization and integration into one system. For a few writers, the term tends to be used loosely to refer to a broad range and great variety of processes and trends, some of which, such as privatization and liberalization, are increasingly escaping control by the nation-state, reflecting a new level of capitalist development in a new set of supranational institutions which have replaced the nation-state (Burbach and Robinson 1999).

The notion of globalization contains a description and explanation of processes and trends that hitherto unfolded at the national level but that over the past few decades have spilled beyond the boundaries of the nation-state. In its most general sense "globalization" refers to the upsurge in direct investment and the liberalization and deregulation in cross-border flows of capital, technology and services, as well as the creation of a global production system—a new global economy. It is in this sense that the term was apparently coined in 1986, in the context of the eighth round of GATT negotiations (Ostry 1990). For the theorists of this process and its many advocates these flows, both in scope and depth, together with the resulting economic integration and social transformation, have created a new world order with its own institutions and configurations of power that have replaced the previous structures associated with the nation-state, and that have created new conditions of people's lives all over the world, including a greater interconnectedness (Giddens 1990; Rosenau 1990; Holm and Sørensen 1995; Therborn 2000).

Globalization as a new phenomenon?

There are several points of dispute about this process, particularly as to whether it represents something "new," a qualitatively different phase in the evolution and development of capitalism, a new epoch, or simply the latest and not necessarily most significant phase in a long historical process.

This issue has both a conceptual and empirical dimension. On the one side it is argued that the trends and developments associated with globalization cannot be equated with the evidence of the internationalization of economic intercourse and the flow of goods, capital, and labor during the late nineteenth century. Several studies have documented that the flows of capital, goods, and labor were higher in the period leading up to the First World War than during the last half of the twentieth century (Dicken 1992). However, advocates of globalization argue that the earlier forms of this internationalization were not accompanied by anywhere near the same degree of economic integration and that it did not result in the creation of an integrated global production system.

As for the new global economy formed over recent decades, the driving forces were different. The entire process of change, globalization theorists argue, has been underpinned by accelerated technological progress, mediated by the growing role of transnational corporations and facilitated by the deregulation and liberalization of markets all over the world (Griffin and Rahman Khan 1992: 59–66). The difference between the past and the present, these theorists assert, is in the technological conditions of this globalization (a revolution in communications technology); its relevant institutional and policy framework (free market reforms, structural adjustment measures); and the degree of systemic integration. The neoliberal program of structural adjustments and policy reforms of the post world war period were designed, and have served, to liberalize the international flow of capital, goods and services, technology, and information. In addition, they have worked to deregulate the associated economic environments and markets.

The myth of the third technological-industrial revolution

If indeed we were living in a new global economy based on the new information technologies, we would expect the introduction of those technologies to have a significant impact on productivity growth. In the past, during the first and second industrial revolutions, when steam power, electricity, and the internal combustion engine were introduced, productivity showed a marked increase. To speak of the information revolution means that the innovations have had a profound effect in stimulating new productive investments, more productive utilization of capital and new ways of stimulating output per capital investment. A comparison of productivity growth in the United States over the past half-century fails to support the argument of the proponents of a third scientific industrial revolution (TSIR). Between 1953 and 1973 productivity grew on an average of 2.6 percent; between 1972 and 1995 productivity grew a mere 1.1 percent (Wolf 1999: 10).

The "information revolution" clearly did not revolutionize production. In fact, it failed to even sustain the previous levels of productivity and was not able to counteract the tendencies to capitalist stagnation that have been operative since the 1970s. Some advocates of the TSIR argue that the real "take-off," of the information revolution should be dated from the mid-1990s, citing the productivity growth of 2.2 percent between the last quarter of 1995 and the first quarter of 1999. While this figure is substantially greater than the rate of productivity between 1992 and 1995 it is still below the growth data for the 1953–1973 period. Moreover, it is very questionable whether the increase in productivity can be attributed to the technological revolution. A recent article by Robert Gordon, which analyzes an increase in productivity between 1995 and 1999, raises serious doubts about the TSIR claims (Gordon 1999a). He argues that almost 70 percent of the improvement in productivity can be accounted for by improved measurements of inflation (lower estimates of inflation necessarily mean higher growth of real output, thus productivity) and the response of productivity to the exceptionally rapid output growth over the three-year period. Thus, only one third of the 1 percent gain in productivity made during the 1995–9 period can be attributed to computerization or the so-called "information revolution"—hardly a revolution (Gordon 1999a).

Even more devastating for the advocates of the TSIR, Gordon provides a convincing argument that most of the increase in productivity attributed to computerization is in the manufacturing of computers! The dramatic improvements in productivity claimed by the TSIR apologists are largely in the production of computers, with little effect on the rest of the economy. According to Gordon's study, productivity growth in the production of computers has increased from 18 percent a year between 1972 and 1995 to 42 percent a year as of 1995. As Gordon sees it, this accounts for all the improvements in productivity growth in durable goods. In other words, the computer has brought about a "revolution" in the production of computers, having an insignificant effect on the rest of the economy. The basic reason is that computers have simply substituted for other forms of capital. According to a recent study, growth in computer inputs exceeded those in other inputs by a factor of 10 in the 1990–6 period (Jorgenson and Stiroh 1999). The substitution of one form of capital for another need not raise productivity in the economy as a whole. The basic measure of a technological revolution is what the authors call "multi-factor productivity," the increase in output per unit of all outputs.

The basic question posed by TSIR theorists is not over whether computers have revolutionized the production of computers but how the so-called "information revolution" has affected the other 99 percent of the economy. According to Gordon's longitudinal study of technical progress covering the period between 1887 and 1996, the period of maximum technical progress as manifested in annual multi-factor productivity growth was in the period from 1950 to 1964, when it reached approximately 1.8 percent. The period of lowest multifactor productivity growth in this century was from 1988 to 1996—approximately 0.5 percent growth (Gordon 1999b)!

Clearly the innovations in the early and middle twentieth century were far more significant sources of economy-wide productivity improvement than the electronic, computerized information systems of late.

Computer manufacturers account for 1.2 percent of the US economy and only 2.0 percent of capital stock (Wolf 1999: 10). While corporations spend substantial amounts on computers it is largely to replace old ones. There is no evidence to back up the claims of the advocates of TSIR. There has been no such thing as the third scientific industrial revolution—at least by any empirical measure of increased productivity in the US economy. Despite the vast increase in the use of computers, the productivity performance of the US economy remains far below the levels achieved in the pre-computer age of 1950 to 1972. In fact, annual multi-factor productivity growth (AMPG) between 1988 and 1996 is the lowest of the last 50 years (Gordon 1999b). Even more significantly, according to Gordon, the rate of growth between 1950 and 1996 has been steadily declining: from 1950 to 1964 AMPG grew approximately 1.8 percent; from 1964 to 1972 it grew 1.4 percent; from 1972 to 1979 it grew 1.1 percent; from 1979 to 1988 it grew 0.7 percent and from 1988 to 1996, 0.6 percent.

The claim of the TSIRs related to a new capitalist era has no basis in any purported third scientific information revolution. On the contrary, one could argue that the new information systems might have a negative effect on productivity insofar as they draw a disproportionate amount of capital away from more productive activities and feed into and reinforce "service" activities, such as financial speculative investments, that hinder productivity growth. At a minimum one could argue that the new information systems are not likely to counteract the long-term systemic propensity towards crisis. We can also argue that rather than being the wellspring of productivity, or the determinant of capitalist growth, the new information systems are subordinate elements of a larger configuration of capitalist institutions—particularly financial—that influence their use and application.

The myth of the new revolutionary information age of capitalism, however, has served several political uses. First, it is an attempt to put an intellectual "technological" gloss on the imperial expansion of Euro-American capitalism. The driving force of what is dubbed "globalization" is imputed to the "revolutionary" consequences of electronic information systems that operate across national boundaries. The information systems approach renders the old Marxist categories of capitalist expansion–imperialism obsolete. The dominance of the new international information systems, according to TSIR, creates a "global economy"—a new global phase of capitalist development. Since we have argued that no such "technological revolution" has in fact taken place, at least as it affects the growth of the productive forces, what can we make of the arguments for a "global economy" and "global corporations"— ambiguous terms that mask the relations of power in the world economy?

At issue in the overseas expansion of Euro-American capital was the need to counteract, and undo, institutional arrangements that were formed in the post-war context of an east–west cold war; movements of national liberation and the desalinization of a large part of the so-called "Third world;" and a labour and capital accord (social contract), supported by the institutions and policies of a Keynesian state in the North and a developmentalist state in the South (Marglin and Schor 1990; Arrighi 1994). Under conditions of an economic and fiscal crisis that beset the system as a whole in the late 1960s and early 1970s, the sweeping reforms of the New Economic Model (Bulmer-Thomas 1996) brought about a counter-revolution in theory and practice, and with it the subversion of the post war world order—and the new Euro-American empire dubbed by then President Bush the New World Order (NWO).

The inevitability of globalization?

Globalization, according to its advocates, has ushered in a new era of late or post-capitalist development, the economic and political dynamics of which have become focal points of a broad range of studies from diverse perspectives (Kenen 1994). So entrenched has this notion of globalization become that even its many critics have succumbed to the suggestion, or claim, that the process is inevitable and thus inescapable in its effects. Accepting this claim some critics argue that the best and only "realistic option"—as Casteñeda (1993) has put it—is to enter into the globalization process under the most favourable conditions available and to adjust to its requirements as needed or possible. This position is most clearly articulated in the World Bank's 1995 *World Development Report* (World Bank 1995a). Among others Keith Griffin, by no means an uncritical globalist, allows for no possible alternative to an adjustment to what cannot be avoided or changed (Bienefeld 1995; Griffin 1995). Against clear evidence to the contrary presented by the United Nations Development Programme (UNDP) with which he is himself associated, Griffin sees a trend towards convergence, which is creating opportunities for some developing countries to participate in the fruits of development engendered by globalization. In this connection, Griffin adopts a view held not only by the economists at the World Bank but by most sceptics and critics of globalization.[1]

---

1 These critics range from scholars of international relations or economic development such as Bello, Korten, Rosenau and participants in a series of antiglobalization forums and

Globalization and the nation-state

The claim of globalization theory about the growing irrelevance of nation-state has also been widely accepted, even by critics. They see globalization as tending to displace the role of the state as the institution creating the conditions of capital accumulation as well as the regulation of capital. Scholars as diverse as Stalker (2000), who provides an ILO perspective on globalization, and Drucker (1993), articulate the widely held mainstream view that globalization has ushered in a new post-capitalist form of development. They argue that the nation-state has retreated from the development process and been replaced by what Robinson conceptualizes as the "internationalized state" (Robinson 1996: 363–80). Some scholars in this connection more plausibly argue for a new system of global governance, a set of institutions that can secure the regulatory conditions of political stability for a global capital accumulation process.[2]

However, not everyone has accepted this notion of a powerless state, unable to resist the erosion of its economic role. Some "realist" analysts of the political dimension of the "globalization" process continue to see the nation-state as a major actor in international relations and its substantive conditions (Holm and Sørenson 1995). Similarly, the notion of a powerless state, whose role and weight in the economy has been diminished by forces of globalization, has been seriously challenged (Weiss 1998). Nevertheless, the prevailing view in academia is that the regulatory powers of the nation-state, and its capacity to make policy, have been seriously compromised and are giving way to a new set of supranational institutions for managing the process or for securing "good governance" (Boyer and Drache 1996).

Globalization in Theory: An Epoch-Defining Shift or Capitalism as Usual?

Supporters of the neoliberal order and the associated Washington Consensus (Williamson 1990) come in two varieties, as do its critics. Among the globalists there remain hard-line voices in favour of an entrenched neoliberal form of free market capitalism such as Shepard (1997: 38–40) and the World Bank (1992). However, the dominant approach is to take the pillars of the neoliberal order, its institutional framework and enabling policy framework, as a given but to recognize the need for a social dimension and to give the development process a "human face."

---

networks—the San Francisco based International Forum on Globalization; the Bangkok-based Focus on the Global South, the PCD Forum, the US-based 50 Years is Enough network for global economic justice, the Third World Network, and the Centre for the Study of Globalization and Rationalization at the University of Warwick.

2   The political dynamics of this process have been the central concern of a number of studies sponsored or published by the US Council for Foreign Relations, such as Ostry, *Government and Corporations in a Shrinking World* (1990), its scholarly mouthpiece *Foreign Affairs*, and the Washington-based Institute for International Economics (for example, Kenen 1994).

The International Labor Organization (ILO),[3] the UN's Economic Commission for Latin America and the Caribbean (ECLAC) and associates of the Washington-based Institute for International Economics typify this approach. However even the IMF has softened its views proposing reforms to the neoliberal model and redesigning the Structural Adjustment Program (Salop 1992).

Critics of the NWO can also be put into two camps. First, there are those concerned with the social dimensions of the globalization process. They tend to focus their criticisms on the uneven distribution of its socioeconomic benefits— and at times its underlying agenda of corporate capitalism. Amongst these reformist critics can be found intellectuals such as Korten (1995) and other participants in the PCD Forum, a consortium of international nongovernmental organizations (NGOs) that have constituted themselves as a watchdog of the World Bank, the WTO and other guardians of the New World Order. Also ranged within this spectrum of liberal reformers are the diverse participants in the antiglobalization Alternative Forum (Griffin and Khan 1992), those associated with the UNDP and its concept of "human development;" Ghai and others with UNRISD (1994) and its concern with the social dimensions of the adjustment process; and Marshall Wolfe (1996), a voice for the Economic Commission for Latin America and the Caribbean (ECLAC).

The reformist critique of the NWO and the process involved in bringing it about—globalization—focus on the fundamental inequalities and inequities in the distribution of society's productive resources and fruits of development as a major problem. Most recognize, as does Sengenberger, Director of the ILO's Employment Strategy Department, that it is the workers who as a class bear a disproportionate share of the social costs of adjustment. To redress this fundamental market-generated inequity, reformist critics of the NWO, for the most part, turn to a Keynesian state-led form of capitalist development, based on a selectively interventionist and socially reformist state.

These reformers argue for a social dimension to development—to alleviate the worst effects of an inevitable process and to protect the poor and other vulnerable groups. They propose a turn towards social liberalism, a reformed neoliberalism, and appeal to the institutions of global capital to reform themselves. In this context, critics also appeal to an emergent "global civil society" coalescing around a global network of international NGOs.

While this school of thought introduces a reformist agenda, it still embraces the idea that there is no alternative to capitalism, the NWO, and the globalization process. Having accepted the idea that there is no alternative, the issue becomes how best to adapt and to insert economies and societies into the process. The issue becomes: what are the most favorable conditions available in order to strike the best deal possible through direct pressure and negotiated concessions? The solution is what Griffin and Khan, Casteñeda and others see as the only "realistic option."

---

3 Werner Sengenberger, Director of the ILO's Employment Strategy Department and the ILO's Working Group on the Social Dimensions of Globalization and Liberalization of Trade (see Foreword to Stalker 2000: xii).

A second group of critics share a Marxist understanding of the nature and macrodynamics of the international capitalist system, although "Marxism" here takes diverse forms.

These critics work from very different theories of the macrodynamics of postwar capitalism and its propensity towards crisis. The general view is that there is an alternative to the existing order and the globalization process and that it should be sought in political terms.

The writers associated with Monthly Review (Magdoff 1992; Sivadandan and Meiksins Wood 1997; Sweezy 1997; Tabb 1997; MacEwan 1999) view globalization as an obfuscating myth, an analysis of an imperialist centred international economy. Another group of left scholars (Du Boff and Herman 1997) view globalization as the latest phase in a long historical process, representing an epochal shift in the nature of capitalism, and as such a systemic (or political) response to the crisis that beset world capitalism in the late 1960s and early 1970s (Amin 1994; Welder and Rigby 1996; Laibman 1997; Brenner 2000a).

In this connection, we propose the concept of imperialism as an alternative explanatory framework of international capitalist expansion and the growing inequalities, and for describing and explaining the process—the concentration of power, property and income in the international system.

Globalization or Imperialism?

The term "globalization" not only serves as description and explanation of what is going on. It refers even more so to a prescription—that certain developments, particularly "the liberalization of national and global markets," will produce "the best outcome for growth and human welfare" and that they are in everybody's interest (World Bank 1995a). In this connection, the notion of globalization is clearly based not on science but on ideology, a manifesto, as it were, of advanced capitalism in which it serves as a shorthand reference to developments and outcomes that are deemed to be highly desirable.

In this connection, the problem is how to generate the requisite support and the "political will" needed to implement the required reforms and policies. The World Bank, in particular, has assumed responsibility in this area, arrogating to itself the task of ensuring that governments all over the world adjust to the requirements of Euro-American multinational corporations and their states.[4]

Another issue in this connection is how to differentiate between reality and appearance. In appearance, there is an unfolding of trends that are leading towards increased integration into one world system. In the process, the nation-state is weakened, hollowed out, forced to retreat from the process of national development and surrender its decision-making power to a new set of international institutions. The reality, however, is otherwise. The state in the Third World actively intervenes to subsidize and attract capital, reduce the role of organized labor, etc. The imperial

---

4   On the World Bank's strategy and its underlying ideology, particularly as relates to the world's workers see Veltmeyer (1997).

state bails out banks, investors, and speculators and provides political pressure to open markets, sends military expeditions to eliminate alternative.

Within the frameworks of both concepts, that of globalization and imperialism, repeated reference is made to the dramatic increase of the international flow of capital, particularly in the form of foreign direct investment (FDI); an associated process of mergers and acquisitions; and the restructuring of capital, viz. its shift towards developing countries, particularly Latin America.[5] However, the economic restructuring associated with the so-called "globalization" process not only has shifted the conditions of a systemic crisis from the North to the South, with a resulting deterioration of economic conditions all across the South and an economic recovery in the North, but has led to a greater concentration of ownership of the world's productive resources. In this connection, Fortune's top 100 transnational corporations (TNCs), 80 percent of which are based in the United States or Western Europe have dramatically increased their control of the world economy (Petras and Veltmeyer 1999). The bulk of technological innovations and direct investments, as well as international trade, are under the direct control of these multinationals, the principal units of Euro-American imperialism. In addition, the 1990s saw a dramatic increase in the takeover, and recolonization, of the strategic sectors of many economies, particularly in Latin America, which, over the course of the decade, took over from East Asia the position of major destination for the growing international flow of productive and speculative capital in the Third World. The growth of direct and equity investment flows is only one, albeit a central, part of the mechanisms of a new resurgent imperialism, a means of securing US hegemony (Petras and Veltmeyer 2000). Also involved are the dynamics and growing integration of world capital markets and the transnationalization of trade.

A recent empirical comparative study by Doremus, Kelley, Pauly and Reich of US, German, and Japanese TNCs found that on the vital issues of investment, research and development the great majority of decisions were taken in the national headquarters of the TNCs (Doremus *et al.* 1998: Ch. 5). With regard to research and development (R&D) of US-based TNCs they show that 88 percent of the total R&D expenditures are made in the "home" country, and only 12 percent of majority-owned affiliates overseas. Technology development remains centralized in the national headquarters of the TNCs. In the other key area of TNC strategy, direct investment decisions and intra-firm trade, the authors find that the priorities of nation headquarters predominate. The authors' findings and conclusions refute the myth of the "global" multinational or transnational corporations demonstrating their ties to the nation-state and their centralized nation-centered decision-making structure. While the TNCs locate production in many countries and divide up operations and production in multiple sites, control and profits are centralized within nation-states. Expansion and control by TNCs has not changed their enduring links to nation-states; nor have their international operations transformed their centralized empire building character. The process of international political and economic expansion and its associated trends and developments has more to do with the dynamics of political and economic power than the transformative effects of new technology. If

---

5   On the dynamics of this process see Petras and Veltmeyer (1999).

there is a driving force to the process it relates to the political and military victories of overseas expansionary social classes and political leaders over their nationalist and collectivist adversaries.

An Alternative Perspective

Globalism as a perspective is deficient at a number of levels and with regards to a number of critical issues. First, as we have seen it is clearly mistaken to view globalization in terms of linear progress based on the introduction of revolutionary technologies and, in these terms to visualize a new form and phase of capitalist development. The process involved is cyclical rather than linear and, notwithstanding the caveats of globalists on this score, not particularly different or new. More to the point, the globalist perspective misreads or ignores the major macrodynamics of the long-term capitalist development process. Whether viewed as a process or alternatively as a project, recent trends and developments can be better grasped in terms of an imperialist perspective.

In these terms, the resurgent international flow of capital, technology, and trade in commodities and services that globalists make so much of is indicative of a process in which US and European capital has not only recovered from the crisis that beset it but that provided the mechanisms of a renewed hegemony. The trend-defining facts related to this process are not in dispute. The issue is how best to interpret them. In the 1990s, the dominant trend was for FDI and other forms of capital to relocate to areas of the world where the spoils are greater—the developing countries of East Asia and, vis-à-vis the United States, Latin America.

The privately owned capitalist corporations that dominate the process are far from being stateless. On the contrary, their headquarters are located either in the United States or in Western Europe. Further, these TNCs have not escaped the regulatory powers of the nation-state. They are supported and led by states that not only pave the way for their international operations but that continue to regulate their operations, working closely together with the TNCs to ensure their success in providing increased returns on invested capital. In this connection, the network of international institutions is an adjunct to the power exercised by the imperial state. The top officials of the World Bank and the IMF are always appointees of the United States for the former and Europe for the latter. Policies are always cleared with their home countries. In this context it is a serious mistake to view the state as obsolete, a hollowed out shadow of its former self, drastically reduced in its role and capacity. Rather, the state has been restructured in the interests of each country's TNCs and its neoimperialist agenda.

Retreat of the State or Resurgence of the Imperial State?

One of the myths of globalization, consumed by scholars across the ideological spectrum, is that it has led to the retreat of the state and a displacement of its former power vis-à-vis capital to an emerging set of supranational institutions at the service of capital. As Tabb (1997) constructs it, the idea of a powerless state vis-à-vis the globalization process is a powerful tool in the service of the status quo. In both intellectual and ideological terms, it gives support to the argument that the officials or occupants of the nation-state have lost control over the instruments of fundamental economic policy and that perforce they are unable to resist liberalizing pressures to open the national economy to the requirements of the imperial centers. The political implications of this position are momentous, dictating as it does the form of national politics and policy-making.

In practical or political terms, the idea of a powerless state not only ignores the continued capacity of the state to regulate capital but it totally ignores the role of the state as a major agency for imperialist expansion and the imperial as well as class character of the state at the center of the system. The international circuits of capital and commodity flows are controlled by TNCs whose headquarters are based in the United States or Europe. Moreover globalization theorists tend to ignore or play down the political dynamics involved in opening markets, overthrowing recalcitrant nationalist regimes and invading countries.

The historical fact is that the countries in Africa, Asia and Latin America have had a long history of several centuries based on imperial ties and relations of exploitation with markets, exchanges and investments dominated by one imperial power or another. Both the current and earlier forms of internationalization in the flow of capital, technology, and trade in goods and services must be understood, and analysed, in this context.

Of late there has emerged a line of analysis that is not structural in approach. Indeed it is antistructural or pos-structural.[6] Through the optics of these studies the macrodynamics of the capitalist system are not at issue. The issue *is* the subjective experience and actions of diverse agents—diverse ways of socially constructing, seeing and being in the world—and interpreting its microdynamics. The context for this form of interpretation is constituted in the search for a community-based and localized form of participatory development that is at once "socially empowering" and "transformative." Advocates of this approach tend to either ignore external structures and processes or minimize their workings and impacts.

A major lacuna in this and other forms of discourse on globalization is in the area of class—an inability to understand (or deliberate avoidance of) the class character of the forces and institutions involved in what is taken as "globalization." One reason for this is the exaggerated focus on impersonal economic institutions. Today, class-based structures and relations operate on a world scale and in such a way that their "objective effects" are clearly visible and recognized even by the defenders of the current world order (Shepard 1997; World Bank 1992). What we find today are the actions of a state-centered system in which the state, that of the US in concert with the states of Western Europe in particular, everywhere projects its political power in support of US capital and its project—the strategic takeover and recolonization of the of world economy and the national states tied to it. This project was advanced in the 1990s with dramatic results. By the end of the decade

---

6   On the various permutations of this poststructuralist or postmodernist approach see Escobar (1995) and Esteva and Prakash (1998). For a critique of this approach see Veltmeyer (1997).

the United States emerged as a hegemonic force, the only super-power in political and military terms, and with strategic control of the major operating agencies of the imperialist system, the bearers of capital and technology and majority membership in the club of transnational corporations and financial institutions.

A survey published by the *Financial Times* (January 27, 1999) of the world's biggest companies based on their market capitalization shows that among the 500 biggest companies in the world, the United States accounts for 244, Japan 46, and Germany 23. Even if we aggregate all of Europe, the total number of dominant companies is 173, far fewer than those owned and controlled by the United States. Thus it is clear that European, not Japanese, capitalism remains as the only competitor to the United States for dominance in the world market. The acceleration of US economic power and the decline of Japan in the 1990s is manifest in the increasing number of US firms among the top 500, up from 222 to 244 and the precipitous decline of Japanese firms from 71 to 46 over the decade. This tendency will be accentuated over the next few years because US-based TNCs are buying out large numbers of Japanese enterprises as well as Korean, Thai, and other firms.

Looking at the largest 25 firms, those whose capitalization exceeds $86 billion, the concentration of US economic power is even greater: over 70 percent are American, 26 percent are European, and 4 percent are Japanese. As for the top 100 companies, 61 percent are American, 33 percent are European and only 2 percent are Japanese. To the degree that the TNCs control the world economy, it is largely the United States, which has emerged as the overwhelmingly dominant power. Insofar as the very largest companies are the leading forces in buying out smaller companies through mergers and the fusion of capital we can expect the US-based TNCs to play a major role in the process of concentration and centralization of capital.

Conclusions

An important issue involved in academic debates focuses on how to view recent trends and developments in the world economy. As an *economic* process, impelled by dynamics of a system, or as a *political* project, the intentional outcome of a consciously pursued strategy (Aulakh and Schecter 2000). In this connection, it has been said, globalization is not a "monolithic, unstoppable juggernaut, but a complex web of interrelated processes," some of which, as Stalker (2000: 10) notes, "are subject to greater control than others." In the same connection, international expansion of Euro-American capital is not as so many see it: a process without a subject and as such irresistible in its logic and inescapable in its effects. To the extent that the international flows of capital and commodities involve a process, it has both a conscious direction and a political agenda: to promote the worldwide interests of a new class of transnational capitalists anchored in the US and Europe. This can best be understood as a form of empire building—imperialism.

The advocates of globalization theory argue for the interdependence of nations, the shared nature of their economies, the mutuality of their interests, the shared benefits of their exchanges (Keohane and Nye 2000). Imperialism emphasizes the domination and exploitation by imperial states and their multinational corporations and banks of less developed states and laboring classes, as well as international competition and cooperation among the rival imperial states and enterprises. In today's world it is clear that the imperial countries are hardly dependent on most of the Third World countries they trade with. They have diverse suppliers; the economic units operating are owned and operated in large part by stockholders in the imperial countries; and the profits, royalties, interest payments flow upward and outward in an asymmetrical fashion. Within the international financial institutions (IFIs) and other world bodies, the imperial countries wield disproportionate or decisive influence. On the other hand, the dominated countries are low-wage areas, interest and profit exporters, virtual captives of the IFIs and highly dependent on limited overseas markets. Hence the imperial concept fits the realities much better than the assumptions that underlie the notion of globalization.

The concept of globalization relies heavily on diffuse notions of technological change accompanied by information flows and the abstract notion of "market forces." In contrast, the concept of imperialism sees the transnational corporations and banks, and the imperial states, as the driving force behind the international flows of capital and tradable commodities. A survey of the major events, world trade treaties, and regional integration themes quickly dispels any technological determinant explanations: it is the heads of the imperial states that establish the framework for global exchanges. Within that political shell the major transaction and organizational forms of capital movements are found in the TNCs, supported by the IFIs, whose personnel is appointed by the imperial states. Technological innovations operate within the parameters that further this configuration of power. The concept of imperialism thus gives us a more precise idea of the social agencies of worldwide movements of capital than the notion of globalization.

According to most advocates of "globalization" theory we are entering a new epoch of interdependency in which stateless corporations transcend national frontiers, spurred by the third technological revolution and facilitated by the new information systems. According to this view the nation-state is an anachronism, the movements of capital are unstoppable and inevitable and the world market is the determinant of the macro–micro political economy.

The result, according to globalization theorists, is a progressive, dynamic, modernizing world of prosperous nations. But the contrast between the premises and promises of globalization theorists and contemporary realities could not be starker. Instead of interdependent nations we have dramatic contrasts between creditor and debtor nations; multi-billion-dollar corporations appropriating enterprises, interests royalties and trade surpluses while billions of workers and peasants reap poverty and miserable existences. Structurally we find that over 80 percent of the major TNCs control their investment, research, and technology decisions out of their home offices in the United States, Germany, and Japan. TNCs are based on worldwide operations but their control is centralized.

Notwithstanding the resistance of the globalists, their basic premises—viz. the claim of inevitability and the notion that it represents a novel development driven by technological change—are suspect. And the same can be said in regards to the denial of possible systemic alternatives to the dominant NWO. In this and other regards we can point to a clear divergence between the grand claims and meager explanatory power of globalism as theory. In this context the notion of imperialism is a more useful tool for grasping the dynamics of the process.

Chapter 3

Civil Society and Good Governance: The Politics of Adjustment

Henry Veltmeyer

The idea of "civil society" has achieved prominence in political and developmental discourse over the past two decades, particularly in connection with successive waves of democratization, beginning in Latin America and Eastern Europe, and spreading across the developing world. In normative terms, civil society has been widely seen as an increasingly crucial agent for limiting authoritarian government, strengthening popular empowerment, reducing the socially atomizing and unsettling effects of market forces, enforcing political accountability, and improving the quality and inclusiveness of governance. Reconsideration of the limits of state action has also led to an increased awareness of the potential role of civic organizations in the provision of public goods and social services, either separately or in some kind of "synergistic" relationship with state institutions.

The idea of civil society was central to the political discourse of the theorists of the eighteenth-century Scottish and French enlightenment. In this context it was used to differentiate a sphere independent of "government" and other distinctly political institutions. In the 1980s the concept of civil society was resurrected by political theorists for similar reasons—to identify a non-political sphere within society—to differentiate this sphere from the state and its associated politics. In this context it was associated with a theoretical discourse on political participation. However, the focus was on nongovernmental organizations (NGOs) formed within not civil society but the "third sector"—a sector differentiated from both the public sector and the private sector of profit-making organizations. The concern here was not political participation but participatory development, models for which were constructed "from above" and "from the outside" and "from below and "from within" —that is with the agency of nongovernmental and grassroots community-based organizations. It was not until the 1990s, in the wake of democratization movement in Russia and East Europe, and in the context of a concern of the official development community to incorporate the private sector into the development process, that a third-sector discourse gave way to a discourse on civil society.

Civil Society, Development and Democracy

The academic discourse on civil society can be put into three ideological categories—conservative, liberal, and radical. On this ideological spectrum liberals see civil society as a countervailing force against an unresponsive, corrupt state and exploitative corporations that disregard environmental issues and human rights abuses (Kamat 2003). Conservatives, on the other hand, see in civil society the beneficial effects of globalization for the development of democracy and economic progress (Chan 2001). As for those scholars that share a belief in the need for radical change, civil society is seen as a repository of the forces of resistance and opposition, forces than can be mobilized into a counter-hegemonic bloc (Morton 2004).

Thus the academic discourse in its diverse ideological currents appears to converge in support of civil society, viewing it generally as an agent for change. The emergence and dynamic rise of civil society organizations in the 1980s and 1990s is offered as proof of the self-organizing capacity of civil society and the virtue of a state that is subject to powerful democratizing tendencies and forces in favor of a democratic renewal. In this process of democratic renewal—or re-democratization—nongovernmental organizations (NGOs) are assigned a predominant role as front-line agents of a more participatory and democratic development, to convince the rural poor of the virtues of alternative community-based or local-level development and the rejection of a confrontational politics of direct action.

NGOs in this context appear as missionaries of the good word about the marriage of convenience between the free market and democratic elections—and the virtues of social democratic action within the spaces available within the power structure as opposed to direct action against it. In this context the NGOs are enlisted by overseas development agencies (ODAs) and governments as partners in the process of "sustainable human development" and "good [democratic] governance"—as watchdogs of state deviancy, as interlocutors and participants in the formulation of public policy and to ensure its transparency (to inhibit or prevent corruption and rentierism). The institutional framework for this more participatory form of development and government would be established by the decentralization of decision-making capacity and associated responsibilities from the national to the local level and the institution of "good governance," that is, a democratic regime in which the responsibility for human security and political order is not restricted to the government and other institutions of the state but is widely shared by different civil society organizations (World Bank 1994b; UNDP 1996a; OECD 1997).

The global phenomenon and explosive growth of NGOs—from some 1000 In 1914 to over 37,000 in 2000 (mostly formed in the 1980s and 1990s) reflects a new policy and political consensus that they are de facto and by design effective agents for democratic change and an important means for instituting an alternative form of development that is initiated from below and within civil society—socially inclusive, equitable, participatory, and sustainable. This consensus view is reinforced by evidence that the NGO channel of ODA is dedicated largely to the purpose of political rather than economic development—to promote democracy in the process of change, to inculcate relevant values and respect for democratic norms of behavior, to encourage the adoption of "civil" politics (dialog, consultations, negotiation)—rather than the confrontational politics of direct action.

The leading role of CSOs in this regard foretells a reworking of "democracy" in ways that coalesce with global capitalist interests and the neoliberal agenda. Indeed, a well-placed development practitioner in the UK has wondered aloud (and put in print) whether the NGOs in this regard has not been used by the community of international organizations as their stalking horse—and, not to put too fine a point on it, as an agent of global neoliberalism or imperialism (Wallace 2003). Global policy forums and institutions such as the OECD's Development Centre, USAID, the World Bank, and the Inter-American Development Bank, as well as operational agencies of the UN such as the UNDP, have actively enlisted the NGOs in the "economic reform process" as "forces of democratization" or agents of "democratic promotion," which, Ottaway notes, is a "new activity in which the aid agencies and NGOs [originally] embarked [upon] with some trepidation and misgivings" but that in the early 1990s "[came] of age" (Ottaway 2003: vi).

Civil Society and the State

In the 1990s the perception of NGOs—as "Trojan horses for global neoliberalism" (Wallace 2003)—also came of age within the policy think-tanks and forums in the US such as the Carnegie Endowment for Peace and the Harvard International Center concerned with the worldwide promotion of democracy. But the effectiveness of NGOs in this regard is not without controversy. Indeed, it has occasioned somewhat of a debate between liberals, generally disposed in favor of the NGOs, and conservatives, who view ODA as a misbegotten enterprise and see NGOs as "false saviors of international development" (Kamat 2003). Radical political economists in the same context tend to view NGOs as instruments, oftentimes unwitting and unknowing, of outside interests, and regard both economic development and democracy as masks for an otherwise hidden agenda: to impose the policy and institutional framework of the new world order against resistance.

This apparent convergence between the Left and the Right in a critical assessment of ODA/NGOs points towards several problems involved in the use of the state as an instrument of political power. From a liberal reformist perspective the state should be strengthened but democratized in the service of a more inclusive and participatory approach towards policy design and implementation. From a neoliberal, politically conservative perspective, however, the state *is* the problem. On the one hand, it is an inefficient means of allocating the productive resources of the system. On the other hand, as Adam Smith argued, it is a predatory device with a tendency to serve special interests and used to capture rents from state-sponsored and regulated economic activities. The officials of the state, it is added by contemporary advocates of this view such as the economists at the World Bank, are subject to pressures that more often than not result in their corruption. The solution: a minimalist state, subject to the democratizing pressures from civil society (that is, groups and organizations able to secure the transparency of the policy-making process).

And what of the state as viewed through the lens of radical political economy? The state from this perspective is an instrument of class rule and by this token the fundamental repository of political power needed to turn the process of national development around—in a socialist direction. In this context, the essence of what is now widely regarded as the politics of the Old Left—or the Old Politics of the Left—is a struggle form state power. Both the political parties and the social movements on the Left tend to be oriented in this direction, albeit in a new political context that has seen the emergence on the Left of a new perspective on a new (postmodernist) way of doing politics—the politics of antipower: to avoid a confrontation and direct against the structures of political and economic power, instead by building on the social capital of the poor to engage in projects of local development within the spaces available within the power structure.

In the academic world the politics of state power are theoretically constructed in these ways. But what about the real world? In this context, and with specific reference to developments in Latin America, the main pattern of political development over the past two decades seems to have been a twofold devolution/involution of state power. On the one hand, the policy andt of political power (vis-à-vis macroeconomic policy) towards Washington-based "international" institutions such as the World Bank and the IMF. On the other hand, various democratic "reforms" has resulted in the institution of the "rule of law" and the decentralization of government from the centre to the local as well as a strengthening of civil society.

The latter development is characterized by, and based on, various forms of partnerships between international organizations and governments, on the one hand, and civil society organizations (CSOs) on the other. And this development was not happenstance. It is based on a conscious strategy pursued by each and all of the major representative organizations of global capital and the new world economic order—the imperial brain trust, as Salbuchi (2000) defines it. Among these organizations can be found the World Bank, the regional banks like the IDB, ODAs such as USAID, the Development Centre of the OECD, and operational agencies of the UN system such as the UNDP, ENEP, FAO and WHO. Each of these organizations since the early 1990s has pursued a partnership strategy with NGOs and other civil society organizations (CSOs), instituting an office to work with them, and officially registering those disposed to work with them in a common agenda of democratic development, poverty alleviation and environmental protection an alternative form of participatory, socially inclusive and "human" (economic and social) development.

In this context, much of the current academic discourse on the role of NGOs in the economic and political development process focus on the issue of improving their organizational effectiveness as well as their accountability—and their "autonomy" vis-à-vis governments and donor organizations. As for the latter, several umbrella organizations within the NGO sector have sought assiduously to ensure greater independence from both donors and the governments that hire "private voluntary organizations" (PVOs) to execute their projects and programs. Generally, however, these efforts have not met with any success. More often than not, as in the case of the US, the major NGOs have met not only resistance on the part of the donor community but also outright efforts to bring NGOs into line. In the case of USAID, in 2003 the director at the time bluntly informed an assembly of NGOs brought together by Interaction, an umbrella organization of NGOs, that they would have to do a better job acknowledging their ties to government, as private contractors of public policy, or risk losing funding. And, research indicates that many of these NGOs in recent years in fact have become increasingly dependent on this funding.

Some studies go so far as to argue that the presumed role of the NGO is a mirage that obscures the workings (and interests) of a powerful state (imperialism), various national elites and the predations of private capital. Hayden argues this from a conservative perspective (Hayden 2002). This chapter, however, argues the same point from a radical perspective on NGOs as agents of an imperialist project—private contractors of governments in the North. Governments in the South, in many cases, are only reluctantly and belatedly moving away from a somewhat skeptical, if not hostile, attitude—born of earlier experiences when NGOs set themselves as watchdogs of the state, particularly in terms of any propensities towards authoritarianism and corruption, with an agenda to promote democracy in its relation to civil society. In the context of widespread authoritarianism, violation of human rights, and other abuses of political power the NGOs throughout the 1980s had no fundamental problem in assuming their intermediary role in the front line of economic and political development. However, in the changed, more democratic context of the 1990s many NGOs began to experience serious concerns that, in effect (by design if not intent) they were advancing the agenda of the donors rather than that of the urban and rural poor, many of whom were not oriented towards alternative development and representative democracy but towards more substantive social change based on direct action and social movements—that is, popular democracy. In this context the major NGOs redoubled their efforts to secure greater autonomy from donors to be able to thereby respond better to the concerns and priorities of the popular movement. As a result, they tend to find themselves caught between a widespread concern to increase their independence from their sponsors and the efforts of these sponsoring organizations to incorporate them into the development and political process as strategic partners in a common agenda.

NGOs and the New Policy Agenda

In the 1980s organizations of international cooperation for development were fundamentally concerned to convert the PVOs into development agencies that could mediate between official aid providing agencies and grassroots communities in the delivery of ODA; and, in the same context, to promote democracy both in the relation of the state to civil society and in the politics of grassroots organizations—"good governance" in the official parlance (BID 1996; UNDP 1996a; Blair 1997; Mitlin 1998; OECD 1997).

In the late 1980s and early 1990s, there occurred a marked shift in practice signaled with a change in discourse—from a "third sector" discourse privileging NGOs to a civil society discourse that was more inclusive, particularly as regards profit-making enterprises and business associations that make up the "private sector" (Mitlin 1998). This shift in discourse coincided with a widespread recognition in official circles of the need to reform the structural adjustment program—to give it a social dimension (a new social policy) and the whole process a "human face" (Cornia *et al.* 1987; Salop, 1992). This change in discourse not only affected community-based development in terms of promoting a partnership between official development associations (donors and governments) and "civil society" organizations. It coincided with a worldwide, and international-level, shift towards the integration of multinational corporations, charitable institutions and UN agencies into public–private–partnerships (PPPs) that supposedly embody civil responsibilities that for-profit enterprises will not pursue. The development role of these PPPs is as current in the discourse as that of civil society.

The dominant political discourse in the 1980s reflected the political dynamics of an ideological shift from a state-centered or state-led development process to a market-led form of development based on the privatization of public enterprise. A "third-sector" discourse in this context represented a concern for an alternative more participatory form of development and politics predicated on neither the agency of the state ("from above") or the workings of the market ("from the outside") but initiated "from below" (within civil society). From the perspective of the ODAs, the IFIs, and governments, however, this discourse was problematic in various regards. For one thing, it was directed against both the market and the state, against public *and* private enterprise. For another, it worked against efforts of the ODAs to incorporate the private sector into the development process. The problem was twofold. One was how to overcome widespread antipathy towards profit-making "private" enterprise—to see it as part of a possible solution rather than as a major problem. Another was to convince the private sector operatives that profits can be made in the process of social development.

In regard to the second problem it remains a concern even into the twenty-first century, making it difficult for the UN's ongoing efforts to establish its "global compact" with the private sector (Utting 2000). As regards the first problem, however, a civil society discourse has proven to be both useful and effective. It has indeed allowed the ODA community to incorporate the private sector into the development project as a strategic partner in the process of economic growth and "sustainable human development." The perceived need for this was established by evaluation studies that suggested that NGOs did indeed provide a useful channel for ODA in regard to political development (promotion of democracy) and capacity-building/strengthening (social capital) but an inefficient means of activating production and employment and providing "financial services." In this regard, the conclusion was drawn that what was needed was a new strategy based on the agency of local governments working in partnership with ODAs and NGOs.

Matters of "Good Governance" and "Alternative Development"

The evolution of CBOs (community-based organizations) or GROs (grassroots organizations) within civil society illustrates the changed environment in which NGOs now operate. For Kamat it also points towards "grave implications" of the new scenario for "development, democracy and political stability" (Kamat 2003: 65). CBOs are locally based organizations that champion a "bottom-up" or "people-centered" approach towards development. They are, Kumar points out, and particularly vulnerable to what he somewhat surprisingly vies as "unexpected patronage" of the donor agencies. What is most surprising is that Kamat sees this patronage as "unexpected." Community-based or grassroots development organizations emerged in post World War II period in response to the failure of developmentalist states to ensure the basic needs of the poor—in the 1970s *the* declared development agenda of the ODAs and associated governments in the North. In this context, as well as a foreign policy concern with the spread of communism and the perceived impulse of some popular organizations and governments to take the road of social revolution towards development, USAID set up, sponsored, and financed a number (some 380 in the 1960s and 1970s) of US PVOs to act as private contractors of the government's agenda foreign policy agenda. A somewhat larger number of community-based organizations in Latin America were similarly financed and sponsored.

In many cases the leaders of these CBOs were, or had been, active in women's or radical left movements, who had become disillusioned with the politics of what would later be defined as the "Old Left." These CBOs generally favored a social rather than political approach towards development, with a concern for social justice and local issues. In this relatively apolitical context these CBOs were aggressively courted by both Northern NGOs and ODAs such as the World Bank that, to some extent, preferred to finance and support these "intermediary" or "local grassroots organizations" directly rather than work through the Northern NGOs. More often than not these CBOs accepted the financial support, if not tutelage, of the ODAs as a necessary evil and betimes even as a virtue (building the capacity for self-help and social capital).

The nature of their work requires CBOs (or "Intermediary Grassroots Organizations" in the World Bank's language) to interact directly with local communities on a daily basis, building relationships of cooperation and trust designed to understand local needs and tailor projects to these needs. The work of such social activists and organizations—identified as "non-party political formations"—often was and sometimes still is looked upon suspiciously by governments in the region, many of which, according to Ottoway, are democratic in form but not in content ("semi-authoritarian") and the target of democratization efforts. In the interest of "strengthening civil society" the ODAs increasingly have turned towards these CBOs rather than the NGOs as their executing agents. The dominant strategy, however, is based on partnership with local governments, CSOs and the private sector: an approach facilitated by widespread implementation of a decentralization policy (Rondinelli, McCullough and Johnson 1989).

The early history of the community development movement in the 1950s and the 1960s signified the emergence of a "pluralist democratic culture" in many developing countries as well as a concern for local development within the framework of liberal reforms of national policy. But the dominant trend was for economic and political development based on the agency of the central government and the state. However, in the new policy environment of "structural" free market reform this incipient democratic culture was cultivated by the return of civilian constitutional rule, and, at another level, by widespread policies of privatization and decentralization. With the retreat of the state from the economy and its social (and developmental) responsibilities it was left to "civil society" to pick up the slack—in the form of emergent self-help organizations of the urban poor and a myriad of community-based and nongovernmental organizations to deal with issues of social and economic development such as health, housing, food kitchens (comedores or communal dining halls), capacity building, and self-employment. The formation of this "civil society" was a predominant feature of the 1980s.

In the environment created by the "new economic model" of neoliberal free market capitalist development, CBOs became a useful, even essential, adjunct of the policies pursued by the donor agencies such as USAID—policies designed to promote the "capacity for self-help." The failure of a state-led model of economic development, combined with conditions of a fiscal crisis and weakened state infrastructure, as well as a decline in state entitlements to the poor, led the donor agencies to channel an even greater share of ODA (official transfers of international resources) through CBOs and a proliferating number of NGOs. In this connection, Gore, on the Vice-presidential campaign trail in 1994, is reported to have stated that within five years (1999) up to 50 percent of USAID would be so channeled. Similarly, *Financial Times* (July 2000) reported that the UK was also increasingly inclined to fund locally based NGOs directly, bypassing its own NGOs such as Oxfam.

The conjunction of a retreating minimalist state and the exponential increase in community-based NGOs led to the conclusion that the phenomenon was analogous to "the franchising of the state" (Kamat 2003: 66). In this context both the donor agencies and the IFIs recommended the privatization of both economic activity and social services—a trend that in any case was already underway—and the allocation of ODA to community-based NGOs for the same programs. Under these conditions the community-based "grassroots" NGOs proliferated as did the Northern NGOs anxious to occupy the spaces left by a retreating state.

The Evolution of Grassroots Community-based Organizations

The influx of external funds, combined with pressure to step into the spaces vacated by the state, forced many NGOs, particularly those that had "grassroots" or were community-based, to restructure their activities in line with a new partnership approach of the ODAs. In the process, according to Kamat, the organizational ethic that distinguished CBOs as "democratic" and representative of the popular will is being slowly undermined. First of all, CBOs generally have an active membership base within the communities in which they work, be they urban slum dwellers or poor peasant farmers. However, these "target" or "client" groups at the local level are themselves increasingly involved in efforts to "strengthening civil society"— incorporating them into decision-making processes at the local level. This form of direct or popular democracy both enthralls the donor agencies and the "social Left" but is also in conveniences the former and embarrasses the latter. On the one hand, it identifies the unique strength of NGOs, which, according to the World Bank, consists in "their ability to reach poor communities and remote areas, promote local participation, and operate at a low cost, identify local needs [and] build on local resources." On the either hand, direct democracy is inconvenient because of "its limited replicability, self-sustainability, managerial ... capacity, narrow context for programs and politicization" (Kamat 2003: 66).

It is in this context that NGOs are being slowly but surely transformed from organizations set up to serve the poor into what the World Bank has described as "operational NGOs"—private contractors of their policies that operate within "poor constituencies" with a more or less apolitical and managerial approach (micro project) but not rooted in or part of these communities. First of all, the implementation of local projects calls for training in specific skills rather than a more general education that involves an analysis of social and economic policies and processes. As a result, NGO after NGO has been forced to adapt a more narrowly economic and apolitical approach to working with the poor than had often been the case. At the same time, local participation in decision-making becomes limited to small-scale projects that draw on local resources with the injection of minimal external funds for poverty alleviation—and that are not predicated on substantial social change in the distribution of, and access to, local and national resources. In this context, local community groups are left to celebrate their "empowerment" (decision-making capacity vis-à-vis the distribution of local resources and the allocation of any poverty alleviation funds) while the powers-that-be retain their existing (and disproportionate) share of national and local resources—and the legal entitlement to their property without the pressure for radical change. In effect, the forced professionalization of the community-based NGOs, and their subsequent depoliticization, represent two sides of the same development, producing a common set of effects: to keep the existing power structure (vis-à-vis the distribution of society's resources) intact while promoting a degree (and a local form) of change and development.

Decentralization and Participation: Empowerment or Depoliticization?

According to ECLAC in its programmatic statement of an alternative to the neoliberal model (*Productive Transformation with Equity*), designed, like the UNDP model of "Sustainable Human Development" published in the same year (*Human Development Report* 1990), to give the Structural Adjustment Program a social dimension and the whole process a human face, "participation" is the "missing link" between the process of "productive transformation" (technological conversion of the production apparatus) and "equity" (expansion of the social basis of this apparatus). The World Bank had recently "discovered" that "participation" is a matter not only of "equity," as ECLAC understood it, but "economic efficiency" (without it projects tended to fail) but of "equity."

This recognition, stated as early as 1989, did not lead the Bank to adopt a more inclusive approach to macroeconomic policy, which, by all accounts, was profoundly exclusive, designed to benefit only those free enterprises that were both productive and competitive).

In any case, the World Bank is in essential agreement with all of the other operational agencies of the UN system that the decentralization of government, if not the state, is an indispensable condition for both a more democratic and participatory form of economic and social (that is, *integral* or *human*) development and for establishing a regime of "good [democratic] governance"—political order on the basis of as little government as possible but rather with what amounts to a "system of social control"—the concertation (or consensus) of civil organizations in society. On this basis, the Bank, like the IDB, has been a major advocate of the policies of decentralization as well as the virtues of local democracy and local development (World Bank 1994b; BID 1996; UNDP 1996a; OECD 1997; Rondinelli *et al.* 1989).

The new emphasis on project implementation at the local level provided by widespread implementation of administrative (and betimes financial) decentralization has had a number of effects. First, it has drawn attention away from the need for large-scale "structural" change in the allocation/distribution of society's productive resources. Development projects are implemented within the spaces available within or left by the structures of economic and political power—ownership and decision-making capacity in regards to society's productive resources. Second, it has resulted in a programmatic focus on individual capacities, minimizing the concern for the "structural" (social and political) causes of poverty, rejecting efforts to deal with them in a confrontational matter action and promoting instead pacific ("democratic") forms of political action: consultation, dialog, negotiations, etc.

This rather apolitical (social?) and managerial (micro project) approach to community development draws on the liberal notion of empowerment in which the poor are encouraged to find an entrepreneurial solution to their problems. In this context, OECD (2007: 30) defines its approach in terms of "helping people of the world develop their skills and abilities *to solve their own problems.*" As noted above, the World Bank adopted a strategy of "empowerment" and "participation"—at least at the level of rhetoric (without any effective or specific mechanisms for bringing about these conditions) in the interest not only of "equity" but also of "economic efficiency."

This entrepreneurial or neoliberal notion of empowerment is altogether different from the critical understanding of it as a form of alternative development promoted by CBOs. In this neoliberal discourse on empowerment the individual, as a repository of human resources (knowledge, skills, capacities to decide and act) is posited as both the problem and the solution to the problem of poverty. Of course, this is congruent with the utilitarian notion of the individual, when freed from government constraints imposed by the state, as an agent of rational choice (to maximize gain and minimize or avoid losses). It diverts attention from the issue of the state's responsibility to redistribute market-generated incomes and the perceived need for radical change not in the direction of the market but away from it.

The earlier "growth with equity" (redistributive growth/basic needs) approach of the liberal reformers in the 1970s was focused on the role of the state as an agency empowered to redistribute market-generated incomes via a policy of progressive taxation, redirecting this income to social and development programs designed to benefit not just the poor but the whole population—to meet their basic needs. However, at the level of the NGOs, this basic needs approach included in fact, if not by design, a policy of conscientization—educating the poor about structural and political issues such as the concentration of economic and political power in the hands (and institutions) of the elite and their own political rights. In the Latin American context *Acción Católica* was particularly oriented this way, its basis being Liberation Theology, implemented at the level of extension work in the form of pastorals. However, from the perspective of the donors this approach was problematic and even politically dangerous (that is, destabilizing) in that it could—

and in different contexts did—turn the poor to reach beyond institutional and policy reform (and "self-help" micro projects) towards more radical forms of change based on collective action, even social revolution.

The issue for the poor in this context was whether they should be empowered as individuals to take decisions related to local "self-help" development (basically how and where to spend poverty alleviation funds) or as part of a collective or community—to take direct action against the structure (and holders) of economic and political power. There is a significant political dimension to this issue. That is, does empowerment of the poor necessarily entail a relative disempowerment of the rich—forcing them to give up some of their "property" (share of society's productive resources and associated incomes) and to share with the poor their decision-making capacity or power? The politics of this question was clear enough, establishing for NGOs the role that they would come to play—not the role they would take for themselves but that which they were cast into as private contractors of public policy.

In the context of actual developments from the 1970s in this regard, the effect, has been not to empower the poor (increase their decision-making control over conditions that directly affected their livelihoods) but rather to depoliticize grassroots organizations of the poor—inhibiting the political mobilizing of forces of opposition to the "system." At most, poor communities have been "empowered" to take decisions as regards to how to spend the miserable and inadequate poverty alleviation funds that come their way. And this in exchange for a commitment to accept the existing institutionality and the macroeconomic policies which support it.

Studies in different countries as well as subsequent practice confirm this practice and the role of the NGOs in regard to it. For example, Mirafab traces the conversion of Mexican NGOs from organizations geared towards "deep structural change through consciousness, making demands and opposing the government" into organizations aimed at an "incremental improvement of the poor's living conditions through community self-reliance" (Kamat 2003: 69). This process was not unique to Mexico. Indeed, in cases too numerous to mention, community-based NGOs moved away from empowerment programs that involved the political organization of the poor based on conscientization (education about unfair government policies or inequitable social structures). Instead, at the behest of the donors, NGOs turned towards a "skills-training" approach to the mitigation of poverty by providing social and economic inputs (social capital) based on a technical assessment of the needs, capacities and assets of the poor.

The dynamics of this conversion process vis-à-vis the role of the NGOs can be summarized as follows. "Operational NGOs"—to use the World Bank's language—that established instrumental relationship with their constituencies in the marginal communities of rural and urban poor allow development experts to proceed as if the demands of the people are already known and predefined—demands such as roads, electricity, midday meals, birth control for women, micro credit and poultry farming, to name but a few. In this context, Kamat (2003: 65) notes, empowerment and participation are simulated by NGOs and their donor agencies even as their practices are increasingly removed from the meaning of these terms, which is to say, they are decapacitated or disempowered in regard to bringing about the changes needed to improve their access to society's productive resources.

The popularity of micro-credit or micro-finance projects in the practice of development can be understood in a context where the state is no longer primarily responsible for creating employment, let alone improving the access of the poor to society's productive resources such as land. In the context of the early 1980s there was a strong push to privatize the means of production and to deregulate markets, liberating the private sector from government constraint as well as emphasizing its role in regards to economic development. In this climate even the state's responsibilities ands funding in the area of social development (education, health and welfare, and social security) were cut back, shifting the former to the level of local governments and cutting back the latter in the interest of balancing the government's national accounts and budget. Empowerment of the poor, as noted by OECD and echoed by USAID and other donor organizations, in this context is defined as and means self-help—helping GROs help themselves.

However, Heloise Weber, in the same context, argues that micro finance and micro credit serve as a "coherent set of tools that may facilitate as well as govern the globalization agenda" (2002: 146). From "the perspective of the architects of global development," she writes, "the microcredit agenda is conducive to facilitating policy changes at the local level according to the logic of globalization ... while at the same time advancing its potential to discipline locally in the global governance agenda."

Rather than assisting the poor in improving their access to society's productive resources, the poor are not assisted in gaining greater access to society's productive resources, such as land (natural resources) financial capital (credit), or physical capital (technology). The poor are expected (with assistance, of course) to build on their own social capital—to enhance their own capacities vis-à-vis their livelihood security, achieving the sustainability of their livelihoods (UNRISD 2000).

Micro-credit programming and projects are well suited to this neoliberal context in which risks are shifted to the individual entrepreneurs, often poor women who are forced to compete for limited resources and opportunities in a very restricted market environment, The promise of livelihood security—and local development—thus translates into optimal utilization of one's own capacities and resources rather than working against the system. In this connection, Kamat (2003: 65) concludes that the "democratization" that NGOs represent is more symbolic than substantive. For the most part they are engaged in producing a particular kind of democracy that coincides with, and can function, within a neoliberal economic context.

In this context GROs that do not function within the "operational NGO" formula for implanting and managing development projects in a technical and professional manner, and that are instead engaged in the politicization of development issues such as livelihood security, health, and education, are delegitimized as anti-national and anti-development—as agents of the agenda set by the donors rather than the local communities. As a point of fact, these organizations, funded and mandated by the multilateral or bilateral donors, are usually concerned with making globalization work for the poor—an agenda adopted by all of the international development associations.

Democracy and Development: A Troubled Marriage

In the 1980s there emerged the idea that economic development, in the context of the globalization agenda of economic liberalization, either required or would bring about a process of political liberalization or democratization. And indeed, subsequent "developments" did appear to provide support to this notion of a marriage of convenience, if not strategy, between capitalism (in the form of the free market) and democracy in the form of free elections (Dominguez and Lowenthal 1996). However, this idea of an organic link between *capitalism* and *democracy*, between economic and political liberalization, was in fact new, a revision of an understanding that dominated the science of political development in the 1950s and 1960s and beyond. In this literature it was frequently argued that authoritarian forms of government, particularly military dictatorships such as the Pinochet regime in Chile, were better able to take the actions that would lead to an economic growth process. In any case, and for one reason or another, this understanding was reversed in the 1980s in the context of a widespread transition from one form or another of an authoritarian state—a widespread process of democratic renewal.

To cite just a few examples of the thinking about the connection between capitalism and democracy before the advent of a neoliberal approach, Walter Galenson in 1959 claimed that "the more democratic a government" the "greater the diversion of resources from investment in consumption." Karl Schweinitz similarly argued that if less developed countries "are to grow economically, they must limit democratic participation in political affairs" (Przeworski 2003: 42).

Joseph La Palombrana, another well-known exponent of the dominant modernization school of political thought, argued that "if economic development is the all-embracing goal, the logic of experience dictates that not too much attention can be paid to the trappings of democracy" (quoted in Przeworski 2003: 42). The conclusion drawn by these and other theorists of political development and policy makers at the time was clear. In the words of Samuel Huntington "political participation must be held down, at least temporarily" (Crozier, Huntington and Watanuki 1975).

At the same time, many of these same scholars assumed, or would argue, that whereas authoritarian forms of government were needed to generate economic growth, they would also self-destruct as a result of their own success. That is, economic development could generate conditions that might allow democracy to take hold. This, in fact, is a basic tenet of political modernization theory—that democratization is the likely end result of societies undergoing a universal process of development. This idea, incipient in many studies on political development in the 1950s, was widely disseminated, even popularized, by Seymour Lipset in his 1960 book *Political Man*. While doubts and concern lingered in the wake of this argument advanced by Huntington, Lipset and others, later "developments" in Chile set their minds at rest. The Pinochet military dictatorship was viewed as a case of the "most sweeping economic reforms in history" and a paradigm of "successful economic reforms." In fact, the "new economic model" constructed by the World Bank as a guide to policies of structural adjustment invoked and imposed in the 1980s and 1990s was based on this experiment in neoliberal economics in Chile. Subsequent developments of a democratic regime (albeit after 19 years of dictatorial rule—the last case of democratic transition in Latin America) and the most successful case of economic liberalization and liberalism in the region proved the point and validated the idea that economic liberalization would result in political democratization.

But the 1960s notion that dictatorships, often if not generally, promote economic development (see also the case of Brazil, Taiwan, and South Korea in this regard) was abandoned in the 1980s in the context of a neoliberal model that equated political and economic liberalization. First, the proposition that (political) democratization and (economic) development tend to go together has turned out to be false. History has simply thrown up for us too many counter-examples. Second, while the first round of authoritarian government experiments with neoliberal economics—in the context of military dictatorships in the southern cone of South America—all crashed and burned, the second round of these experiments was instituted by a series of democratically elected regimes formed under conditions of region-wide debt crisis that provided the World Bank and the IMF the leverage needed to push governments in the region to use the "new economic model" as a guide to economic policy reform.

In the space of a few years (1983 to 1989) virtually all regimes, mostly democratic in form, either out of conviction or (more often) under duress, turned towards a program of free market structural (neoliberal) reforms. At the turn into the next decade, with the last of the generals having returned to their barracks, those few governments that had not turned neoliberal did so, implementing—in the case of holdout countries (Argentina, Peru, and Brazil)—some of the most radical programs of structural adjustment seen to that date.

In each case it might appear that a process of democratic renewal led to economic liberalization at the level of macroeconomic policy. However, the sequence of developments, and the dynamics involved, do not support neoliberal thought. What can be concluded from a brief review of historical developments in the region is that the international financial institutions in the early 1980s were in a position to impose the Washington consensus on macroeconomic policy and, at the same time, to push for a renewal of democracy in the region—democracy defined at two levels: a respect for the rule of law and the virtue of free elections in the constitution of regimes; and the strengthening of civil society as a means of providing greater accountability of elected officials and public participation in the formulation of public policy. In regard to the former, the historic record shows a relatively dismal record in generating the expected economic growth and greater success, albeit not intentionally, in generating movements of political protest against neoliberal policies. As for the latter, the historic record points towards a mixed record manifest in the emergence of "semi-authoritarian" regimes that adopt the "form" of democracy but disrespect its content.

Argentina under the presidency of Carlos Menem and Brazil under Fernando Cardoso, as well as Chile under various post-Pinochet democratic *concertación* regimes, at different points (in the 1990s) were viewed as paradigm cases of successful economic development brought about by a democratic regime on the basis of the Washington consensus on macroeconomic policy. That is, they are viewed as good examples of a trend towards the marriage of liberal democracy and free market capitalist development in the broader context of globalization. The experience of these countries, as well as Mexico towards the end of the 1990s, laid to rest the notion of a necessary trade-off between democracy and development, although, it has to be said, the flames of lingering doubts have been rekindled by developments in Argentina after 1998 (five years of the country's deepest and most severe economic and political crisis) and the experience of countries that are in a process of transition from socialism to capitalism.

In regards to this process of transition the problem—for neoliberal thought vis-à-vis the organic link between capitalism and democracy—is that after a decade of democratic reforms and untrammeled free market capitalist development, Russia and Eastern Europe have failed to recover a level of economic development achieved in earlier decades within the institutional confines of a socialist model. At the same time, several countries in Asia, notably China, have made explosive advances in the level of economic growth—with growth rates, in the case of china, of 10 percent per annum sustained for over a decade—on the basis of a model of capitalist development but within the framework of a non-democratic form of political development. Indeed, the experience of China has revived the specter of modernization theory—that economic development is best advanced on the basis of a non-democratic form of government. That is, China has revived the idea that it is possible to embark on a program of economic liberalization without at the same time provoking or turning towards a similar process at the political level. Despite the continuing, at times heated, rhetoric on this issue both in academic and "official" policy-making circles, the jury, as it were, is still out, although it could be pointed out that China, having made the judgement that the country could be inserted into the global economy under favorable conditions and a positive outcome, has turned towards a capitalist model of economic development without liberalizing either the political system or, more to the point, the economy.

As for countries in other parts of the "developing world" that have undergone a process of democratic renewal, and that have instituted all the trappings of liberal or representative democracy at the national level, the promoters and guardians of democracy have discovered that, in many cases (ranging from Venezuela in South America to Senegal in Africa), democracy is encountering a new challenge: the emergence of semi-authoritarian regimes that pay lip service to the forms of democracy while disregarding its substance in practice.

For a number of scholars, such as those connected to the Carnegie Endowment for Peace and the *Harvard International Review*, the emergence of so many fragile democracies, failed states, and semi-authoritarian regimes in the Third World represents a "development dilemma": "democracy or bust" (Chan 2001). The dilemma is this. On the one hand, as noted by Amartya Sen, winner of the 1998 Nobel Prize for Economics, "the most important thing that ... happened in the twentieth century [was] democracy." On the other hand, the value of democracy to many developing countries is by no means clear. Democracy and development are not necessarily correlated and the proposed marriage between elections (democracy) and the free market (capitalism) might very well not work; in fact, in some situations it might be dysfunctional.

The possible dysfunctionality of combining democracy and capitalist development arises precisely in the context of widespread implantation of the new economic model. In this context, the experience of many countries with democracy and capitalism has been nothing less than disastrous. In Argentina, the result was a country pushed to the brink of financial crisis and a situation of economic regression rather than development. Nevertheless, the experience of so many developing countries in the 1990s does not argue for an abandonment of democracy as a preferred form of political development. In fact, the problem is that this form of development—the institution of democratic regimes—combined with pressures arising out of efforts to join the globalization project, allowed for an assault on the capacity of these states to make policy and on their efforts to institute democracy.

In this regard, there is clear and substantial evidence that macroeconomic policy for many of these countries was set and designed in Washington and imposed on these regimes as a condition for accessing the financial resources of the global economy. In addition, the policy of privatization implemented under these conditions has in a number of cases not only diminished the capacity to advance a process of economic and social development but also resulted in a process of denationalization policy as regards control over the country's stock of natural resources. In effect, decision-making in critical areas were transferred to international organizations and financial institutions that are profoundly undemocratic in that they are not in the least representative of the populations affected by their policies and actions, their actions are far from transparent, and they are not accountable to any electorate.

In this context, Chan (1991: 23) argues that "developing nations themselves must determine the best form of governance and the best economic policy that will drive their economies forward." The problem is that this would require a substantial change in the behavior of institutions that at one level insist on good democratic governance but that at a different level they undermine the institution of substantive (as opposed to formal) democracy. That is, the issue is not the failure of regime leaders to respect the form but not the substance of democracy; it is the contradictory workings of international institutions set up and controlled by the self-appointed guardians of the "New World Order." "As Przeworski notes, under conditions that prevail in the global economy, the marriage of democracy and free market capitalist development provides a flawed blueprint" for action by the regimes governing developing countries. It might very well be that these regimes would prefer a different development path or an alternative institutional and policy framework for their national development.

NGOs and the Imperial Agenda

The institution of a democratically elected regime and the rule of law are parts of the democratization/good governance strategy currently pursued by many developing countries under the aegis of the World Bank and other international development organizations. Other critical dimensions of this strategy include: (1) effecting a change in the power relationship between civil society and the state; (2) strengthening "civil society" in regard to its capacity to participate in the formulation of public policy; and (3) empowering the poor via the accumulation of their "social capital."

The major institutional or structural means for bringing about democratization in this form has been the decentralization, a policy instituted by many countries across the world in the 1980s. Decentralization has taken diverse forms but most generally involves a delegation of government responsibilities and policy-making capacity from the center to lower levels of government. Ironically, it was Pinochet in the early 1970s who pioneered this policy, as well as the package of "sweeping economic reforms" used by the World Bank to construct its neoliberal program of structural adjustment reforms. It was in regard to this policy of decentralization that Pinochet spoke of "teaching the world a lesson in democracy"—what the Bank (World Bank 1989b, 1994b) came to define as "good governance:" rule by social consensus based on the participation of people and local communities in decisions that relate to conditions directly affect them. At issue in this policy is "popular participation," conceived of by ECLAC as "the missing link" between the neoliberal concern with "productive transformation" and the principle of "equity" promoted by structuralists and social reformists. In the 1980s this notion of "popular participation" would be enshrined in the notion of "good governance" as well and treated as a fundamental principle of project design and the delivery of both development assistance and government services. Popular participation in these optics and Bank programming is seen as a matter not only of "equity" but also of "efficiency" as well as "good governance."

Behind this notion of "good governance" is the concern to establish the political conditions needed to implement the new economic model of free market capitalist development—to ensure the capacity and the political will of national governments to "stay the course" (structural adjustment, globalization) and thereby the stability of the new world economic order. And, of course, even more important, are the operational and political conditions needed to subjugate the local (national) economies and "emerging markets" to the dictates of global capital in its corporate and financial forms. This is the agenda of US or Euro-American imperialism. As we have shown, it is this agenda that defines the ideology of globalization and the agency of organizations involved in the international development project. Both globalization and development as geo-strategic "meta-projects" can be unmasked as disguised forms of imperialism, which raises serious questions about the role of NGOs in the process.

Our conclusion is that these organizations have played, and continue to play, an important role in advancing the imperialist agenda. These "civil society" (or "nongovernmental") organizations have been formed in both the "third sector" of voluntary associations (PVOs) and the "private sector" of profit-oriented capitalist enterprises. In the 1970s many PVOs were converted into frontline "development" agencies—to spread the good word about the virtues of social and political reform, and to offset growing pressure for revolutionary change; to provide a nonsystematic alternative in the form of rural integrated development micro projects. In the 1980s, in a different context (an external debt crisis, implementation of a new economic model, privatization and state reform, democratization), a rapidly growing and proliferating sector of NGOs were enlisted in the "war against poverty" as agents of (popular) democracy and (alternative) development—as partners in the enterprise of economic, social, and political development; and, in the process, as bearers of the virtues of a nonconfrontational approach towards social change.

In the 1990s this process was consolidated, creating conditions that would facilitate the workings of Euro-American imperialism. A critical factor in this consolidation was the creation, at the level of the state, of a series of client regimes committed to a neoliberal model of capitalist development and globalization. However, another factor, just as critical, was the incorporation of "civil society" into the process of development and democratization. One part of "civil society," organized in the form of social movements, engaged the political project of opposition to neoliberalism and globalization—mobilizing the forces of resistance into a counter-hegemonic bloc and opposing the imperialist agenda. However, another part of "civil society," in the form of nongovernmental development organizations, has been complicit with Euro-American imperialism, providing it an important ideological and political service. In this regard the actual intent of these NGOs is not the issue. In many cases the individuals involved in these organizations believe that they are in acting in the interest of the local communities, providing "the poor" essential services and benefits. The issue is whose interests, in fact, are served by their "actions" as agents of "development." On this point we need say no more.

PART 2
The Regional Macrodynamics of Globalization

Chapter 4

Denationalizing Mexico:
The World Bank in Action

John Saxe-Fernández and Gian Carlo Delgado-Ramos

To reflect on the processes of economic internationalization requires a serious effort to identify the specific agents involved as well as to gauge the weight and effect of their actions. These agents or agencies include the capitalist states at both the center and the periphery of the world capitalist system (hereinafter CCSs and PCSs), the multinational corporations (MNCs) that roam the world in search of profit-making opportunities and the international organizations that dominate the world economy. An indispensable step in this analysis is to elaborate a "situational frame" that allows us to delineate the relations of domination and subordination that exist at this level.

After taking this first step we proceed towards a deconstruction of the workings of the US imperial state in Mexico via the agency of the World Bank. The secular empire of the World Bank group of international financial institutions (hereinafter the WBG) is analyzed in some detail with regard to efforts to exploit and gain control of one of Mexico's largest pools of strategic productive resources and wealth. The processes of privatization and denationalization involved in these efforts could be analyzed in terms of the major assaults made in recent years against Mexico's agricultural production, its water resources and other areas of the country's biodiversity. In this paper, however, we concentrate on the World Bank's imperial strategy with regards to Mexico's oil resources and associated petrochemicals industry.

The operations of the World Bank in Mexico can be categorized and periodized in two phases, the second of which roughly corresponds to the implementation of the "new economic model" (neoliberalism) in the wake of "the debt crisis" (1982–3). With regard to the first phase, we focus on the political dynamics of the conditionalities attached to World Bank loans—and the political leverage gained over government economic policy by these means. We first examine some paradigmatic examples of World Bank loans in the first phase of Bank operations in Mexico. We then proceed with the documentation, and analysis, of some of the World Bank's principal Mexican operations in regard to the privatization and denationalization (extranjerización) of resources that are of vital economic and political importance. This analysis relates to the second phase of World Bank operations. In the interest of brevity we limit our discussion here to the production of oil and the associated petrochemicals industry.

In the conclusion we provide some final considerations on the impact of the World Bank's operations in Mexico on behalf of the US imperial state.

A Situational Frame: A Matter of Analysis

At issue in our analysis is the persistence of assymetrical relations of imperialism and colonialism that after Bretton Woods were maintained but took on a new or different form, preserving operations of economic exploitation between the center and the periphery while the formal institutions of colonial rule were generally abandoned. Thus, with reference to the *modus operandi* of the World Bank group of institutions[1] and associated institutional "actors" such as the Inter-American Development Bank (IDB), the Global Environmental Facility (GEF) and the Economic Commission for Latin America and the Caribbean (ECLAC), we will undertake a critical analysis of the role of these institutions in inducing a process of denationalization of Mexico's strategic assets in the guise of "privatization." We explore this process in the geoeconomic and political context of Mexico, and with particular reference to the sociopolitical and military–strategic outcomes of this denationalization process, categorized by James Petras, an American political sociologist, as a "cogovernment."

Petras (1987: 28–30) distinguishes between three types of relations that exist between the WBG and peripheral capitalist or "Third World" states—relations of (1) subordination; (2) convergence on the basis of unequal and coerced agreements; and (3) negotiation and resistance.[2] This categorization corrects a number of the epistemological vices characteristic of the euphoric, abstract, and deterministic discourse on "globalization," enabling him to reincorporate the power equation as an indispensable frame of reference in the study of economic internationalization and, at the same time, to analyze the changing correlation of changes in the correlation of internal and external forces.

This perspective can be contrasted with that of those theorists who view "globalization" as if it unfolds in a power vacuum—as the result of the automatic, if hidden, workings of the "free market." A countercurrent to this conventional or mainstream approach proceeds by identifying the instruments of state and class wielded from the imperial power in the North via what Costa Rican ex-president Rodrigo Carazo terms the World Bank's "*country managers* in the South" (Saxe-Fernández 1999: 9–68; 2001). In these terms one of the the aims of this chapter is to expose the relations of power inherent in, and the political–institutional parameters of, what is widely known as "globalization."

In this context it makes sense to ask whether there exists any empirical basis for the widespread notion of a self-regulating world economic system that is beyond political control. Alternatively, does it make sense to speak and write of national economies across the world that have been inserted into the system by means of

---

1 The WBG is organized by region (East Asia and the Pacific, South Asia, Sub-Saharan Africa, Middle East and North Africa, Europe and Central Asia, Latin America and the Caribbean) and is composed of the World Bank itself (the International Bank for Reconstruction and Development), the International Development Association (IDA), the International Finance Corporation (IFC), the Multilateral Investment Guarantee Agency (MIGA) and the International Center for Settlement of Investment Disputes (www.worldbank. org).

2   See also Saxe-Fernández (1989: 7a–8a).

the automatic processes of the "world market?" Is it possible to view markets and production systems, and the world economy overall, as essentially self-regulated? If these questions can be answered in the affirmative then the regulatory mechanisms of the state, both in the North and in the South, vis-à-vis the operations of the MNCs are increasingly obsolete or irrelevant (Saxe-Fernández *et al.* 2001: 12–13; Petras 2001: 33–85; Bellamy 2002: 1–16). One would have, in effect, a world of weak or powerless states, dominated by the global reach and economic power of stateless corporations.

Nevertheless, both historically and in the current context, international economic transactions have always taken place within a "cauldron of power" centered on the relationship between, on the one hand, the CCSs and their instruments of hegemonic projection such as the WBG of international financial institutions, and, on the other, the MNCs (Kolko and Kolko 1972; Magdoff 1978). In this context, far from being "stateless" virtually all the MNCs operate across the world from a home base in a nation-state (Hirst and Thompson 1996; Doremus *et al.* 2000; Petras and Veltmeyer 2001).

As Harry Magdoff (1978: 183) has put it: "it is necessary to recognize that each capitalist firm relates to the world system through, and must eventually rely on, the nation state." At issue is an imperial state that regulates and protects its MNCs, providing them all manner of subsidies whether these be charged to the public purse or take the form of pressures exerted through diverse financial or economic, political or diplomatic channels—or the projection of military power. This point is made by Diaz-Polanco (2002: 59) in the following terms:

> it is not the free development of the market that determines politics, but it is politics (via the formidable weapon of the nation-state) that defines the direction and behaviour of markets. It is not ... the impersonal forces [of the market] but powerful interest groups, with their human and contingent aims that make decisions, project and implement strategies of capital ... the so-called "globalization" is in reality a political project that is clearly designed [within the centre of power] and that allows the holders of this power to use their preeminent position in the countries at the centre and on the periphery, and its international financial institutions, to impose their policies and appropriate wealth and use of the nation-state.

The history, evolution and current behavior of the WBG validate this perspective. It is worth noting in this regard that after World War II, the United States and its principal European allies considered it inadvisable to maintain the form of political colonialism that had hitherto characterized the international economic system. However, it was necessary to substitute for this system another that permitted the continuation of imperialist control over, and exploitation of, the natural resources and markets of capitalism's peripheral areas. To this purpose they designed a new international economic architecture that would secure the avoidance of another "great depression," the nodal point of the complex causality of World War II and the likely cause of another. The fundamental motivation behind US foreign policy, then as now, was to place the rest of the world under the dominion of institutionalized principles that reflect its economic and geostrategic interests. The IMF and the World Bank were designed for this purpose, as was the World Trade Organization

(WTO) some 50 years later. These Bretton Woods institutions were so designed, via the voting mechanism, that Washington could dominate their policies and foment programs that would facilitate the growth of its "private sector." Those mechanisms were meant for the mutual protection and enhancement of their strategies. For this "reason" membership in the IMF is a prerequisite for incorporation into the World Bank. The architects of this system, according to Joyce and Gabriel Kolko:

> designed [these institutions] not merely to implement disinterested principles but to reflect the United States control of the majority of the world's monetary gold and its ability to provide a large part or its future capital. The IBRD (BM) was tailored to give a governmentally assured framework for future private capital investment, much of which would be American. (Kolko and Kolko 1972: 16)

Although these instruments—to which GATT (the General Agreement on Tariffs and Trade, now the WTO) would be added—were designed as a substitute for the pre-war colonial system and in no way was it intended to transform the system in such as a way as to deny the new hegmonic power (the US) and its allies access to the natural resources, cheap labor and markets of "the South." Indeed the system was so designed as to mantain for the countries "at the center" (North) a favorable balance in terms of international transfers of "productive resources" and economic surplus. And, as argued by the economists at ECLAC,[3] this was particularly the case for the United States vis-à-vis Latin America and the Caribbean (González-Casanova 1999; Saxe-Fernández and Núñez 2001: 87–166).

The end of the *belle epoque* by the end of World War II led to the weakening and collapse of colonial institutions based on the principles and institutions of British "free trade" (the forced exchange, by the colonies, of raw materials, for imperial manufactured goods), making it impossible to maintain colonialism in its traditional form and, as indicated, leading to the elaboration of new mechanisms of economic exploitation. "The only solution," as noted by Edward Goldsmith (1999), "was to open our markets to the countries in the Third World, incorporating them into the industrial system within the orbit of our commerce." This, he added, "was the essence of the Bretton Woods conference."

In Bretton Woods as well as subsequent summit meetings, to set in motion a worldwide process of financial reorganization, Washington characterized the resulting institutions as "multilateral" or "international" when in reality they were fundamentally conceived of as an important part of the *Pax Americana*, and, as such, a means of exercising a specific form of "selective bilateralism." In this agenda, the United States also consolidated its projection of the dollar as the major international currency and standard of exchange (Kolko and Kolko 1972: 84).

The idea was to create a complex of "international" institutions, whose control by the United States was guaranteed by means of an internal voting system based on the principle of "one dollar, one vote." The case of the IMF is illustrative. According to Section 2-c (Adjustment of Quotas), Article III (Quotas and Subscriptions) of the

---

3   Variations on this argument formed the crux of the theory constructed by exponents of what came to be known as "Latin American structuralism"—a school of thought initiated by, and still associated with, ECLAC.

Agreements of the IMF, "an 85 percent majority of the total voting power shall be required for any change in quotas." Because of the capital that it has contributed, the US can count on 17.16 percent of all the votes (Borón 2001: 46). In contrast, China and India, with more than a third of the world population, barely have a 4.88 percent of the voting power. As a result, the United States can block any actions that it sees as contrary to its interests and, at the same time, it can count on the support of "allies" on a "quid pro quo" basis. Moreover, as a crucial aspect of the IMF is the formalization of impunity vis-à-vis the national and international normative system. Section 3 (Immunity from Judicial Process), Article IX (Status Immunities and Privileges) of the *Agreements of the IMF* reads as follows: "The Fund, its properties and its assets, wherever located and by whosoever held, shall enjoy immunity from every form of judicial process except to the extent that it expressly waives its immunity for the purpose of any proceedings or by the terms of any contract." According to Section 9 of the same Article, "All Governors, Executive Directors, Alternates, members of the committees, representatives ... advisors of any of the foregoing persons, officers and employees of the Fund: (i) shall be immune from legal process ... except when the Fund waives this immunity" (www.imf.org).

In effect, we have here a "New International Order" in which, as explained by former Secretary of the Treasurer, Henry Morgenthau, "international trade and international investment can be carried on by businessmen on business principles" (Senate Committee on Banking and Currency, Bretton Woods Agreement, cited in Kolko and Kolko 1972). The specialists of the Department of State at the time were emphatic in their recognition that this state of affairs could only be achieved on the basis of institutions that operated with the principles "of free trade and private enterprise, the conceptual nucleus of the foreign policy of the United States" (Kolko, 1974: 698). And, they added, "this [foreign policy goal] was incompatible with an extensive growth of state property and with commerce in state hands."

These principles have been maintained to this very day as evident in the IMF"s webpage (http://www.imf.org/external/about.htm): "since the IMF was established in 1946, its purposes have remained unchanged but its operations—which involve surveillance, financial assistance, and technical assistance—have developed to meet the changing needs of its member countries in an evolving world economy."

The aforementioned has led to a policy of the privatization and decentralization of strategic national assets, including "natural assets" such as biodiversity and water. It is the International Finance Corporation (IFC), within the World Bank system, together with the Global Environmental Facility (GEF), that has been the major "actor" in this regard. As noted on the GEF (http://www.gefweb.org): "the World Bank, in its role as a GEF implementing agency, should play the primary role in ensuring the development and management of investment projects. ... The World Bank draws upon the investment experience of its affiliate, the International Finance Corporation (IFC) ... to promote investment opportunities and to mobilize private sector resources."

We have here the institution of the IFC, as part of the WBG, as an agent for articulating relations of cooperation among various international "partner" institutions including the MNCs and "host" nation-states with their governments. The IFC, in effect, has positioned itself, as of the 1980s, as the launching platform for projects not only of privatization but of the denationalization of the strategic assets of countries on the periphery. In this context, it operates in a very convoluted manner to hide the true beneficiaries of its program. The IFC "promotes sustainable private sector development primarily by a) financing private sector projects located in the developing world b) helping private companies in the developing world mobilize financing in international financial markets c) providing advice and technical assistance to businesses and governments" (www.ifc.org).

The IFC's actions are organized and implemented through diverse interconnected working "clusters" and "sub-clusters." Invariably, at the end of this "clustering" process the primary, if not exclusive, beneficiaries are selected, usually US- or EC-based, MNCs.[4]

The World Bank in Mexico

A review of the World Bank's major operations in Mexico demonstrate in concrete form the operational principles of US imperialism synthesized above. These operations can also be found in other PCSs, particularly in Latin America where facilitating or enabling conditions for the penetration of US capital have been generated by close to two decades of neoliberal policies. These conditions threaten to deepen under Plan Pueblo Panama (PPP) and the proposed formation of a Free Trade Area [in] the Americas (FTAA).

It is possible to distinguish two major phases of the World Bank's operations in Mexico. The first dates from the launching of the Bank to the mid-1970s and the beginnings of the 1980s; it relates to the import substitution model of industrial development. The second represents the neoliberal model, implemented under conditions of a widespread "debt crisis" (in 1982), based on what has become known as the "Washington Consensus" (Williamson 1990).[5]

The impact of the World Bank and related institutions on the structure and intra-institutional dynamics of Mexico's economy were extended and deepened throughout the 1980s with the growth of the national debt and the servicing of this debt by the government. Undue influence on the dynamics of government policy

---

4   For example, the BPD Water and Sanitation cluster includes MNCs such as Vivendi, Ondeo (Suez) and Thames Water. In the BPD Natural Resources cluster we have Conservations International, USAID, IDB, UNEP, UNDP, GEF, and WTO; in the BPD Global Road Safety Partnership, 3M, Daimler-Chrysler, Ford Motor Co., and Royal Dutch/Shell Group. In the "Best practices in dealing with the social impacts of oil and gas operations" cluster are: BP Amoco, Chevron, Conoco, Exxon Mobil, Shell, Conservational International, and the World Wildlife Fund.

5   In both periods the economic and financial characteristics of World Bank supported projects indicate systematic efforts to promote the interests of the CCS, particularly the US state. The Executive Briefs on government loans and debts elaborated by the Nacional Financiera focused on the 1970s but the analysis and conclusions are compatible with the first phase of World Bank operations in Latin America. Contrary to the experience in Asia it relates to the import substitution model based on, *inter alia*, a high level of dependence on FDI, private bank loans and, consequently, on the WBG and MNCs in the design of national policy.

applied particularly to the IMF at the macroeconomic level and the WB in regard to sectoral programs. This influence was particularly strong in regards to the Secretaries of State and in the executing agencies vis-à-vis new loans.

In the first phase of Bank operations (up to the 1982 crisis) projects were managed and supervised by the Fideicomiso of the Banco de Mexico and later by Banxico; others were managed by the National Fund for Tourism (Fondo Nacional para el Turismo), the Secretary of Agriculture and Water Resources (Secretaría de Agricultura y Recursos Hidráulicos), the Secretary of Ports and National Railways (Ferrocarriles Nacionales de México), the Federal Electric Power Commission (Comisión Federal de Electricidad), the secretary of Budgeting (Secretaría de Programación y Presupuesto), Fertilizantes de México, the National Bank of [Public] Works (Banco Nacional de Obras), Nafinsa, the Rural Bank (Banco Rural), and so on.

Loans always include commission payments, a formal and legally established procedure in international agreements. Within the framework of international law, they refer to stipulated amounts (generally a percentage negotiated on the basis of the total amount of capital borrowed) to be paid once the operation is approved— although the project in question has not been approved by either the executive or the legislature of the host country. Thus, even though approved funds have not been disbursed, the "loan" begins to incur interest and generate profits for the creditor, the cost of which is added to the total amount of the debt owed. In this way, the WBG (World Bank, IMF, IDB, etc.) receives both a commission and interest payments on top of the money borrowed, as negotiated by the Executive and invariably approved by the Legislature. We can add to this the mechanisms used by the Bank to *jinetear* ("jockey") the amount borrowed, paid out in *tramos* ("tranches"),[6] for other investments. *Tramos* are also functional for the power exercised by the Bank over the PCS because of the "conditionalities" and performance schedule attached to them.

In the first phase the emphasis was on construction or the improvement of communications infrastructure as part of the Bank's effort to promote North– South trade and the position of the MNCs in this trade, particularly in the US's Latin America's periphery. The hegemony of the CCS in this phase is manifest in the dominant position of their MNCs in regard to both exports and domestic markets. Unlike Asia where national firms, on the basis of domestic savings and investment strategy dominated the home market, in Latin America these markets were dominated by the MNCs (Petras and Veltmeyer 1999).

Returning to the Mexico case, loans for infrastructural loans and for other activities in agriculture, mining, industry, services, housing, etc., tended to have a national component, generally 50 percent. But in each case the participation creditor country enterprises, principally from the United States, is part and parcel of the "conditionalities" attached to the lines of credit extended—and facilitated—by the Bank. Thus the World Bank not only directed how and where borrowed money was

---

6　By *a jinetear* (jockeying) we refer to the speculative or productive use of funds *no erogados de un préstamo dado*. Thus, while the Bank charges interest on the total amount owed, the debtor actually disposes of only a part of the funds.

to be used but it set parameters on the investment and use of public funds derived from taxes collected from the Mexican population. This is also a characteristic of developments in the second phase (see below) but with even greater intensity.

Some pradigmatic examples of World Bank loans (first period)

In May 1972 the Secretariat of the Navy sought funds of US $42 million to upgrade port facilities. The project, approved by the Bank, includes the purchase of dredging equipment; storage, warehousing and communications systems; loading and fire protection equipment; and consulting services and personnel training (World Bank n.d.). The Bank's participation in the funding (820 ME) was in the form of a $20 million loan. Its agreement commission, in this case, was US $429 million; the interest rate 7.25 percent; and interest payments (up to March 1977) were US $9,650 million.

It would not be incorrect to suggest that the central concern in this and other cases was not to stimulate development in the debtor country but to strengthen various private interests in the creditor country, in this case, the United States. Although the dominant paradigm was "import substitution industrialization," all equipment acquisitions were made through creditor country MNCs. Of the group of foreign enterprises that directly benefited in this way—including Seadrec Ltd Dubigean Normandie, Sumimoto, Shoji Kcuslea, Ltd—six were American, one was English, one French, one Canadian, one Swiss and one Japanese. Collectively these MNCs received US $15,480,249 in loan funds.

As for the various railway "projects" approved and funded by the World Bank in the same period they were not generally directed towards their indirect control—and the privatization of FNM—as was the case throughout the 1980s and 1990s. The aim, instead, was to ensure the modernization of the system and increased capacity vis-à-vis commerce between Mexico and the United States; that is, Mexico's exports of minerals, petroleum and other raw materials, and its importing of goods manufactured in the United States.

The World Bank's "Second Railroad Loan" (June 1972) of US $75 million was not paid off for another 25 years but by September 1977, five years into the loan, had already generated close to US $53 million in interest payments. Into the 1990s the government was still meeting interest payments of US $125 million even though the Bank itself pushed for the dismantling, privatization, and denationalization of state enterprises. As in most of the Bank's pre-privatization "loans" funds directed towards the national railroad system were designed to privatize (and denationalize) profits and to socialize (nationalize) the costs. For a bonus, the Bank in this case favored Motorola Communication Division (US), Sidney Steel Corp. (Nova Scotia), Nippon Electric (Japan), and la empresa maderera Hondumex, a forest products company registered in Honduras.

The World Bank's "third Railroad Project" loan (11232 ME) for US $100 million was negotiated in 1976, with the last "tranche" payment set for November 2000. The agreement commission was US $2,526,000 and interest payments were US $16,258,000. Beneficiaries included 35 US-based MNCs, six Japanese, two English, one German and a Dutch one. The World Bank doled out to these MNCs a total of US

$94 million, including US $3 million for Missouri Pacific Railroad; US $21 million for Nippon Electric; US $2.3 million for NAB International; US $4.9 million for Koyo International; US $16.6 million for Sidney Steel; US $3.3 million for Breuco Inc; US $6.8 million for Multisystems Inc; US $6.8 million for Fruit Grower. Most of the remaining funds went to scores of small or medium-sized firms, mostly American.

A paradigmatic case of World Bank loans, under the rubric of "import substitution" in the industrial sector was 1205 ME, negotiated by Banxico and designed to "finance fixed assets and feasibility studies for Mexican industrial firms that produce goods and services for exports [and thus[reduce imports [for the country]." The project, financed with US$50 million, was signed in April 1976, with a grace period of two years and ten months, and the last "tranche" of capital between February 15, 1979 and August 15, 1992. The interest rate for the loan was 8.5 percent and interest payments were set at US $15,133,000, with another US $732 million in the form of an Agreement Commission. Two thirds of the firms favored with a "contract"—collectively worth US $37 million—were US-based MNCs. With the participation of over 300 firms the actual amounts involved per firm is not large, but everything indicates that the aim of the Bank was to inhibit development of a national sector of machine tooling and railroad stock, displacing Mexican firms in the industry with foreign ones and opening up spaces for MNCs in the domestic market. The World Bank program, in effect if not by design, served to promote US and European Community exports and to create conditions for the concentration of capital and the virtual dismantling of the national industry in machine tools and metallurgy. Under NAFTA, initiated on January 1, 1994, the same day on which the Zapatistas exploded onto the national—and world—scene, this "development" would be accelerated.

Another interesting case involved FERTIMEX, a *paraestatal* or state enterprise in the agricultural sector, whose privatization was brought about with the considerable "aid" of the WB. The loan (1112 ME) for FERTIMEX I was for US $50 million. It was negotiated and signed in May 1975 with a grace period of three years and eight months and a final "tranche" payment in July 1989. It was directed towards the construction of diverse plants to produce the basic ingredients for fertilizers. One example is the urea plant in Coatzacoalcos, Veracruz, with a capacity of a half a million metric tonnes annually. Another is in Salamanca, Guanajuato, with an annual production capacity of 330,000 metric tonnes.

A central notion behind FERTIMEX I and most infrastructure loans, as shown above, is not only to stimulate MNC operations but also to promote small and medium firms in creditor countries. In this case, 100 percent of equipment and materials, valued at an estimated US $33 million, together with all engineering and consulting services, as emphasized in the document, were "imported" from "outside the country." In this case the beneficiaries (of US $30 million in contracts) included 111 US firms; seven others were Italian, three of them German, three Japanese, one was from Israel and one was French.[7]

---

7   Principal beneficiaries include: General Electric, Krupp Industrie, PHB Forder Technic, Petro Valves, Nuovo Pignone, Snamprogerry, Foster Wheeler Energy Co, F. Peroni, FMB, V. Machinefabreci Lewes Refrigeration.

The given examples not only provide indications of the role played by the World Bank in the *sui generis* "import substitution" model in this period. They also point towards the role played by the Mexican state in the context of the drive towards "globalization" (to insert Mexico into the process) and, as noted by Fernando Fajnzylber (1983), "the absence of an effective leadership [within the Mexican capitalist or political class] in the construction of a potential endogenous industry capable of adapting, innovation and competing internationally in a broad range of production sectors."

The "development option" for the great part of Mexico's "political class," members of which historically have shown themselves all too keen to exploit any opportunities for personal enrichment, has been relegated to denationalized programs and economic strategies based on external debt financing and indebtedness), FDI, bank loans (*los empréstitos*), and the so-called "forces of the market." In this context no country in the region, not even Chile, currently the darling of the free marketeers, in its *modus operandi* (client relation with foreign capital and CCS) has managed to produce overall positive results.

These "developments" in Mexico and Latin America contrast markedly with similar developments in Japan, South Korea, and other "rapidly growing countries" in South East Asia. In these countries high levels of economic growth and "development" were achieved on the basis of a highly interactive relationship between the "private sector" and the state, with strategic planning generally undertaken by the latter and imposed on the former or implemented under conditions of shared interests (Saxe-Fernández 1998a: 120–38). From this we should not infer the absence of corruption, personal enrichment, speculation, and profoundly inequitable owner-worker relations in these countries. The relevance of the comparison between countries in Asia and Latin America consists in the fact that in the case of the Asian elite we have an "establishment" of national capital with characteristic vices and advantages. As to Mexico's elite, we have a new oligarchy whose reference group and psychosocial identification is with the Anglo-American "way of life."

As Carlos Monsivais, the well-known writer and political commentator of Mexican affairs, has observed, the behavior of this oligarchy can be characterized as one of "willing subservience" and thus integrally "anti-national." Large elements of this elite have responded to the siren of American "culture" (opportunities for personal enrichment—for "making it") by a willingness to appropriate any crumbs (*migajas*) left by Americans in their economic "operations" in Mexico and, in this context, to be content with even a marginal participation in the "wealth" or economic surplus generated in the process of capitalist development of the country's "productive resources." The result? In addition to the huge transfers of wealth outside of the country, the concentration of the remaining "wealth" in the hands, pockets, and banks of the country's elite—and poverty for the immense majority of the population. According to the National Statistics Agency (Instituto Nacional de Estadística, Geografía e Informática) and the Bank of Mexico (1994), in 1984 the poorest decile of households received only 1.7 percent of national income (the GNP), a share that was reduced to 1.6 percent by 1989 and 1.5 in 1992 (Saxe-Fernández 1994: 333). At the same time, the share in national income of the richest decile of families rose from 32.8 percent in 1984 to 37.9 percent in 1989 and 38.2 in 1992.

In this context World Bank loans reinforced tendencies within Mexico's elite—and elites in the rest of Latin America—to accept a subordinate position within the structure of North–South relations. In the same context diverse proposals for intraregional economic integration and the construction and consolidation of regional trading blocs have not fared well.

The failure of schemes for regional integration can be attributed to various factors, including an inversion of priorities vis-à-vis commerce and the currency. The general weakness of national monetary and financial instruments, and the absence of regional ones, a situation that in part has been encouraged by the World Bank and the IMF, and in part by Latin America's indigenous "oligarchy," have not allowed for any effective endogenous regional development planning or institutions. In the face of this situation, and with the growing power of the euro, the WBG has promoted the replacement of national currencies with the US dollar (as in Panamá, El Salvador and Ecuador). This "situation" and "development" both anticipates and makes more likely the eventual adoption of a Latin American Free Trade Area (LAFTA), which most observers see as an arrangement designed to benefit, above all, the US economy. In fact, some see it as a new form of colonialism, based as it is on a structure (relations of dependency) that favors the MNCs.

Mexico's path towards industrial nationalism staked out by the State as of the late 1930s under the rubric of "the [Mexican] Revolution" was synthesized by Lombardo Toledano in the slogan "to nationalize is to decolonize." The influence exerted by the World Bank in its Mexican "operations" over the past two decades can be seen in the modification in this slogan made by José Angel Conchello, former Partido Acción Nacional (PAN) senator: "to privatize is to recolonize." This formula expresses succinctly developments in the next phase of the Bank's Mexican operations.

The period after 1982: Co-government with the World Bank

The installation of a regime dominated to an astonishing degree by international creditors, in the context and as a result of negotiations arising out of Mexico's debt crisis in 1982 involved a frontal attack against the as yet fragile pivots of Latin American nationalism, and, as have noted, a major campaign to provide private (and foreign) interests greater access to the country's productive resources.

With the added newly acquired leverage of debt renegotiation mechanisms, and of the associated "conditionalities," the World Bank campaigned for greater influence over the levers and deployment of state power vis-à-vis the economy. The result: a form of co-government formed between state officials and the WBG, who installed their own functionaries in the design of "national" development plans, and in preparation of the national budget, accounting procedures, and management of the economy. In relatively short order, the World Bank, the IMF, and other international organizations such as the Inter-American Development Bank (ADB), extended their intervention from trade policies to those involving mining, biodiversity and water, the "restructuring" of the energy sector (oil, natural gas, electric power), transportation (railways, airports and highways), heavy industry, agriculture and fertilizers, financial deregulation, employment retraining and "human resource development," housing construction, social assistance and the vaunted "war against poverty" (World Bank 1989a).

In each of these areas the Bank intervened with its "loans" and thus with its missions of technical evaluation, control and supervision. Between 1982 and 1990 the Bank's sectoral loans were increased to US $11,500,000 and each Department of State (*Secretaria*), each state enterprise—and private ones—formed an ongoing relationship with the Bank, whether this relation be direct or indirect, or one of evaluation and supervision—or control. This relationship, in its diverse permutations, seen by the Bank as one of "partnership," persists to this day.

At issue is the denationalization (*extranjerización*) of the decision-making process, with profoundly negative implications—economic, sociopolitical, constitutional, and with regards to national sovereignty and national security. Also at issue is the de facto or virtual co-government formed in the process of a "double conditionality." We refer here to a twofold synergizing process involved in the institution of NAFTA in 1994 and subsequent (and ongoing) efforts to extend "free trade" to the entire hemisphere. On the one hand, there is the cross-fertilization that exists between the conditionalities (stabilization measures) imposed by the IMF on the government's macroeconomic policy and the conditionalities (structural adjustment reforms) applied by the World Bank to different economic sectors. This could be viewed as an "external synergy." Then we have the same structure reproduced within each organization in the context of its program operations. A matter of internal synergy.

The dynamics of this process are clearly illustrated in the regime and administration of de la Madrid (1982–8), which took Mexico's economy on a neoliberal path. First, there was the declaration by the Mexican government in 1982 that it would not be able meet its debt repayment obligations. It was this declaration and the underlying situation, conditions of which were also present elsewhere in the region, particularly in Argentina and Brazil, that provoked the "debt crisis" and led the IMF and the World Bank to align their policies vis-à-vis the requirement for both macroeconomic stabilization and structural adjustments to the economy. Second, the loans arranged by the Bank and the Fund were conditioned on the acceptance by the government of a new set of economic policies—and an agenda set by the country's creditors. Specifically, the trade policy loans arranged by the Bank, on condition that the government meet the requirements set out in the Letter of Intent signed with the IMF, were designed to open up the Mexican economy and to liberalize trade—and integration into the US economy. This "development" was induced by means of the following operations: TPL 1 (Loan 2745 ME) and TPL-2 (Loan 2882 ME) as well as two export loans. In 1989, the President of the World Bank talked of the instrumental effects of these loans in the following terms: "most promising ... import barriers have been dramatically reduced for agricultural inputs such as machinery, pesticides and other high technology products" (Conable 1991: 74–5).

The loans in question, totaling a million dollars, were very "persuasive" in causing the government to adjust its trade policy to the requirements of the United States and the agenda of the creditors. For example it has allowed the highly subsidized surplus production of US grains (wheat, corn) and other agricultural products to be shipped to Mexico, with drastically negative effects on Mexico's agriculture. In 1988, 4900 tariffs on US exports as well as the need for export licenses were entirely eliminated. In this regard, the President of the World Bank (1989) pointed out that:

the Mexican government fulfilled its obligations and commitments according to the operations stipulated in both loans. It liberalized over three quarters of its internal production and licensing. Less than a quarter is left under state control, in some agricultural and food products, petroleum and its derivatives, automobiles, some electronic products, pharmaceuticals and a few others.

He added:

> [T]he trade policy loan was a major breaking point. By this means the World Bank managed to finance the introduction of the process of trade reform. The second loan was oriented towards maintaining this opening within the parameters established by the first and it had a series of objectives, that the Mexican government must meet for funds in the second phase to be freed.

By means of just a few millions of dollars this "breaking point" changed the internal dynamics of the Mexican government as well as the "correlation of forces" involved in the relationship that had existed between two very unequal economic and political systems. It also established a very different trading relationship, a commercial opening without reciprocity, based on what could well be viewed as a new form of imperialism, a system dominated by the United States.

In this regard, consider that in 2000 the World Bank estimated Mexico's GNP as US $574.5 billion, while the GNP of the United States was US $9.9 trillion (World Bank n.d.). Mexico's annual per capita income, measured in terms of a seriously overvalued peso, was in the order of US $5,070 while in the United States it was US $ 34,260. These figures indicate a ratio of 17 to one between the size of the two economies but on a per capita basis this ratio is reduced to 6.5. But this statistical procedure does not reflect the actual or real dimensions of the asymmetry between the two economies. This would require a different perspective, based on a comparison of the two countries' stock of accumulated wealth (assigning value to all manner of assets—natural, physical, financial—including highways, railroads, industries, real estate, automobiles, etc.). By this measure it is estimated that the ratio of difference between the United States and Mexico rises to an order of 250 to 300. With an asymmetry of this magnitude it is not possible to have a type of relationship that would permit serious negotiations leading to a mutuality of national interest, particularly if one party to these negotiations (the United States) has at its disposal such a disporportionately large arsenal of weapons, instruments, and agents, including the World Bank and the IMF. At issue is a power structure with its inevitable relations of domination and subordination, (neo)imperialism and (neo)colonialism, between two sets of economic interests.

Mexico's Oil in the Bank's Crosshairs

With the exhaustion of reserves of petroleum, natural gas, coal, and other sources of energy in the United States, and a concomitant and growing dependency on external sources of supply, the interest of both Washington and the World Bank in the western hemisphere's hydrocarbon reserves and associated industries has intensified, particularly over the last two decades. Consider that in 1958 the American geologist King Hubbert elaborated a statistical methodology that permitted him to predict a serious shortfall in domestic reserves and supply of oil in 1970. A more refined form of this methodology has been applied by other geologists for other areas of the world (Deffeyes 2001). The results indicate reserves of anywhere from 1.8 to 2.1 billion barrels, which suggests that the wave of world production of conventional (cheap) sources of crude oil would crest either in 2001 or 2003/4, with a persistent decline thereafter in production levels—and a dramatic repercussion on the world capitalist economy geared to the production and consumption of oil (Deffeyes 2001: 4).

In the context of this problem the reserves and supply of oil in the region, particularly in Venezuela and Mexico, have increased in strategic importance to the United States, which, as a result, has pursued a series of strategies designed to improve and secure access of its MNCs to these hemispheric reserves. The Bank's campaign for Mexico and other countries in the region to structurally adjust their economies— to liberalize trade and the movement of investment capital; to deregulate private economic activity; and, above all, to privatize ownership of productive resources and enterprises—has also been brought to bear on the problem. As of the 1980s, the parastal Petróleos Mexicanos (Pemex) has been targeted by the World Bank for privatization. Using the argument or excuse of the need for "efficiency," the World Bank in its *Country Strategy Paper—Mexico* (1995b: 110) instructed the Mexican government as to the need to increase "the participation of private initiatives in the hydrocarbon sector as much to allow companies [the MNCs] to compete against Pemex as the sale of Pemex's assets, which promise to bring enormous advances in efficiency."

Although the World Bank over the course of little more than a ten-year campaign has achieved substantial "advances" in regard to its privatization strategy—under the presidency of Carlos Salinas de Gortiera the privatization of up to 1200 state enterprises, including de facto privatization of some of Pemex's important activities— it does not consider the "end result" to be satisfactory. Its "objective" is to secure the privatization and denationalization of Pemex, particular its most profitable sectors such as petrochemicals.

Without a doubt the United States' agenda includes the privatization (and de-nationalization) of Mexico's oil industry. The aim of the United States government vis-à-vis securing the privatization of Mexico's oil industry is manifest, inter alia, in the World Bank's privatization agenda and in the effective in situ control by US-based enterprises of Pemex operations. The Bank's strategy revolves around five measures conceived by its technocracy and outlined in the Bank's "Hydrocarbon Strategy Paper" (1995: 98–113) as a "roadmap" that the Mexican government should follow. This roadmap includes the following steps:

- allow risk contracts for oil exploration and development
- allow a majority interest of foreign investment in petrochemicals
- break up Pemex into separate enterprises and under competition
- subject Pemex to both domestic and foreign competition
- privatize Pemex.

Three of these steps have been incorporated into an argument made by the Bank in favor of privatization in diverse documents and published by the Heritage Foundation in terms of the following justifications:

- That Pemex does not invest sufficiently in exploration, in development or in petrochemicals.
- That Pemex should be dismembered, broken up into separate and independent entities, each operating independently and with profit criteria, permitting domestic and foreign competition, and resulting in greater efficiency.
- That privatizing Pemex totally would allow Mexico to pay both its external and domestic debt.

These three justifications are fallacious. First, the Mexican government imposes irrationally high taxes, representing 95 percent of profits, that are directed towards debt service and other nonproductive expenditures, so that there is scarcely enough left to maintain the immense infrastructure of Pemex, which covers the whole national territory. During López Portillo"s six-year term as president direct taxes paid by Pemex were equivalent to 61 percent of its total exports. Under de la Madrid they were pushed to 84 percent and during Salinas's term (or reign) taxes charged to Pemex rose to an irresponsible 158 percent of its export earnings (Manzo 1996: 51).

Second, under the auspices of the World Bank, Salinas Gortieri and Zedillo implemented a process dubbed by the United States as a "divestiture" that, in effect, constituted a partial dismemberment of Pemex. The big oil companies, however, at the same time went in a different direction (Tanzer 1993; Gachúz Maya 2000: 64–114). They pursued a strategy of vertical integration to increase their capacity to coordinate decisions on the production, refining and marketing of oil. The "divestiture" of Pemex was designed to create small and inefficient companies that would be vulnerable and easily dominated by the stronger MNCs that would at some point "reintegrate" them within their vertical structure. This was the apparent and largely successful aim of the Bank.

As for the Bank's third "argument," it is worthwhile remembering that Michael Tanzer has demonstrated that if Pemex were privatized, say for US $150 billion as proposed by the Heritage Foundation, the investment would necessarily be foreign: DuPont, Exxon-Mobil, Shell, Amoco, etc. Since the profit expectation of these corporations is at a minimum 20 percent the Mexican economy would likely yield an annual "export" of $30 billion in the form of capital (Tanzer 1993). Such a privatization would have a devastating effect on the Mexican economy and the national treasury, constituting as it does the principal source of financing of the federal budget as well as an important source of "unconditioned" profits. The future contributions of the oil industry to the country and its people would not remotely compare to the value (US $30 billion) of the resources lost each year to the new owners of these resources. If the privatization were fully achieved it would undoubtedly generate conditions of a crisis, both political and social, that would compare with the crisis that has engulfed Argentina under similar conditions (having pioneered the policy of privatization and, in the 1990s advancing further in this direction than any other country in the region, Argentina has been portrayed as the model of privatization). The privatization of Pemex would entail enormous social, economic, and political costs for the Mexican population, with few benefits; most of the benefits would be siphoned out of the country into the accounts of the MNCs and their investors, managers, and directors.

Returning to the recipe synthesized in the Bank's roadmap for the privatization of Pemex, the Bank is very clear as to the parameters under which Pemex should operate as a parastatal enterprise. First, Pemex should:

> extend [to the private sector] competitive contracts for exploration and development of each oil field so that the biggest would yield higher rates of profit (ground rents) because the extraction of the resource would be cheaper ... For Pemex, these contracts would commit the firm to pay the same earnings and taxes as the private firms, and to offer, in addition, incentives for risks taken. (World Bank 1995b: 102)

At present the Vicente Fox government is proceeding with this guideline or directive in terms of the Multipler Service Contracts (MSCs) prepared by the Bank for its predecessor but modified in the search for legislative approval. Formally an MSC implies the implementation of a project and tasks set by Pemex although financed by the "private sector," both "national and foreign," in different areas, including the exploitation of oil deposits under the responsibility of Pemex Exploración y Perforación, one of the operating subunits created in Pemex's "divestiture."

To a considerable extent MSCs are oriented toward the promotion of "integration" into the monopoly sector. In the words of Senator Cantón Zetina:

> given their size, the technical requirements and economic capacity of the enterprises participating in the bidding are oriented towards foreign capital, contravening various articles of the Constitution and Mexican laws ... it violates art. 134 ... given that these contracts raise the final cost of the work and services and, thus there is no taking advantage of the lowest cost available. Also, our country will not benefit from the wealth generated given that this ends up in the country of origin of the [invested] capital. (cited in Rocha 2002: 1, 10)

In the Preliminary Version of the Terms and Conditions of the Project elaborated by Pemex's consultants, all of whom are American, the "rights" of those party to the contract, mostly MSCs, include:

- free access to the contract zone and existing hydrocarbon installations and duty free use of these installations
- use of any sand, gravel (*grava*), soil (*suelo*) and water in the public domain
- employment of workers and personnel, both national and foreign
- import of any needed goods, services, and equipment
- freedom to buy or contract any national service or equipment
- finance operations in any way decided on, and the contractor [Pemex] will place no duties [either] on reserves [or] hydrocarbon production
- use of the hydrocarbons produced in the contract zone as energy in the field in conformity with permitted operations.

The concession granted of 20 years differs from the norm of five years; this led deputy (member of Congress) Rosario Tapia to argue that

> The contractee is practically given a piece of national territory to do whatever up to the extraction of gas and the construction of treatment plants. ... It entails a massive surrender of resources. We are returning to the risk contracts of a century ago that had provoked the oil expropriation [by the state]; they are riskless risk contracts because they [the wells] are perfectly located. (cited in Carriles 2001: 43)

In the case of the basic petrochemicals industry—the second point on the Bank's roadmap—its "deregulation" was effected according to the directions, timetable and needs of foreign interests. The program, initiated in 1986, had as one of its principal objectives the participation of private enterprise (including foreign) in the sector, which is constitutionally reserved for the State. According to Bank documents the program was designed to:

- Limit the role of Pemex as the sole producer of basic petrochemicals (de la Madrid and Salinas complied to the letter of this condition with a strategy elaborated by the Bank to have basic petrochemicals reclassified and placed on a "secondary" list. Also, the Bank insisted on the "flexibilization" of pricing policy in regards to basic petrochemicals).
- Permit the private sector to import basic petrochemicals and provide fiscal incentives.

Pemex is considered a "serious impediment"—strategic, political, commercial, and entrepreneurial—by the World Bank and the oil and gas industry in the United States. In unpublished World Bank documents it is viewed as "an obstacle to the development of the petrochemicals industry," and, therefore, according to the Bank's president, the Mexican government:

> should face swiftly the problem that affects the dominant position of the parastatal in the industry ... [even worse] the private international firms *cannot achieve vertical integration* because of Pemex's control over basic chemicals ... [while] Pemex's plans for expansion results in possible foreign investors viewing Mexico as a market of short duration (World Bank, 1995b: 102; emphasis added).

The Bank also notes that in 1989 the Mexican government in finally agreed to apply:

> in this sector a Plan of Action that would include the following fundamental measures: (i) limit the exclusive right of the parastatal [Pemex] to produce a maximum of 25 basic chemicals and to define an initial list of "secondary" petrochemicals open to private sector participation; and (ii) foment a program of cooperative agreements between the private sector and Pemex.

The plan to privatize the petrochemicals sector has accelerated as a result of the chronic underfinancing and decapitalization to which it has been subjected, this to the point that many of the petrochemical complexes are in ruins or chatarra (steel garbage). The fact is that Pemex's petrochemicals infrastructure has been taken to what the Bank terms the "selling point." In addition, the reclassification of basic petrochemicals as secondary has been extended to include oil fields. As President Vicente Fox is fond of saying, "the table has been set."

It is worth remembering that with the alienation of the petrochemicals sector, the country has lost control and usufruct rights over the sector with the greatest capacity to add value to the country's natural resources. According to calculations made by Engineer Rafael Decelis, for a barrel of oil to undergo the various steps in the process of transformation not only adds considerable value to the product—up to US \$700 barrel—but it involves a similar increase in employment generation. Considering the growing unemployment and widespread poverty, surrendering these fruits of development is irrational.

In regard to the third ingredient in the Bank's recipe for change—Pemex's administrative reorganization—its goal has been the eventual dissolution of the parastatal, subjecting it to a process of divestiture—dismantling it as if it were a "monopoly" operating in the normative context of anti-monopoly legislation in the United States. In this case, and without regard for the Constitution which places the oil industry under the exclusive control of Pemex, the Bank's roadmap proposes to pave the road for the privatization of Pemex by breaking it up "into competitive units, each of which would be of the size of a big private transnational firm" (World Bank 1995b: iv, 109–110).

Following this signpost, the government of Salinas Gortieri "reorganized" Pemex into four "decentralized" units (1) Pemex-Exploration and Production; (2) Pemex-Refining; (3) Pemex Gas and Basic Petrochemicals; and (4) Pemex-Petrochemicals, with a coordinating holding (non-operating) company named Pemex Corporativo that, according to one of the "options" presented to the government by the Bank, will eventually disappear in a process of further divestiture: "each subsidiary enterprise will be divided, perhaps, into four independent enterprises. ... The Corporation Pemex will cease to exist" (World Bank 1995: 109).

With the view of Pemex's eventual disappearance, the Bank has proposed the establishment of an institutional apparatus similar to what exists in the United States vis-à-vis the hydrocarbon sector, an entity that is, and would be, subject to the power and influence of the industry in the country. According to the World Bank, the Mexican government should proceed with the establishment of a bureaucratic apparatus that would be in charge of the administration of hydrocarbon resources—a Federal Hydrocarbon Agency ("authority") that would be independent from Pemex. Such an agency would be responsible for exploration and production, negotiate and sign exploration and production in all existing and future sites, supervise the implementation of investment commitments contracted by Pemex and subsidiary private enterprises, and serve as a depository of information—as is the case, for example, with the Land Commission in Oklahoma and the Texas Railroad Commission (World Bank 1995b: 109).

The World Bank, Pemex and workers

During Salinas' presidency, the Bank, by means of a hydrocarbon sector loan, fomented a program of "administrative modernization," a key element of which was the "flexibilization" of the Collective Contract signed between the Oil Workers Union (Sindicato de Trabajadores Petroleros) and the government as well as a massive downsizing of the labor force. The Bank had induced a similar development in the railway sector as part of a region-wide campaign for labor reform (see Chapter 5 below). In 1989 Pemex had a workforce of 280,000; by 1998 this force was reduced to 121,000. However, the "restructuring" of 150,000 jobs in the areas of drilling, construction, maintenance, and general service did not, as announced, result in "greater organizational, functional and productive efficiency." On the contrary. The Bank "prepared" (softened) Pemex so that the international oil companies would take over precisely those areas most affected by the downsizing of both the technical personnel and workers. For example, drilling operations were given over to the private international companies without establishing for them minimal requirements such as the use of Mexican inputs, services, and labor. Not only were the adopted measures in flagrant contradiction of the Bank's rhetoric in this regard, but union sources indicate that it was inevitable that the restructuring would not result in any reduction of management or in any unit labor power costs (Gachúz Maya 2000: 17–118).

As a result of "decentralization" into four separate units, the number of administrative and management personnel grew disproportionately as the production and technical workers were let go. For example, in 1982, when Pemex produced 1.4 billion barrels a year, it had a management staff of 203. In 1995, with a lower production level by 117 million barrels, the number of management positions grew to 1255; that is, the divestiture arranged by the Bank resulted in the addition of 1052 new managers, vice-managers, subdirectors, and executive directors, with a corresponding layer of supervisors, heads of department, heads of section and support staff (document cited by Gachúz Maya 2000).

Another major objective of the Bank has been to stimulate exploration and the drilling of wells with the aim of increasing the export of crude oil to the United States, and notwithstanding evidence of serious overproduction vis-à-vis refining capacity and the overexploitation of reserves, which has caused irreversible damage to the wells. According to Walter Friedeberg, former Pemex manager: "the data indicate that the damage to wells [was] caused by immoderate exploitation. In Tabasco-Chiapas average production per well from 1995 to 1998 dropped [significantly]. The decline has been even more dramatic in offshore fields in Campeche. There average production per well fell to below one half former levels. The average per well of light crude in the region declined by two thirds" (cited in Shields 1996: 32; see also Gachúz Maya 2000: 120–1).

According to the Bank, however, the overexploitation of wells does not exist or is not a factor. At the beginning of Zedillo's government in the early 1990s the Bank, with criteria diametrically opposed to those used in available technical reports, but consonant with the interest of the United States in the increase of exports from Mexico, proposed the extension of private investment "risk contracts" to the end of expanding production for exports (World Bank 1995b: 99).

With the government of Vicente Fox and with Muñoz Leos, former Dupont CEO at the head of Pemex, the exploitation of crude and exports were increased in the context of what the Company Union, the Unión Nacional de Trabajadores termed "the silent privatization" of Pemex (Rocha 2002). According to this source, each month an average of 179 workers, "de confianza" and unionized, are fired; exploration and drilling contracts are awarded by Pemex to foreign companies; and management positions are occupied by private sector executives. It is anticipated that 4,000 professionals and technicians, and over 30,000 workers, will be let go, leaving Pemex "without a cadre of professional and experienced personnel." As for management personnel they come from firms such as Dupont, Negromex, ICA, Resistol (Rocha 2002: 1, 10).

It appears that the new senior management personnel are also remunerated with exorbitant salaries and benefit packages. To pay the salary of a new manager without experience in the industry Pemex fires four experienced workers. Pemex pays a private foreign consultant, whose function precisely is to help move Pemex towards disintegration, US$1500 a day. Alberto Rocha (2002), in this regard, notes that:

> it is made clear that the firing and pension programmes are a complemenary part of the project that Pemex's project for the participation of big foreign capital in the oil industry via the *Pidiregas* and Multiple Service Contracts (MSCs). ... The participación of foreign firms ... is headed by *Degoller McNaughton,* the *Scotia Group, Dowel Schlumberger, Halliburton, Drilling Fluids de México* and *Zapata Internacional*—all TNCs. They are given all the facilities to do their "work" and charge millions of dollars even though to date there have been no [concrete] results.

With the help and means of the Public Enterprise Reform Loans the correlation of forces within the Federal Government and the parastatals, of which Pemex is the biggest, has been changed in favor of the "reformers" or "privatizers" (World Bank n.d.). In the case of Pemex, this is reflected in the acceptance of its divestiture, something that would have been impossible in an earlier, more nationalistic and populist political climate.

The administrative dismemberment of the strategic state enterprises (Pemex, Ferrocarriles Nacionales and the Comisión Federal de Electricidad), as emphasized above, has been promoted by the Bank, in its roadmap as a step towards privatization—and denationalization. Although they have occasioned little debate there are immediate and ultimate consequences of this surrender to outside interests of the country's major productive resources. They will require a lot of further study—and collective action.

Final Considerations

The World Bank's intervention in Mexico's economy can be traced back to the mid-1970s. The presence of the Bank, via the power derived from its loan conditionalities and synergies, was a determinant factor in the privatization of the railroads and, as we have shown, in the de facto privatization of the petrochemical sector in Mexico's oil industry, which, together with electric power, is reserved by the Constitution for the state. The actual role of the Bank in this regard can be observed in the equally disturbing way in which Mexico's geographic and territorial spaces have been managed and its usufruct given up; the sacking of strategic resources of immense strategic importance such as water and biodiversity; and the exploitation of the knowledge and labor power of the population—all in the interests of the MNCs, which are protected and promoted by the World Bank functioning as an instrument for the projection of the imperial power of the United States and its "European allies."

The documents cited and analyzed in this chapter show that the Bank has virtually served as an American political party, that works from both inside and outside the country to influence and direct the actions and policies of the Mexican government, in the process constituting itself as a virtual "co-government."

This "co-government" involving the WBG is a matter that remains, for the most part, outside the realm of public awareness and debate. The problem is that it has been instituted under conditions of what has been described as "stealth imperialism" (Johnson 2000), the power of which resides precisely in it being undetected and unable to be located. This situation, highly functional for the Bank's privatization– denationalization scheme, is well understood by Bank officials. For example, in the Bank's 1995 *Country Strategy Paper—Mexico*, the reader can easily follow the foot- and thumb-prints of the WBG in the corridors of state power from one *sexenio* (presidential regime) to another, in this case from Salinas to Zedillo. In the World Bank's *Office Memorandum* dated 1995 that accompanies the document, classified as "confidential" and "for official use only," there appears the following request:

> Please take note that much of the material in these documents is highly sensitive for the Mexican government. The Bank agreed with the stipulation that as a condition of [preparing this document] that the texts would be kept confidential and would not be processed by the Bank beyond its actual informal state. We ask for the [reader's] consideration in helping us keep to this agreement. In this spirit, we also ask that any external enquiries in regard to these documents be directed towards this División.

The documents in question are "unclassified" and "sensitive" precisely because they outlined the role of the Bank in delineating the heuristic principles and parameters of Mexico's "national agenda," particularly with regards to the design and implementation of the federal budget. For one thing, they clearly raise the question of who is the "the power behind the power"—who makes policy in the context of a peripheral client state. In this context, the Bank has assiduously worked to create in Mexico a cadre of local country managers who are disposed, if not compelled, not to act in the national interest but to advance the interests of the imperial power in the North, particularly as regards the design and execution of the federal budget. It is clear that we have here a case of the "power behind the throne" in regards to major policy issues, which is only possible with the control over the instruments of state power and with the acquiescence of a key part of the ruling circle. This acquiescence is secured by the spoils left by the foreign actors and given to their local country managers as a reward for facilitating the "Mexico Purchase," an old colonial practice (Saxe-Fernández 2002).

We hope that the data and analysis presented in this chapter will stimulate and contribute towards an urgent political debate in other countries, especially in terms of the urgent need to review similar tendencies and reflections of the Mexico model in Canada and the United States. For this we hope to have opened up in public, legislative, and judicial spheres, and for political parties, discussion of the mechanisms that have to be established in order to render accounts with the sacking of the country's wealth and productive resources, and of the profoundly negative impacts of the measures involved on large sectors of society.

In Mexico, the Bank's policies of pillage and denationalization, implemented by the Bank and its country managers, constitute a veritable "class war" whose campaigns have not been limited to any particular arena but ranges from the economic and political to the diplomatic–military and the ecological–social. Nevertheless, we are not in the face of a monolithic power that allows for no alternatives. The process involved, full of cracks and contradictions, has generated, among other things, an enormous reservoir of social discontent within sectors most affected by the policies of empire. This discontent, and associated forces of opposition and protest, is manifest in, and has been mobilized by, social movements, both those advocating peaceful methods and armed force, that have surfaced all across the country.

In this political context, the forces of protest and opposition threaten to destabilize the co-government regime. For its part, the Mexican "oligarchy" has responded to this threat by pouring oil on troubled waters—an explosive mix that blew up in the Zapatista uprising in Chiapas on January 1, 1994.

In the Zapatista uprising we see a population, deeply aggrieved, reacting against the loss of hope and desperation. But their ongoing struggle is not just to live with dignity, for social and cultural identity, to establish their right to the land, and manage their own resources in the collective interest of their population and communities. The struggle today is to ensure that these rights are given to and enjoyed by following generations. This struggle began within various nuclei of the most aggrieved indigenous communities and peasants (for example, the Ejército Zapatista de Liberación Nacional) but it has been joined by a growing number of diverse social groups and organizations (the Frente Zapatista de Liberación Nacional). Such a social construction of oppositional forces will eventually be dissipated unless they can form a movement capable of taking over the state. State power is essential for the realization of any popular project to assume national control over the country's resources and wealth.

If we do not join this struggle and commit ourselves to this project, and from within our own space—according to our capacities and condition—to help consolidate the participation of all affected social classes, to construct a consciousness that will permit and lead to actions that might revert the situation lived by so many in Mexico and Latin America, the possibility of a peaceful way out of this situation is greatly reduced.

In the case of NAFTA what is needed is a renegotiation of the agreement that, in addition to securing the national interest in each of the three countries, also includes mechanisms for correcting the asymmetry of relations that exists between Mexico and the other two countries—an asymmetry conceded by the Mexican government under conditions that need to be changed. At the same time, it is of critical importance to the Mexican people that the expropriation of their productive resources via privatization be reverted.

To this end, freedom of access to relevant information and studies such as this are critical factors in the formation of a class consciousness that might mobilize the population at large and provoke discussions as to the direction that the country (Mexico) should take—a direction geared to the public interest rather than in pursuit of the geostrategic interests of an imperial state or the personal enrichment of the oligarchy. NAFTA, like the other projections of US imperial power in the pursuit of hegemony—Plan Colombia, Plan Puebla Panama (and its "green" version, the Mesoamerican Biological Corridor) and the Free Trade Area of the Americas (FTAA)—can be viewed as acts of "brutal aggression" and concessions made on the backs of the Mexican people.

Chapter 5

Crisis and the Retreat from Globalization in Asia

Walden Bello

During the annual spring meetings of the WB and the IMF in April 2006 Sebastian Mallaby, the influential economic columnist of the *Washington Post*, made this observation:

> A few years ago, anti-globalization rioters were clogging the streets, disrupting meetings of the world's multilateral organizations. Today, something more serious is afoot. The protesters have mercifully vanished, but international institutions are in disarray. Anti-globalization may have lost its voice, but so has globalization. (Mallaby 2006)

Noting that "trade liberalization has stalled, aid is less coherent than it should be, and the next financial conflagration will be managed by an injured fireman," he concluded that "the great powers of today are simply not interested in creating a resilient multilateral system."

In fact, globalization has not only "stalled," as Mallaby puts it; it is going into reverse. And it is not just the key institutions of global economic governance such as the World Bank, the WTO and the IMF that are in crisis but the deeper structures and processes of what was formerly seen as an inevitable phenomenon. What was seen, by many people on both the Left and the Right, as the wave of the future—that is, a functionally integrated global economy marked by massive flows of commodities, capital and labor across the borders of weakened nation-states and presided over by a "transnational capitalist class"—has retreated in a chain reaction of economic crises, growing intercapitalist rivalries and wars. Only by a stretch of the imagination can the US under the George W Bush administration be said to be promoting a "globalist agenda."

Globalization was no mirage. But in retrospect, rather than being a new, higher phase of capitalism, it was in fact a reaction to the underlying structural crisis of capitalism, something that was masked in the early 1990s by the collapse of the centralized socialist regimes in Central and Eastern Europe. Fifteen years on, globalization seems to have been a desperate effort by global capital to escape the stagnation and disequilibria overtaking the global economy in the 1970s and 1980s rather than the Brave New Phase in the capitalist adventure promised by Margaret Thatcher when she coined her famous slogan TINA—that is, "There is no alternative" to capitalism. The promise of globalization, like the promise of the New Economy with which it was associated, was largely stillborn.

The crisis of globalization and overaccumulation is one of the three central crises that are currently eroding US hegemony. The other two are the overextension of US military power and the crisis of legitimacy of liberal democracy. All three have been discussed in *Dilemmas of Domination: the Unmaking of the American Empire* (Bell, 2005). This chapter is an effort to extend and deepen the analysis one of these crises: that of overaccumulation.

The End of the Long Boom

The period from 1945 to 1975 was marked by relatively high growth rates as Keynesian policies institutionalized the reinvigoration of capitalism that had been brought on by the state-led war economies during the Second World War. Also known as the Fordist model of production, the post-war capitalist economy involved significant state intervention and regulation and rested on a class compromise between Big Capital and Big Labor—a compromise that was expressed in relatively high wages that translated into expanding demand that fueled growth. Most of the newly independent countries also adopted varieties of state-assisted capitalism. The result was what is now seen in retrospect as the "long boom" of the international economy.

To some analysts this boom was a manifestation of the "A Phase" of the so-called Kondratiev Wave, where growth was triggered partly from the civilian application of technologies developed during the Second World War in key industries such as aviation, metals and information technology.

The long boom came to an end in the 1970s; one of its main manifestations was the "stagflation" or stagnation-cum-inflation—a phenomenon that was not supposed to occur in Keynesian economic theory—that overtook the Northern economies, in particular the US economy. The period of state-supported "import substitution industrialization" also ran into trouble in the South, with stagnation, inflation, and massive indebtedness combining to reverse trends on the reduction of poverty and inequality.

From the early 1980s on competition rather than synergy or complementarity became the principal aspect of the relations among the key Northern economies. The key cause of this development was capitalism's classic crisis of overproduction, overinvestment, and overcapacity, meaning the emergence of too much productive capacity globally relative to global demand, resulting in a decline in the rate of profit. Also contributing to stagnation was the end of the profitable exploitation of the new technologies of the post Second World War era, leading the international economy to the so-called "B Phase" of the Kondratiev Wave, the main features of which were, as Wallerstein pointed out:

> the slowdown of growth in production, and probably a decline in per capita world production; a rise in rates of active waged work unemployment; a relative shift of loci in profits, from productive activity to gains from financial manipulations; a rise of state indebtedness; relocation of "older" industries to lower-wage zones; a rise in military expenditures, whose justification is not really military in nature but rather that of countercyclical demand creation; falling real wages in the formal economy; expansion of

the informal economy; a decline in low-cost food production; increased "illegalization" of interzonal migration. (Wallerstein 1996: 28)

Growth in one center economy became dependent on recession in another, and with the generalized adoption of floating exchange rates after the Nixon administration abandoned the gold–dollar peg in 1971, currency manipulation became a key instrument of competition, with the US, for instance, seeking to reflate its economy by pushing the revaluation of the Japanese yen. This made Japanese imports to the US more expensive in dollar terms and made production in high-wage Japan increasingly noncompetitive, forcing the Japanese to shift a significant part of their manufacturing operations to South East Asia and China.

Monetary manipulation, via the high interest rate regime initiated by Federal Reserve Chief Paul Volcker in the late 1980s, while directed at fighting inflation, was also geared strategically at channeling global savings to the US to fuel economic expansion. One key consequence of this momentous move was the Third World debt crisis of the early 1980s, which ended the boom of the economies of the South and led to their resubordination to the Northern capitalist centers. As Carlos Diaz Alejandro put it:

> What could have been a serious but manageable recession has turned into a major development crisis unprecedented since the early 1930s mainly because of the breakdown of international financial markets and an abrupt change in the conditions and rules for international lending. (Ocampo 2006: 79)

Latin America, for instance, changed from being a net capital importer, enjoying positive net resource transfers of 2–3 percent of GDP, into a net capital exporter, hemorrhaging net negative transfers of 4–5 percent of GDP. In an effort to regain "international competitiveness," the US and UK, under Ronald Reagan and Margaret Thatcher respectively, adopted neoliberal, free-market policies aimed at ending the Keynesian class compromise, rolling back state participation in and regulation of production, reducing protectionism in trade policies, and ending capital controls. The result was an increase in inequality in the key Northern economies, but without their regaining the high growth rates of the first two decades after the war that neoliberal economists had hoped for.

The search for profitability amid stagnation pushed the US and the other center economies, via the World Bank and the IMF, to resubordinate the economies of the South through pro-market structural adjustment policies. The dismantling of developmental states in much of the South deepened and consolidated the comprehensive crisis of the developing world that was ushered in by Volcker's high interest rate regime.

The trend towards global stagnation was striking. Angus Maddison's statistical work—regarded as the most reliable—shows that the annual rate of growth of global GDP fell from 4.9 percent in 1950–73 to 3 percent in 1973–89, a drop of 39 percent.[1] The United Nations confirmed this trend, estimating that world GDP grew at an

---

1 Angus Maddison, cited in Crotty (2002: 25).

annual rate of 5.4 percent in the 1960s, 4.1 percent in the 1970s, 3 percent in the 1980s, and 2.3 percent in the 1990s.

The decline in corporate profitability that accompanied this trend was equally striking, with the profit rate of the largest 500 US transnational corporations falling drastically from \$4.70 in 1954–9 to \$2.04 in 1960–9 to 75.30 in 1980–9, 72.64 in 1990–9 and 71.92 in 2000–02. (O'Hara 2006: 27). Behind these figures, notes Philip O'Hara, is the specter of overproduction: "Over-supply of commodities and inadequate demand are the principal corporate anomalies inhibiting performance in the global economy" (O'Hara 2006: 27).

Clinton and the Globalist Project

The reign of the Democratic Party led by Bill Clinton appeared to portend a break with this pattern of low and erratic growth. The US economy moved into an eight-year boom that many interpreted as a sign that it had become a "New Economy" impermeable to the cycle of boom and bust. The administration embraced globalization as its "Grand Strategy"—that is, its fundamental foreign policy posture towards the world. The accelerated integration of production and markets, based on a faith in the efficacy of minimally regulated markets, was felt to play to the strengths of US corporations. As the director of intelligence of the National Security Council saw it: the US would benefit immensely from this shift because it is well placed to thrive in a globalized political economy. Indeed, a globalized society of market states plays into and enhances American strengths to such a degree that it worries some states that the United States will become so dominant that no other state will be able to catch up to it (O'Hara 2006: 145).

The dominant position of the US allowed the liberal faction of the US capitalist class to act as a leading edge of a transnational ruling elite in the process of formation—a transnational elite alliance that could act to promote the comprehensive interest of the international capitalist class. It appeared to demonstrate this capacity when it pursued the strong dollar policy, one that was meant to revive the economies of Japan and Germany, even if this was not in the short-term interest of many US corporations that had to compete against cheaper Japanese and German products. Thriving markets in Japan and Europe, however, were ultimately beneficial for US capital in terms of providing healthy, expanding export markets, and this is what the Clintonites had as a strategic aim (Brenner 2002: 127–133).

The Clinton conjuncture was captured by Stephen Gill when he called attention to the emergence of a "neoliberal historical bloc that practices a politics of supremacy within and across nations" (Gill 2003: 120). Gill called this a politics of supremacy instead of hegemony because this historical bloc was able to gain only a fragile legitimacy for the globalist project. Thus, while neoliberal globalization brought about "a growth in the structural power of capital, its contradictory consequences mean that neoliberalism has failed to gain more than temporary dominance in our societies" (Gill 2003: 120).

Achieving hegemony and not simply supremacy was nevertheless a major concern, and a major thrust of the Clinton administration was geared towards institutionalizing the emerging neoliberal global order; that is, to make its functioning independent of the coercive power of the hegemon. Its crowning achievement in this area was the founding of the WTO in 1995. A product of eight years of negotiations, but negotiations conducted principally between the US and the EU, the WTO was the most ambitious effort to codify trade rules in order to consolidate a free-trade regime globally that responded to corporate profitability. The WTO was the key project of what Gill called the "New Constitutionalism," that is, the "legalization" of neoliberal principles in order to make a relapse into the old protectionism very difficult, if not impossible (Gill 2003: 131–5).

Meanwhile, the IMF sought the dismantling of capital controls worldwide by making capital account liberalization one of its articles of association. The IMF and the WTO, along with the World Bank, were seen by the transnational class alliance as the key pillars of the system of global governance of the neoliberal global order. At the Singapore Ministerial of the WTO in 1996 the challenge of the future was defined by the three agencies as the achievement of coherence—the technocratic integration of their policies and their co-management of the global economy in the direction of freer and freer capital and commodity markets.

Finance Capital and its Contradictions

The transnationalisation of production via the outsourcing of different phases of the production process was expected to be the central dynamic of the era of globalization. But, in fact, the dominant dynamic of global capitalism during the Clinton period— one that was the source of its strength as well as its Achilles' Heel—was not the movement of productive capital but the gyrations of finance capital.

The centrality of finance capital was a result of the declining profitability of industry brought about by the crisis of overproduction. By 1997 profits in US industry had stopped growing. Financial speculation, or what one might conceptualize as the squeezing of value from already-created value, became the most dynamic source of profitability. The "financialization" of global capital that drove the Clinton period's eight-year boom had several key dimensions:

- Elimination of restrictions dating back to the 1930s that had created a Chinese Wall between investment banking and commercial banking in the US opened up a new era of rapid consolidation in the US financial sector.

- The creation of a whole host of new financial instruments, such as derivatives, which monetized and traded risk in the exchange of a whole range of commodities. The 1990s ushered in a "world where practically anything can be traded, from weather predictions to broadband Internet connections to forecasts involving the housing market" (Berenson 2006: 44). Enron exemplified the firm that detached itself from producing and trading on any one commodity to trading and profiting on risk in a large number of unrelated commodities.

- The creation of massive consumer credit to fuel consumption, with much of the source of this capital coming from foreign investors. While stimulating the economy in the short run, this created a dangerous gap between the consumers' debt and their income, opening up the possibility of consumer collapse or default that would carry away both consumers and their creditors— a possibility that has been a constant preoccupation of the IMF.

• The salient role of the stock market in driving growth, a phenomenon labeled by Robert Brenner as "stock market Keynesianism." Stock market activity drove, in particular, the so-called technology sector, creating a condition of "virtual capitalism" whose dynamics were based on the expectation of future profitability rather than on current performance, which was the iron rule in the "real economy." The workings of virtual capitalism were exemplified by the rapid rise in the stock values of internet firms such as Amazon.com, which by 2001 had not yet turned a profit. Once future profitability rather than actual performance became the driving force of investment decisions, Wall Street operations became indistinguishable from high-stakes gambling in Las Vegas, leading some observers to coin the term "casino capitalism."

• The elimination of capital controls among economies, to enable speculative capital to move quickly to take advantage of differentials in value of currencies, stocks and other financial instruments. This resulted in the emergence of a truly unified global capital market, whose operations were, thanks to the advances in information technology, carried out in "real time." Special targets of capital account liberalization in the 1990s by the IMF and the US Treasury Department were the Asian economies, which Northern finance capital was eager to enter in order to get its share of their seemingly endless growth. Yet, even before the decade was over, the contradictions of global financial capital had caught up with it.

Perhaps most dramatic was the bursting of the Wall Street bubble in 2000–01, which ended speculation that the US had developed a recession-proof "New Economy." The dizzying rise in market capitalization of non-financial corporations, from \$4.8 trillion in 1994 to \$15.6 trillion in the first months of 2000, represented what Robert Brenner called an "absurd disconnect between the rise of paper wealth and the growth of actual output, and particularly of profits, in the underlying economy" (Brenner 2002: 192). But the law of gravity was not to be defied. With the profitability of the financial sector dependent on the actual profitability of the manufacturing and industrial sector, stock prices had to fall back to their real values. An astounding \$7 trillion in investor wealth was wiped out in the collapse of 2001–02. This massive loss of paper wealth represented the rude reassertion of the reality of a global economy crippled by overcapacity, overproduction and lack of profitability. With the mechanism of "stock market Keynesianism"—that is, reliance on speculative activity in the financial sector to drive growth—"broken and perhaps beyond repair" (Brenner 2003: 20) the economy plunged into recession in 2001 and 2002, and crawled into an era of weak and jobless growth.

Speculative crises marked the deregulation of finance capital in different parts of the world, and one crisis in one market touched off another in another market in an increasingly unified global market. The rush of speculative investors into Mexico forced a real appreciation of the Mexican currency, provoking a massive current account deficit as Mexican exports got more expensive in foreign markets and foreign imports cheaper in Mexico. This triggered a speculative attack on the peso that had investors in panic cashing their pesos for dollars, leading to the devaluation and collapse of the Mexican economy in 1994.

Essentially the same dynamics unfolded in East Asia in 1997. One hundred billion dollars in speculative capital flooded into the region between 1994 and 1997 as countries liberalized their capital accounts. Seeking a quick and high return, most of this money went into choice sectors such as real estate and the stock market, resulting in overinvestment and a chain reaction of economic dislocations.

Smelling crisis in the air, hedge funds and other speculators targeted the Thai baht, Korean won, and other currencies, triggering a massive financial panic that led to the drastic devaluation of these currencies and laid low Asia's tiger economies. In a few short weeks in the summer of 1997 some $100 billion rushed out of the Asian economies, leading to a drastic reversal of the sizzling growth that had marked those economies in the preceding decade. In less than a month, some 21 million Indonesians and one million Thais found themselves thrust under the poverty line (Chomthongdi 2000: 18, 22).

The Asian financial crisis helped precipitate the Russian financial crisis in 1998, as well as financial troubles in Brazil and Argentina that contributed to the spectacular unraveling of Argentina's economy in 2001 and 2002, when the economy that had distinguished itself as the most faithful follower of the IMF's prescriptions of trade and financial liberalization found itself forced to declare a default on $100 billion of its $140 billion external debt.

Financial volatility promised to continue in a world where, despite a chain reaction of speculative crises, there was no serious move to re-regulate finance capital's central role in the new global economy. As Robert Rubin, Clinton's Secretary of the Treasury, asserted in 2003, "Future financial crises are almost surely inevitable, and could be even more severe. The markets are getting bigger, information is moving faster, flows are larger, and trade and capital markets have continued to integrate ... It's also important to point out that no one can predict in what area—real estate, emerging markets, or whatever else—the next crises will occur" (Rubin and Weisberg 2003: 296).

Globalization, it seems, has stalled while multilateralism has unraveled. Paradoxically, while financial integration advanced, the integration of production that would create one borderless world economy marked by weakened states and under the direction of one dominant transnational faction of the international capitalist class stalled. As Hirst and Thompson demonstrated in their classic work *Globalization in Question*, truly global TNCs are relatively few, with most continuing to have the bulk of their production and sales in national or regional markets rather than spread out globally (Hirst and Thompson 1996).

While states in the South were weakened by structural adjustment programmes, states in the North, particularly the USA and those in Europe, remained significant economic actors tied to advancing the interests not of an increasingly fragile alliance of transnational capitalist fractions but of the more nationalistic or more regionally oriented sections of their national capitalist classes. This was also the case in China, where the power and influence of the Chinese state over economic activities grew rather than diminished with China's integration into the international economy.

Despite much speculation about the consequences of outsourcing, what was taking place was not so much the emergence of one functionally integrated global economy but a process that was pretty much along the lines of what David Held and Anthony McGrew described as the "sceptical" position: while relocation of industrial facilities and outsourcing of services escalated, what was occurring was not the advent of a qualitatively new stage of capitalism but "an intensification of linkages between discrete national economies ... [wherein] internationalization complements rather than displaces the predominantly national organization and regulation of contemporary economic and financial activity, conducted by national or local public and private entities" (Held and McGrew 2002: 40).

The stalling of the structural processes of globalization at the level of production was accompanied by a deep crisis of legitimacy of the much vaunted multilateral system that was supposed to govern global production, trade, finance, and development.

The IMF, the agency that was supposed to be the lynchpin of the global financial system in the new global order, was undergoing a severe crisis of legitimacy. The Fund never recovered from the Asian financial crisis, when it "lost its legitimacy," as one former IMF staff member put it (Dennis De Tray, Comments at luncheon sponsored by the Carnegie Endowment for International Peace, Washington DC, April 21, 2006). The Fund suffered three devastating hits during the crisis.

First, it was seen as being responsible for the policy of eliminating capital controls that many of the governments of East Asia followed in the years preceding the crisis.

The second hit was the widespread perception that the multibillion rescue packages assembled by the IMF for the afflicted countries did not actually go to rescuing the economies but to paying off foreign creditors and speculative investors. Citibank, for instance, though heavily overexposed in Asia, did not lose a cent in the crisis. These scandalous developments led to strong criticism of the IMF, even from free market partisans such as George Shultz, Secretary of State under Richard Nixon, who said that the Fund was encouraging "moral hazard," or risk-free investment and lending, and should therefore be abolished.

The third blow to the Fund sprang from the results of the stabilization programs it pushed on the crisis economies. With their wrongheaded emphasis on cutting back on government spending in order to fight the wrong enemy—inflation—these programs actually accelerated the descent of these economies into recession. In a manner similar to the way Volcker's high interest rate regime impacted on the indebted Latin American countries in the early 1980s, the IMF turned what should have been a manageable crisis into an economic catastrophe. The Asian governments were all the more bitter since the Fund, colluding with the US, had, at the height of the crisis, vetoed the creation of an "Asian Monetary Fund" that would have provided loans with relatively loose conditions that would have allowed them to surmount the crisis.

The Fund went from one institutional disaster to another. The Russian financial crisis in 1998 was attributed partly to its policies, as was Argentina's economic collapse in 2002. By 2006 the IMF, according to the Governor of the Bank of England, had "lost its way" (Woods 2006: 2).

The World Bank, the second pillar of the global multilateral order, was also under assault after a decade of failed reform under Clinton appointee James Wolfensohn, who sought to make the Bank the spearhead of the neoliberal transformation of developing countries. Structural adjustment programs that it had imposed on over 90 developing countries and post-socialist economies and co-managed with the IMF resulted most often in more poverty, more inequality, and stagnation. A commission appointed by the US Congress called for devolving the Bank's lending operations to other organizations after finding out that, by the Bank's own assessments, the failure rate for its projects in the poorest countries was 65–70 percent and 55–60 percent in all developing societies (Meltzer 2000). The Bank was also accused of abetting corruption in Indonesia and Kenya. And when George Bush appointed Paul Wolfowitz as head of the Bank to replace Wolfensohn in 2005, the move led to further erosion of the Bank's multilateral image, since Wolfowitz, former US deputy secretary of defense, was widely seen as one of the key architects of the war in Iraq and his appointment was regarded as a move to tie the Bank more closely to the USA's strategic policies.

Perhaps the most serious threat to the multilateral order was that to posed to the WTO, which had been described by one former director general as the "jewel in the crown of multilateralism." The outlook for the WTO a decade after its founding was much less rosy. A de facto alliance between developing countries resistant to further trade liberalization and civil society networks critical of the subordination of social and environmental concerns to corporate trade, plus increasing competition between the US and the EU, triggered the dramatic collapse of the third ministerial of the WTO in Seattle in 1999 and the fifth ministerial in Cancun in 2003. A third collapse in Hong Kong was barely averted in December 2005, but the unraveling of a desperate effort to arrive at a deal that would conclude the Doha Round of negotiations among the so-called G6 in July 2006 practically ensured this outcome. With its authority fading, the future of the WTO as the main engine of corporate-driven free trade was in doubt, as was the future of neoliberal globalization.

Reflecting the worries of the establishment, *Washington Post* commentator Sebastian Mallaby laid out a bleak picture for the future of the multilateral system after the spring 2006 meetings of the World Bank and the IMF:

> The troubles at the IMF, World Bank, and World Trade Organization are paradoxical. It is not that the underlying forces of globalization have gone limp; it's that nobody wants to invest political capital in global institutions. Trade is expanding, and bilateral trade deals sprout like weeds; but governments don't find the multilateral Doha talks to be a congenial setting in which to reduce tariffs. Equally, aid is expanding; but too much of the new money is flowing through uncoordinated bilateral channels rather than through the World Bank. International financial flows continue on a massive scale; but countries don't seem interested in sustaining the IMF in its historical role as the insurer against crises. (Mallaby 2006)

Persistence of Overproduction

The chain of crises since the last years of the Clinton era have been, in the view of many analysts, a reassertion of the underlying crisis of overaccumulation and underconsumption that was papered over by the superficial boom in the US, Asia, and Europe in the first part of the 1990s. On this, there is an interesting convergence between Marxists and the IMF, a point noted by analyst Ho-fung Hung (2006). As Raghuram Rajan (2005), the director of the IMF"s research centre, put it recently: "I see the problem as the world investing too little. The current situation has its roots in a series of crises over the last decade that were caused by excessive investment, such as the Japanese asset bubble, the crises in Emerging Asia and Latin America, and most recently, the IT bubble. Investment has fallen off sharply since, with only very cautious recovery" (Rajan 2005: 3–4).

Overcapacity was in fact a constant feature of the New Economy, even at its height. The crisis was particularly severe in the core industries. In the US the computer industry's capacity was rising at 40 percent annually, far above projected increases in demand. The world auto industry was selling just 74 percent of the 70.1 million cars it made each year, creating a profitability crunch for the weakest players, like former giant General Motors, which lost $10.6 billion in 2005 (*New York Times* 2006: C1). In steel excess capacity neared 20 percent (Crotty 2002: 24). Crotty here estimates this excess capacity in volume terms to be an astounding 200 million tons, so that plans by steel producing countries to reduce capacity by 100 million tons by 2005 would still leave "a sizeable amount of capacity which ... would not be viable." And, according to the former General Electric Chairman Jack Welch, "there was excess capacity in almost every industry" (Shilling 1998: 177). By the turn of the century, the gap between global capacity and sales was, said *The Economist* (20 February 1999: 15), the largest since the Great Depression.

Globalization and financialization were mechanisms designed to escape the inexorable pressures of overaccumulation and overproduction. In fact they worsened it. The spur to overcapacity provided by hothouse finance was strikingly evident in the telecommunications industry, where aggressive Wall Street financial intermediaries linked capital-flush investors with capital-hungry techno-entrepreneurs, all three interests united by a naïve faith in a high-tech boom that they expected would go on and on. The supply of capital rather than real demand was driving investment decisions, and the telecom firms "were soon laying tens of millions of fiber-optic cable across the [US] and under the oceans" (Brenner 2003: 20). By Spring 2000 the market capitalization of telecom firms had reached $2.7 trillion, close to 15 percent of the total for non-financial corporations. The result of this overcapitalization was a "mountainous glut: the utilization rate of telecom networks hovers today at a disastrously low 2.5–3 per cent, that of undersea cable at just 13 per cent" (p. 27).

Not surprisingly, profits plunged drastically from a peak of $35.2 billion in 1996, the year the industry was deregulated, to $6.1 billion in 1999, and then to –$5.5 billion in 2000. Once the darlings of Wall Street dealmakers like Salomon Barney Smith and Merrill Lynch, the telecom firms led the way to high-profile bankruptcy: Global Crossing, Qwest, and Worldcom.

Overaccumulation and the China Problem

But probably the most serious single factor worsening the global overcapacity and overaccumulation crisis was a development that was one of the main achievements of the globalist project: the integration of China into the international economy.

On the one hand, China's 8–10 percent growth rate per annum has probably been the principal stimulus of growth in the world economy in the past decade. In the case of Japan, for instance, a decade-long stagnation was broken in 2003 by the country's first sustained recovery, fueled by exports to slake China's thirst for capital and technology-intensive goods; exports shot up by a record 44 percent, or $60 billion (Riding China's coattails," *Business Week*, 50). Indeed, China became the main destination for Asia's exports, accounting for 31 percent while Japan's share dropped from 20 to 10 percent. As one account pointed out, "In country-by-country profiles, China is now the overwhelming driver of export growth in Taiwan and the Philippines, and the majority buyer of products from Japan, South Korea, Malaysia, and Australia" (*Straits Times* 2004: 12).

On the other hand, China became a central contributor to the crisis of global overcapacity. Even as investment declined sharply in many economies, particularly in Japan and other East Asian countries, in response to the crisis of excess capacity, it increased at a breakneck pace in China. Investment in China was not just the obverse of disinvestment elsewhere, although the shutting down of facilities and sloughing off of labor was significant not only in Japan and the US but in the countries on China's periphery like the Philippines, Thailand, and Malaysia. China was significantly beefing up its industrial capacity and was not simply absorbing capacity eliminated elsewhere. At the same time, the ability of the Chinese market to absorb its industrial output was limited.

A major actor in overinvestment was transnational capital. Originally, when transnational corporations (TNCs) moved to China in the late 1980s and 1990s, they saw it as the last frontier, the unlimited market that could endlessly absorb investment and endlessly throw off profitable returns. However, investment in many cases turned into excess investment because of China's restrictive rules on trade and investment, which forced transnationals to locate most of their production processes in the country instead of outsourcing only a selected number of them. This is what analysts termed the "excessive internalisation" of production activities by transnationals.

By the turn of the millennium the dream of exploiting a limitless market had vanished. Foreign companies headed for China not so much to sell to millions of newly prosperous Chinese customers as to make China a manufacturing base for global markets, taking advantage of its inexhaustible supply of cheap labor. Typical of companies that found themselves in this quandary was Philips, the Dutch electronics manufacturer. Philips operates 23 factories in China and produces about $5 billion-worth of goods, but two-thirds of their production is not consumed in China but exported to other countries (United Nations 2003: 45).

The other set of actors promoting overcapacity was local governments which invested in and built up key industries. While these efforts are often "well planned and executed at the local level," notes analyst Ho-fung Hung (2006), "the totality of these efforts combined ... entail anarchic competition among localities, resulting in uncoordinated construction of redundant production capacity and infrastructure."

The result is that idle capacity in such key sectors as steel, automobile, cement, aluminum, and real estate has been soaring since the mid-1990s, with estimates that over 75 percent of China's industries are currently plagued by over capacity and that fixed asset investments in industries already experiencing overinvestment accounts for 40–50 percent of China's GDP growth in 2005 (Hung 2006).

The State Development and Reform Commission projects that automobile production will more than double what the market can absorb by 2010 (Hung 2006). The impact on profitability is not to be underestimated if we are to believe government statistics: at the end of 2005 the average annual profit growth rate of all major enterprises had plunged by half and the total deficit of losing enterprises had increased sharply by 57.6 percent (Hung 2006).

Excess capacity could have been overcome had the Chinese government focused on expanding people's purchasing power via a policy of income and asset redistribution. Doing so would have meant a slower process of growth but a more stable one. China's authorities, however, chose a strategy of dominating world markets by exploiting the country's cheap labor.

Although China's population is 1.3 billion, 700 million people—or over half—live in the countryside, earning an average of just $285 a year. These people serve as an almost inexhaustible source of cheap labor. Because of this reserve army of rural poor, manufacturers, both foreign and local, have been able to keep wages down. The negative social and economic impacts of this strategy are well described by Ho-fung Hung:

> Under the post-Tiananmen consensus among the ruling elite, the Communist Party single-mindedly pursues rapid economic growth without directing much attention to the alleviation of social polarization. Class, urban—rural, and inter-regional inequalities expanded hand in hand with the economic miracle. Poverty spreads and intensifies in the rural inland area and the old bastions of state industry are besieged by extensive unemployment. The peasants-turned-workers in the coastal boom towns are not doing much better. Owing to the colossal size of the pool of surplus labor and the "despotic factory regime" under the auspices of the party-state, industrial wage growth amid China's economic miracle is dismal in comparison with the growth of manufacturing wages in other East Asian NICs during their miraculous moment. During the most explosive phase of takeoff, South Korea and Taiwan remained modestly equalitarian societies ... In contrast, China's gini-coeffcient has ascended from 0.33 in 1980 to more than 0.45 today. The pattern of income distribution in China's development is more reminiscent of the Latin American experiences than the East Asian ones, so much so that some begin to forewarn of the "Latin Americanization of China". (Hung 2006)

Aside from being potentially destabilizing politically, this wealth concentration in a few and the relative immizerization of the vast majority impedes the growth of consumption relative to the phenomenal economic expansion and great leap of investment. This has meant, among other things, an exacerbation of the crisis of overproduction in that a significant amount of China's industrial production has been dumped on global markets constrained by slow growth.

The Global Macroeconomic Picture Today

The accumulation of crises rooted in persistent overproduction culminated in the stock market collapse, recession, and weak recovery-cum-jobless-growth of the US economy in the first term of the George W. Bush administration. In the past few years the global economy has been marked by underinvestment in most key economic regions apart from China and by persistent tendencies towards stagnation. Weak growth has marked most other regions, notably Europe, which grew annually by 1.45 percent in the past few years. It is increasingly marked by a circular relationship. On the one hand, its growth has increasingly depended on the ability of American consumers to continue their debt-financed spending spree to absorb much of the output of China's production brought about by excessive investment. On the other hand, this relationship in turn depends on a massive financial reality: the dependence of US consumption on China's lending the US private and public sectors billions of dollars from the reserves it accumulated from its yawning trade surplus with the US. Parenthetically, this relationship is ironic since, notwithstanding its opportunistic alliance with China in the "war on terror," the Bush administration identified China as a "strategic competitor" in its 2002 National Strategy Paper.

Reflecting the worries of the IMF about global overproduction, a Fund official called attention to the "excessive dependence of global growth on unsustainable processes in the United States and to a lesser extent in China." He noted: "Perhaps the central concern has to be about consumption growth in the United States, which has been holding up the world economy" (Rajan 2005). Consumption-led growth, which entailed a current account deficit of 6.25 percent of the US's GDP and 1.5 percent of world GDP, was sustained mainly by the US's ability to pull in 70 percent of all global capital flows, much of them from China, as noted above (Rajan 2005). It was helped along by tax cuts for the rich and massive deficit spending that led to the evaporation of the federal budget surplus accumulated during the Clinton years. Much of the deficit spending went on defense expenditures, resulting in defense-related production accounting for 14 percent of GDP growth in 2003, although it represented only about 4 percent of the gross domestic product of the US. "Growing global imbalances" was the IMF's euphemism for the chain reaction of overproduction, underinvestment, and reliance of global growth on volatile financial flows sustaining consumer expenditure in the US. The disruption of these flows, coupled with higher energy prices, it warned, posed the possibility that they would "slow abruptly, taking away a major support from world growth before other supports are in place" (Rajan 2005).

End of the Long Wave?

Consumption-driven growth—the volatile driver of the tepid growth of the so-called "Goldilocks" economy—was, in the view of the Fund, unsustainable. So was overinvestment in China. These two factors were conditioned by a third: to many observers, the resumption of stagnation and listless growth were not only manifestations of a medium-term structural crisis but underlined the broader, degenerative long-term trend referred to earlier that had begun in the late 1970s—the B Phase or downward trend of the Kondratiev Wave. The crisis of overproduction was both a cause and an effect of the exhaustion of the profitable exploitation of technologies that had been the driver of growth in the immediate postwar era.

Contrary to forecasts by analysts who saw information technology as the core of a long-wave upswing in the first decade of the twenty-first century, the productivity gains from information and communications technology have been disappointing and certainly are insufficient to propel an upswing. Following David Gordon, Philip O'Hara has argued that the much vaunted information revolution of the 1980s and 1990s—the so-called driver of the New Economy—was actually a "pale imitation of a major technological revolution compared with the applications of electricity, the automobile, the airplane, chemicals, telephone, radio, television, sanitation, and plumbing in previous phases of capitalist development" (O'Hara 2003: 496).

The jobless growth of the recent "recovery" under Bush, in which productivity gains have come not from new applications of information and communications technology but from the shedding of labor, would seem to support this claim. The contradictory trends of the past few years may be the prelude to deflation, a deeper recession, and perhaps even a depression, as the world enters the tail end of the current long wave of capitalist expansion.

Bush and the Retreat from Globalization

The Bush administration's foreign economic policies must be seen partly as a response to the inability of globalization to surmount the crisis of overaccumulation and long wave-related exhaustion plaguing the US and global economies. Indeed, it is a retreat from globalization conceived as a project of functional integration of the global economy across national borders, led by a transnational capitalist elite, and governed by multilateral institutions that "constitutionalize" neoliberal, pro-corporate economic principles.

But this retreat from globalization takes place within a broader, momentous shift in Washington's Grand Strategy, thanks to a reconfiguration of the ruling bloc brought about by the Bush II ascendancy. The key elements of the Bush II paradigm appear to be the following. Unlike the Clinton administration and even the Bush senior administration, the Bush II people aggressively put the interests of US corporations ahead of the common interest of the global capitalist class, even if severe disharmony is the outcome. Their project is the unilateral assertion of power of the US elite rather than the construction of a system of shared power within a US-led global elite that was the thrust of the Clinton globalist project. Bush's political economy is very wary of a process of globalization that is not managed by the US government to ensure that the process does not dilute the economic power of the US. After all, a truly free market might victimize key US corporations, compromising US economic interests. Thus, despite its free market rhetoric, this is a group that is very protectionist when it comes to trade, investment, and the management of government contracts. It seems that the motto of the Bushites is protectionism for the US and free trade for the rest of the world.

The Bush approach towards the developing world is marked by the increasing resort to naked force to impose radical structural adjustment or free market policies. The administration is not content to leave the task to financial coercion by the IMF, World Bank, and the private banks. Iraq and Afghanistan are experiments in this enterprise of militarized economic adjustment. Moreover, although this ominous trend began before Bush, there is under his administration an intensification of "accumulation by dispossession," as David Harvey calls the latest stage in the privatization of the commons (Harvey 2003: 1–42). Through mechanisms like the imposition of "patent rights" via the WTO's Trade Related Intellectual Property Rights Agreement (TRIPs), US corporations seek to privatize the fund of commonly shared knowledge and technology passed down through the generations of farming communities in the South by restricting the use of genetically modified seeds developed at the end point of this communal process. TRIPs also allows corporations to restrict the natural processes of the communal diffusion of knowledge via patents, thus making industrialization by imitation—the traditional route to industrialization, all but impossible.

The Bush inner circle is strongly skeptical about multilateralism. They fear it since, although multilateralism may promote the interests of the global capitalist class in general, it may, in many instances, contradict particular US corporate interests. The administration's growing ambivalence towards the WTO stems from the fact that the US has lost a number of rulings there—rulings that hurt US capital—while not bringing about the expected openings for US exports in both Northern and developing country markets.

For the Bush people, politics is key, not only in the sense of using state power to repay political favors to corporate interests but, even more importantly, in the sense that for them, strategic power is the ultimate modality of power. The neoconservatives and nationalists who command enormous power in the administration see economic power as a means to achieve strategic power. Economic arrangements, like trade deals and the WTO, are judged less by their adherence to free trade than by the extent to which they contribute to the strategic power of the US. Given their emphasis on strategic power, the Bush elite has put the emphasis on disciplining the South via military force instead of relying only or mainly on structural adjustment programs imposed by the IMF or the World Bank.

While economic and related factors, such as control of oil, are certainly important in accounting for the US invasion of Iraq, they are not primary: the US expedition was meant mainly as an "exemplary war" whose purposes reached far into the future—to teach countries of the South the costs of defying the US and to warn potential rivals like China not to even think of challenging Washington militarily.

While the Bush administration is dedicated to advancing the interests of US capital as a whole, it is especially tied to the interests of what might be called the "Hard Economy." This is in sharp contrast to the Clinton administration, which was closely tied, via Treasury Secretary Robert Rubin, to Wall Street, the most internationalist section of the US capitalist class. The interests closest to Bush are either tied to government leaders by direct business links, as is the case with the oil industry (Bush and Cheney count as its special sons), or consist of those that can only subsist with massive subsidies from the government, like the steel industry and agribusiness, or those which often operate outside the free market and depend instead on secure government contracts that run on "cost-plus" arrangements. These latter kinds of firm make up the powerful "military industrial complex" that is really the most powerful bloc among corporate lobbyists in Washington today.[2] Not surprisingly, since many

---

2   One of the best analyses of the hard capitalist interests that are the 'mass base' of the Bush regime is Juhasz (2006).

of the interests supporting Bush are not subject to the market, they regard the free market and free trade as no more than rhetorical weapons to be deployed against external competitors and not taken seriously as an operating principle.

Key Economic Policy Thrusts

If the foregoing form the fundamental perspective of the Bush administration, then the following prominent elements of recent US economic policy make sense.

- *Achieving control over Middle Eastern and Central Asian energy resources* While this did not exhaust the war aims of the administration in invading Iraq, it was certainly high on the list. The invasion in part was aimed at potential European competitors. But perhaps the more strategic goal was to pre-empt control of the region's resources in order to limit access to them by energy-poor China, which, as noted earlier, is identified as a strategic competitor in the 2002 National Security Strategy paper, notwithstanding its serving as an ally in the "war on terror" (Meiksins Wood 2003: 145).

- *Aggressive protectionism in trade and investment matters* The Bush administration has, in fact, not hesitated to destabilize the multilateral trading order in order to protect US corporate interests. In addition to pushing for massive farm subsidies and raising steel tariffs, it defied the Doha Declaration that health should take priority over intellectual property claims. Responding to its powerful pharmaceutical lobby, the administration sought to limit the easing of patent controls to just three diseases. Since the Doha ministerial, in fact, Washington has put less energy into making the WTO a success. It prefers to pour its efforts into bilateral or multilateral trade deals, such as the Free Trade of the Americas (FTAA) or the Central America Free Trade Agreement (CAFTA). Indeed, the term "free trade agreements" is a misnomer, since these are actually preferential trade deals designed to severely disadvantage parties outside the agreement, like the EU.

- *Incorporating strategic considerations into trade agreements* Former US Trade Representative Robert Zoellick has stated explicitly that "countries that seek free-trade agreements with the United States must pass muster on more than trade and economic criteria in order to be eligible. At a minimum, these countries must cooperate with the United States on its foreign policy and national security goals, as part of 13 criteria that will guide the US selection of potential FTA partners." New Zealand, a government committed to free trade, has nevertheless not been offered a free trade deal because it has a policy that prevents visits of ships carrying nuclear weapons.[3]

---

3   'Zoellick says FTA candidates must support US foreign policy', *Inside US Trade*, 16 May 2003. This article summarizes an 8 May 2003 speech by Zoellick.

- *Manipulation of the dollar's value to shift the costs of economic crisis to rivals among the center economies and regain competitiveness for the US economy* The 25 percent fall in the value of the dollar relative to the euro within a relatively short period of time in 2002–03 was not the result of market forces but of conscious policy. While the Bush administration issued denials that this was a beggar-thy-neighbor policy, the US business press saw it for what it was: an effort to revive the US economy at the expense of the EU and other center economies, in order to counter the stagnationist pressures of the crisis of overaccumulation. With a falling dollar, US products could be competitively priced vis-à-vis foreign products in the US market as well as in foreign markets. The Bush policy was a reversal of the Clinton administration's strong dollar policy and a return to the weak dollar policy of another nationalistic administration, the Reagan presidency.

- *Aggressive manipulation of multilateral agencies to promote the interests of US capital coupled with a renewed reliance on bilateral aid as a means of forcing change on poor countries* While instrumental employment of a multilateral agency may not be too easy to achieve in the WTO because of the strength of the EU, it can be more readily done at the World Bank and the IMF, where US dominance is more effectively institutionalized. Despite support for the proposal from many European governments, the US Treasury recently torpedoed the IMF management's proposal for a Sovereign Debt Restructuring Mechanism (SDRM) to enable developing countries to restructure their debt while giving them a measure of protection from creditors. Already a very weak mechanism from the point of view of developing countries, the SDRM was vetoed by the US Treasury in the interest of US banks.[4]

In another example of intensifying conflict between the EU and Washington over the use of the IMF, the USA prevented the Fund from exerting significant pressure on Argentina when the latter threatened to unilaterally devalue its $100 billion private debt, owed mainly to European bondholders, on grounds that it opposed a bailout of the latter.

Even before Paul Wolfowitz was appointed head of the World Bank in 2005 the Bush administration was already moving to make it a more pliable instrument of its bilateral aid and development initiatives, including the radical privatization effort known as the Private Sector Development (PSD). Nancy Alexander's account of how this came about is instructive: Initially, most of the Bank's Board of Directors opposed the PSD Strategy's proposal to launch a third generation of adjustment focused on investment and to privatize services, especially health, education, and water. Gradually, outright opposition dissipated as Board members described the hard, uncompromising, "you're with us or against us" attitude of US officials. The PSD Strategy, which was finally approved by the Board on February 26, 2002, calls for a radical transformation of the form and functions of the World Bank group

---

4   For the sharpening conflicts between the US Treasury Department and IMF officials over US unilateralist moves, see Bullard (2002).

in order to promote the private sector. The Bank is now promoting investor rights while, at the same time, liberalizing and privatizing services, especially in low-income countries where regulatory regimes are generally weak to nonexistent.[5]

Perhaps even more important, the US lassoed the World Bank and the IMF to provide public finance for its so-called reconstruction efforts in both Afghanistan and Iraq. This is using international taxpayers' money to stabilize economies devastated by US wars. The World Bank, in particular, is not only being harnessed to provide money but to implement a blueprint of radical privatization in close cooperation with consultants and agencies of the US government. This trend is likely to intensify.

Instead of multilateral aid, bilateral aid in the form of grants has become the main conduit of US aid policy. Bilateral grant aid, Bush's foreign policy people argue, is more effectively controlled and thus tailored for one's purposes. "Grants can be tied more effectively to performance in a way that longer-term loans simply cannot. You have to keep delivering the service or you don't get the grant," said John Taylor, undersecretary of the Treasury (Bello 2005: 170–3).

The most ambitious new bilateral aid program unveiled by the administration was the Millennium Challenge Account (MCA), which called for a $5 billion increase in US aid, in addition to the average of $10 billion now regularly appropriated. To qualify for aid under the new program and for aid to continue flowing once a country had qualified, it had to get passing grades on 16 criteria that included trade policy, "days needed to start a business," inflation, budget deficit, control of corruption, rule of law, civil liberties, and immunization rate (Soederberg 2004: 295). The World Bank would provide assessments of the eligibility of countries for aid, as would conservative private nongovernmental organizations like Freedom House and the Heritage Foundation. The aid process itself would be conducted like a business venture, as the State Department makes clear:

> The MCA will use time-limited, business-like contracts that represent a commitment between the US and the developing country to meet agreed performance benchmarks. Developing countries will set their own priorities and identify their own greatest hurdles to development. They will do so by engaging their citizens, businesses, and governments in an open debate, which will result in a proposal for MCA funding. This proposal will include objectives, a plan and timetable for achieving them, benchmarks for assessing progress and how results will be sustained at the end of the contract, delineation of the responsibilities of the MCA and the MCA country, the role of civil society, business and other donors, and a plan for ensuring financial accountability for funds used. The MCA will review the proposal, consulting with the MCA country. The Board will approve all contracts.

The aim of this radical right-wing transformation of the aid policy is not just to accelerate market reform but, equally, to push political reform along narrow US-preferred lines, making the other center economies as well as developing countries bear the burden of adjusting to the environmental crisis. While some of the Bush people do not believe there is an environmental crisis, others know that the current

---

5 Nancy Alexander, "The US on the world stage: reshaping development, finance, and trade initiatives," Citizens' Network on Essential Services, Washington, DC, October 2002.

rate of global greenhouse emissions is unsustainable. However, they want others—specifically the EU and Japan—to bear the brunt of adjustment since not signing the Kyoto Protocol on Climate Change means not only exempting environmentally ineffecient US industry from the costs of adjustment, but hobbling other economies with even greater costs. Raw economic Realpolitik, not fundamentalist blindness, lies at the root of Washington's decision not to sign.

Conclusion

Overaccumulation or overproduction has been the specter that has hovered over the global economy since the 1970s. Neoliberal adjustment via structural adjustment and other contractionary programs merely worsened the crisis in the 1980s. Globalization and financialization during the Clinton period appeared to be a successful response in the 1990s as the central capitalist economy, the US, embarked on an eight-year-long boom. However, they merely added to contradictory pressures that broke out in a chain reaction of financial crises from the mid-1990s onwards and culminated in the recession that inaugurated the Bush administration in 2001.

A major casualty of these developments has been the phenomenon of globalization. At the structural level the much-vaunted relocation of industrial facilities, outsourcing of services, and decline in trade barriers have not resulted in a functionally integrated global economy where nation-states and their institutions are ceasing to be central determinants of economic affairs.

At the "superstructural" level the system of multilateral institutions that was supposed to govern and manage the system has been unraveling. Over the past few years, as a reaction to the overinvestment of the 1980s and 1990s, underinvestment has been the trend in most key economies. Growth has depended mainly on sustained consumer spending in the US to absorb China's massive production, with US demand being sustained by the flow of global savings from China and other key capitalist countries. This circular relationship is unfolding amid a momentous change in the paradigm of the US elite that can only, in the long run, worsen the crisis of overaccumulation.

Washington is currently dominated by a faction of the US ruling class that is intent on increasing the strategic power and hegemony of the US. The exercise of force, particularly against dissident forces in the South, is the main currency of this administration. In terms of meeting the global crisis of overaccumulation, the strategy of this faction has not been the Clintonite one of coordinated transnational response among allied capitalist elites but of forcing the burden of adjustment onto other center economies, while competing with them to exploit the developing word more intensely via new innovations in "primitive accumulation" such as TRIPs.

The conflicts between the EU and the US over agriculture in the WTO, over adherence to the Kyoto Protocol, over the debt problem of developing countries, over the value of the US dollar and over the policies of the IMF are manifestations of growing inter-capitalist and inter-imperialist competition. Added to policy conflicts such as differences over Iraq, Palestine, and Israel, these conflicts have spelled an end to the politico-economic Transatlantic Alliance which had sustained the hegemony of the Western capitalist bloc since the end of the Second World War.

A question of profound importance is how the US–China relationship will develop. Washington today has a grudging de´tente with China thanks to the necessity of enlisting it as an ally in the war against terror. But probably less compelling as a rationale for alliance to an elite that values the strategic supremacy of the US above all is the current economic dependence of the US on China's lending and its turning out of commodities to meet US consumer demand. With strong pressures from within its ranks and from the Pentagon to act towards China as a strategic enemy, the future of the grand economic bargain of the two key pillars of the capitalist global economy hangs in the balance.

The global economy being held hostage to geopolitics on the part of two political leaderships that value the accumulation of strategic power above all is not the future that corporate-driven globalization was supposed to deliver.

Chapter 6

Globalization and Counter-Globalization in the Caribbean

Norman Girvan

I would like to suggest that a distinction be made between the *substantive meaning* and the *ideological use* of the term "globalization." The linking of different regions of the world through transcontinental circuits of capital, trade, and production started towards the end of the fifteenth century and was a result of European maritime and mercantile expansion. In that sense substantive globalization has been taking place for 500 years and the very existence of the contemporary South is one of its historical products.

But the widespread use of the term belongs to the 1990s; a popular and journalistic expression of the ideology of neoliberalism applied to the post Cold War world. Globalization has become shorthand for an allegedly irreversible process towards the formation of world economy, society and culture driven by technology and the transnationalization of capital. Reduction and eventual elimination of barriers to the movement of goods, services, and capital across national borders is held to be at once inevitable, necessary, and universally benign. Here we will refer to the "globalization project" of the 1990s, meaning (1) the package of neoliberal practices that governments are required to adopt; (2) the multilateral institutions responsible for policing and enforcing these practices; and (3) the legitimating theory and ideology.

Globalization in Context

To set this project in context, we need briefly to review the turbulent events of the previous two decades. The abandonment of the Bretton Woods system at the beginning of the 1970s was to have major long-term consequences, for it established a framework in which currency speculation and its offshoots became major sources of profit for international finance. The OPEC price increases of 1973 further fueled the growth of the eurodollar market, which found profitable opportunities for international lending to both surplus and deficit developing countries. Hence the external debt of the South grew rapidly, and, together with a decline in commodity prices in the second half of the 1970s, led to a sharp deterioration in its bargaining power towards the end of the decade.

The beginning of the 1980s saw the Keynesian consensus in the North replaced by the new orthodoxy of neoliberal monetarism, reflected in the Thatcher/Reagan administrations. The subsequent interest-rate shocks imposed in the US and elsewhere in the name of a monetarist anti-inflation strategy threw the South into a severe debt crisis that started in Mexico in 1982 and continued throughout the 1980s. It provided the lever by which the Northern-dominated international financial institutions were able to impose severe neoliberal policy conditionalities on much of the South. The measures centered on devaluation, privatization and trade and investment liberalization.

By 1986, with the South in retreat and disarray, UNCTAD (United Nations Conference on Trade and Development) had been eclipsed by GATT (General Agreement on Tariffs and Trade) as the main forum for international trade negotiations. The agenda shifted from effecting structural reforms in the international trading system for the promotion of development, to lowering barriers to trade and investment for the promotion of market-led growth. The growth in new information and communications technologies also led to the determined—and successful—bid by the US to include services and intellectual property in the Uruguay Round of the GATT negotiations. At the same time, each of the three capitalist centers intensified efforts to strengthen its position itself vis-à-vis the other two. The European Community made plans to transform itself in to the European Union. Japan continued to consolidate itself as the center of an Asia-Pacific economic zone; while the United States initiated talks for the creation of North American Free Agreement (NAFTA), which would lead towards to the FTAA (Free Trade Agreement for the Americas) project of the 1990s.

The collapse of Eastern European socialism and the USSR was the catalyst for the conversion of trade and financial liberalization into a truly global project. The one large remaining non-capitalist economy, China, was busily adopting market-oriented reforms and opening up to direct foreign investment, though not to full "globalization."

The Globalization Project of the 1990s

The globalization project of the 1990s therefore had a coherent political, institutional, theoretical, and ideological basis, a set of prescribed practices, and a convenient and easily recognized label. We see *ten* features as central:

1. A world economic order centered on the Triad of US–EU–Japan, under the political and military leadership of the US;
2. The World Trade Organization (WTO), dominated by the Triad, as the chief global institution for negotiating, codifying and enforcing neoliberal practices in interstate economic relations;
3. The construction of regional blocs or free trade zones by each member of the Triad in order to strengthen its position vis-à-vis the other two; the strongest being the EU;
4. In regional North–South trade agreements (NAFTA, FTAA, Lome), replacement of the principle of non-reciprocal preferences to assist the development of weaker partners with that of reciprocal trade liberalization to promote trade expansion and market-led growth, in line with WTO provisions;

5. Promotion of a package of neoliberal policy measures with assumed universal applicability. These include privatization, financial deregulation, trade and exchange rate liberalization, fiscal and monetary orthodoxy, labor market reform, and social welfare reform;

6. The alleged loss of national economic sovereignty flowing from the imperative for all governments to adopt standard neoliberal measures in order to maintain competitiveness and attract investment capital;

7. The attainment of "global competitiveness" as the benchmark by which all countries and producers, regardless of their resources or level of development, are to be evaluated through participation in the global market place (the "level playing field");

8. The growth of global telecommunications—computer networks, satellite TV and the internet—as the technological infrastructure in the globalization of finance, production, marketing, and patterns of consumption;

9. The consolidation of huge concentrations of private capital—transnational corporations and institutional investors—as the dominant players in world production, trade and finance; and finally

10. A triumphalist ideology, marked by the assumption that there is no other way to organize the world, as summed up in the phrase "the end of history." This is receding as a result of the present global financial crisis (Halimi 1998).

Counter-globalization

We use the term "counter-globalization" to refer broadly to that body of opinion that is critical of market-oriented, corporate-led globalization, and to social movements that advocate alternative ways of managing national economies and international exchange. Counter-globalization does not necessarily imply a retreat to a world of autarchic national entities—though some elements within the broader movement may embrace such a position. It accommodates the fact that the world community is being brought closer together by rapid advances in info-communications technologies as well by the growth of international transport.[1] To that extent the degree of national barriers to international exchange on which the post World War II order had been erected had become impossible to sustain by the 1990s.

What is questioned is the assumption that global market liberalization will work to the benefit of all, inducing weaker economies to become more competitive, generating equitable all-round economic growth, and leading to desirable social and environmental outcomes with minimum government intervention and no need for social management. This is contradicted by the fact that international markets are skewed against the poorer countries of the world, by the evidence on widening income

---

1   For instance, the cost of an international telephone call fell by 90 percent between 1970 and 1990, maritime transport costs fell by more than two-thirds between 1920 and 1990, and operating costs per mile of airline transport fell by 60 percent between 1960 and 1990. Global telecommunications traffic grew by 80 percent per year in the 1980s. By 1997, the internet was being used by at least 50 million people and growing rapidly (UNDP 1997a: 83).

inequalities among nations, and by the rapid pace of environmental degradation. In the words of the UNDP's 1997 *Human Development Report*:

> Globalization is ... proceeding apace, but largely for the benefit of the more dynamic and powerful countries of the North and the South. The loss to developing countries from unequal access to trade, labour and finance (is) estimated ... at $500 billion a year, 10 times what the receive annually in foreign assistance. (UNDP 1997h: 87)

Among the findings highlighted in this and other issues of the Human Development Reports are that in international financial markets, real interest rates are four times higher for poor countries as for rich countries (17 percent compared to 4 percent). Eighty-three percent of foreign direct investment goes to rich countries, and three-quarters of the remainder goes to ten developing countries, mostly in East and Southeast Asia and in Latin America. The countries with the poorest 20 percent of the world's people receive just 0.2 percent of international commercial lending (UNDP 1992: 48; UNDP 1996b: 9).

Developed countries impose the highest trade barriers on goods in which developing countries have the greatest competitive advantage: textiles, clothing, and footwear. The cost to the developing countries of these barriers has been estimated by the IMF at $50 billion per year (UNDP 1994: 66).

Domestic agricultural subsidies and price supports by the industrial countries cost the developing and formerly centrally planned economies approximately $22 billion a year in foregone export revenues (UNDP 1992: 48; UNDP 1994: 67).

Cumulative terms-of-trade losses by the developing countries amounted to $290 billion between 1980 and 1991 (UNDP 1997a: 84).

The share in world trade of the world's poorest countries, with 20 percent of the world's people, has declined from 4 percent to less than 1 percent from 1960 to 1990 (UNDP 1996b: 9).

Although the net benefits from the GATT Uruguay Round agreements are estimated at $212–510 billion per year, the losses will be concentrated among countries that are least able to afford them: Sub-Saharan Africa will lose up to $1.2 billion per year, and the Least Developed Countries (LDCs) $600 million (UNDP 1997h: 82).

The poorest 20 percent of the world's people saw their share in world income decline from 2.3 percent to 1.4 percent in the past three decades, while that of the richest 20 percent grew from 70 to 85 percent. The ratio of the shares grew from 30:1 to 61:1 (UNDP 1996b: 8). The assets of the world's 358 billionaires exceed the combined annual incomes of the 2.5 billion people who comprise the poorest 45 percent of humankind (UNDP 1996b: 8)

Global warming has already become a serious problem; 20 countries already suffer from water stress; a sixth of the world's land area is now degraded; deforestation has reduced the wooded area per 1,000 inhabitants by 36 percent since 1970; world fish stocks are declining; and wild species are becoming extinct at 50–100 times the natural rate (UNDP 1998: 4).

Counter-globalization therefore challenges the neoliberal assumption that markets are "free and fair"—that is impersonal, devoid of institutional context, equitably structured, and immune to the exercise of corporate power. This assumption is the theoretical underpinning of free trade negotiations in the WTO/EU–ACP/FTAA contexts. Hence the issues of *market information, market transparency, market regulation and market structure reform* become relevant for international negotiations. Similarly, the principle of *gradated differentiation of treatment of countries and groups of countries* according to their ability to compete effectively in an open trading environment needs to be retained and reinforced as in integral part of international trade arrangements.

Heightened pressures on all producers everywhere to become "globally competitive" are an established fact due to the spread of info-communications technologies and the conclusion of the Uruguay Round. The issues are: Competitiveness to what end, and by what means. Competitiveness for the world market achieved at the cost of increasing unemployment, social exclusion, poverty, and inequality is questionable. Heightened efficiency that results from equipping the poor and marginalized with education, skills, health care, and economic assets, and in doing so reduces poverty and social exclusion, is to be welcomed. The need is to make global markets supportive of poverty reduction and human development, rather than to sacrifice the latter to the needs of the former.

This calls into question the validity of the practice of blanket trade liberalization and its underlying theoretical principle, which relates to the universal applicability of market-oriented, private-sector-led growth. The relevant practices would appear to be selectivity and sequencing of trade liberalization, complemented by strategies to build up technological and managerial capabilities among producers at the micro level and to empower the poor and the marginalized. In terms of theory, it questions the universalistic presuppositions of neoliberal thinking.

Universalistic thinking holds that all economies obey certain universal laws of economics and correspondingly that the policies that guarantee economic success are essentially the same in every country. Epistemologically, universalism is rooted in the claims of neoclassical economics to be akin to the natural sciences, especially physics. The opposing view is that economic processes are embedded in specific social contexts. The world community exhibits wide diversity in history, institutions, culture, social structure, economic structure, and politics. Hence the functioning of markets, the nature of entrepreneurship, and the capacity of the state machinery varies from country to country. Accordingly, questions related to the role of "market vs. state" cannot be determined outside of a specific context in time and place. Each country will need to find the combination of mechanisms—state and market—and organization (state versus private sector enterprises, cooperatives, civil society or nongovernmental organizations [NGOs], community-based or grassroots organizations) that works best given its historical legacy and its specific economic, social, institutional, and cultural setting. What succeeds in one country may fail in another, and vice versa. This is more so when issues of social and human development, equity, and ecological sustainability are to be addressed; for these require the inclusion of civil society in governance and economic management.

To work out a suitable blend of market, state and civil society in economic management, countries need to have room for experimentation and social learning in a supportive global environment. Universalistic neoliberalism will be replaced with respect for diversity and acceptance of the principles of *pluralism, particularity* and *learning*. Balancing this against the need for a minimum set of standards and rules to govern international economic exchange is a matter for international negotiation.

To summarize, counter-globalization questions the theory, the ideology and the practices of neoliberal globalization. It draws on a wide range of social forces: governments of disadvantaged countries in the South; labor unions in the North who fear the loss of jobs to low-wage locations in the South; projectionist lobbies in the North; environmental groups and community organizations. A major factor is the emergence of North–South counter-globalization coalitions of citizens' groups and other NGOs. The NGO Forums on the World Bank/IMF and the NGO mobilization against the Multilateral Agreement on Investment (MAI) negotiations are clear indications of the growth of this social movement, using new information technologies—especially the Internet—to great effect. Other examples include the World Forum on Development Alternatives (DAVOS), and the Citizen's Public Trust Treaty. Here we may write of "the globalization of counter-globalization."

In general these organizations advocate an alternative order based on the principles of equity, social justice, democratic participatory governance, and ecological sustainability. This should apply both within and among nations. However counter-globalization is not necessarily a united, coherent body of opinion and political action. There are contradictions among NGOs and between NGOs, governments, and labor unions. This produces a pattern of "shifting coalitions" around specific issues, e.g. the MAI, NAFTA, the IMF, and the Convention on Global Climate Change. It represents so far a kind of global social movement in the making. Its potential for the future is significant, given the global scope of problems such as poverty, the subordination of women, and ecological degradation; and given the powerful tools available to the movement from global communications technologies.

Impact of the World Financial Crisis on Globalization

The world financial crisis of 1997–8 has been a major blow to the current globalization project. There is a broad consensus that it came about largely as a result of the unrestricted, unregulated, and unmonitored inflow of "hot" money to these countries from the early 1990s through 1996, following strong pressure for capital account liberalization from the US. This was followed by a massive turnaround in 1997–8 that often had little to do with underlying conditions in particular countries ("contagion of emerging markets" effect). To that extent even prominent proponents of the neoliberal orthodoxy are being forced to re-examine their position and concede a greater role for government regulation of financial systems.

To survive therefore the globalization project will undoubtedly undergo theoretical and policy modification. The purely market-oriented version will probably be shaded into one that recognizes a role for global financial regulation, similar to the national regulation of financial systems in the advanced capitalist countries. This may work against the immediate interests of speculative capital. But it will assist the globalization of production and long-term investment by providing a more stable and less risky global economic environment. It would approximate what might be called a regime of "globally managed neoliberalism."

But the social and political effects of the crisis will be much more difficult for the pro-globalization forces to manage and control. Tens of millions of people have been thrown into poverty and unemployment in some of the world's most populous countries, unleashing social movements and political forces that blame international finance and its corrupt local allies for their plight. Several countries are now experimenting with unorthodox measures, such as capital controls, and limiting foreign access to domestic capital markets. The eventual outcome of political developments in countries such as Russia, Indonesia, and Malaysia is impossible to predict. But it seems likely that the states most severely impacted by the crisis will become more nationalistic and assertive with regard to the globalization project. This will provide an example to others. China, for its part, had always managed its participation in the globalization project very carefully, refusing to engage in capital-account liberalization or to float its currency.

The immediate effect of the current crisis, therefore, has been to weaken the globalization project. However, the longer-term effects could be to weaken it or to renovate it, depending on how effectively the various actors develop strategies to defend and extend their interests. The North (i.e. governments and capital) has yet to come up with a coherent consensus plan. The positions advanced in the search for consensus in the reform of the International Monetary/Financial System include the following:

1. Greater information, transparency, monitoring and surveillance of short-term flows; reform of domestic regulatory systems in developing countries (supported by the US, the IMF and the World Bank);
2. The IMF to become lender of last resort (proposed by Fischer, Chief Economist at the IMF);
3. For the IMF to become the World Central Bank (proposed by George Soros); and
4. Controls to be placed on short-term capital flows (proposed by UNCTAD, leading voices in the EU and Japan; already adopted by some Asian developing countries).

The US, for obvious reasons, opposes any move to institute controls and regulation on short-term capital flows, a position that is finding growing support in the EU, and Japan and in the developing world. There is a multitude of contradictory interests to reconcile—among the US, the EU, and Japan, between finance capital and industrial capital, and between different fractions of finance capital. It may take a full-blown world depression to push the North towards making drastic revisions in current arrangements.

In any case the South needs to insert itself more effectively into this debate, with well-thought out proposals of its own. Strengthening of the IMF role in world finance, for instance, would not necessarily be in the interests of the South, as that organization is controlled by the North and is still wedded to neoliberal principles.

Position of the South

As mentioned before, the South as a negotiating bloc (G77, Non-Aligned Movement or NAM) has been in retreat since the tide turned against it in the run-up to the WTO.

It has been further fractured through "regionalization" of North–South negotiations in the EU–ACP, NAFTA, and FTAA contexts, and by the rapid growth of East Asia vis-à-vis the rest of the South, followed by its equally dramatic collapse.

The reality is that the South is a far more heterogeneous group of countries than it was 30–40 years ago, when the "Third World" was conceived. This is so whether the reference point is level of per capita income, dependence on primary commodities, degree of industrial and technological development, incidence of poverty among the population, social and political structures, or ideological orientation. (Size has always been a major point of differentiation.) To the extent that there is a common factor, it lies in the generally (though not uniformly) subordinate relationship of the countries of the South with the capitalist centers in international trade, technology and finance and in the negotiations governing these processes. In other words "the South" is defined by *the nature of power relations in the international system.*

This also calls into question the concept of the "South" as a cohesive bloc with common interests across a whole range of specific issues, and concerned exclusively with relations on the inter-state level. It may be more realistic to think of a *series of coalitions* organized around specific common interests shared by particular groups of states and civil society organizations. Already this development is under way at the level of NGOs. At the inter-state level within the South, the realities of differentiation are evident in the existence of the group of Small Island Developing States (SIDS) for the purpose of environmental negotiations, in the grouping of LDCs, and in associations of primary commodity exporters.

However, global trade negotiations are still structured on the presumed cohesiveness of the South as a group, with the three regional subgroups of Asia, Africa, and Latin America and the Caribbean. It is not at all clear that this is the most appropriate structure for purposes of negotiation. Each regional subgroup contains countries whose interests are often contradictory. China, India, Brazil, and Indonesia, for instance, are large states with a considerable degree of industrial development. They have much more in common with one another than they do with sub-Saharan Africa, or with the small countries of Latin America and the Caribbean. Therefore we could envisage, for example, a coalition grouping of small states, of large states, of manufacturing exporters, of primary commodity exporters, and of LDCs. This Caribbean, as a collection of small and mini-states, needs therefore to review its position within the wider setting of the South and the broad currents of the counter-globalization movement.

Globalization in the Caribbean

The context in which Caribbean countries have been impacted by globalization is characterized by:

- *Small size.* The 28 entities of the insular Caribbean have an aggregate population of only 36 million; 22 have populations of less than one million.

- *Dependency.* Trade dependency ranges from to and averages. Most countries specialize in a narrow range of goods and/or services exported to a narrow range of metropolitan markets (US, EU, Russia), relying on EU trade preferences in the case of traditional agricultural products. Financial dependency is evident in the degree of foreign financing (commercial and concessional) for government capital expenditure and sometimes for recurrent spending.

- *Fragmentation.* Twelve entities are dependent territories of the four colonial powers—Britain, France, the Netherlands, and the United States. The independent states comprise English-speaking (12), Spanish-speaking (2) and French- and Dutch-speaking (one each). There is no single integration grouping for the insular Caribbean. The Caribbean Community (Caricom) includes all the English-speaking states and Suriname and has admitted Haiti, but Cuba and the Dominican Republic (DR) are not members. Cariforum comprises Caricom and the DR but excludes Cuba, and is not a true integration grouping since its functions are limited to coordinating trade and aid negotiations with the EU. The Association of Caribbean States (ACS) includes all the insular Caribbean plus the littoral states in Central and South America from Mexico to Venezuela, most of which belong to other integration groupings (i.e. Nafta, SICA (Central American Integration System, Spanish: *Sistema de Integración Centroamericana*, and the Andean System).

Globalization, therefore, has generated strong cross-currents within the region. Differences in production structures and external association have sometimes resulted in contradictory short-term interests among countries and marked divergences in economic policy. There is a growing interest in regional cooperation, but this will need to address the formidable obstacles arising out of the wide economic differentiation among countries, and the legacy of political and linguistic fragmentation. Below we discuss this in terms of the issues of policy convergence, external relations, and regional cooperation.

Policy Convergence

All Caribbean states have instituted market-oriented policy reforms of one kind or another in the past two decades. But the changes have varied widely and have resulted in marked policy divergence in some areas of macroeconomic policy. Within Caricom this is most evident in exchange rate policy, where Guyana, Jamaica, and Trinidad-Tobago have instituted floating rates and no capital controls whereas Barbados and the ECCB (Eastern Caribbean Central Bank) countries have maintained fixed rates with restrictions on capital movements. The DR and Haiti also have floating exchange rate regimes whereas Cuba follows a two-tier system. There are also differences among countries in the degree of privatization and of trade and financial liberalization. In general, the countries with the most severe debt and adjustment crises in the 1980s have gone the farthest in embracing neoliberal policy reforms (with the notable exception of Cuba). This may constrain the readiness of their governments to adopt a critical stance vis-à-vis the underlying principles of globalization as expressed in external negotiations.

Jamaica's experience in the 1990s is a noteworthy example of the risks of blanket adoption of neoliberal policy reforms. After undertaking a series of stabilization and structural adjustment programs between 1977 and 1990, the Jamaican Government decided to lift all remaining exchange controls, deregulate the financial system, and float the currency. The Jamaican dollar lost 70 percent of its value over a 12-month period, and inflation in 1991 topped 80 percent. In order to stabilize the exchange rate and stem the inflationary spiral, the Jamaican authorities have issued huge amounts of government paper have been issued, at high real interest rates. In recent years these policies have succeeded in stabilizing the exchange rate and cutting inflation to single digit levels, but at a high economic and social cost. Economic growth during the 1990s, has been minimal; the ratio of internal debt to GDP grew from 35 percent in 1990 to 46 percent in 1997. Debt servicing now absorbs 80 percent of government revenue and 70 percent of government expenditure, four-fifths of this being for internal debt. A financial sector crisis beginning in 1997 has so far cost the government the equivalent of 45 percent of the GDP in financial interventions. Hence, deregulation of the currency and financial system has lead to a situation in which monetary and fiscal policy is hostage to the maintenance of price stability, severely prejudicing government provisions for human development and the achievement of economic growth.

External Relations within the Caribbean

The majority of Caribbean countries are unique in the developing world in having enjoyed one-way preferential trading arrangements with both the EU under Lome and the US under the Caribbean Basin Initiative (CBI). Now both of these arrangements are being undercut by the requirements of multilateral, reciprocal trade liberalization under the terms of the WTO Treaty. Cuba of course lost its preferential trade arrangements with the USSR and other CMEA (Council for Mutual Economic Assistance) countries after 1989.

The impact of the WTO is both direct, stemming from the requirements of the WTO Treaty itself; and indirect, due to the requirements of "WTO compatibility" in the renegotiation of the Lome agreement and in the FTAA negotiations. In fact it is the latter that is posing the most immediate competitive challenges to Cariforum and CBI countries. An additional complicating factor in the negotiations is that Cariforum countries are allied with African and Pacific countries in the ACP Group under Lome and with Central American countries in the Small Country Group within the FTAA negotiations. There is also the issue of "cross-compatiblity" between the terms of the FTAA and post-Lome arrangements.

The EU, Lome and Cariforum

The EU is proposing to make radical changes in its trade and aid relationship with the ACP after the current Lome Convention expires in the year 2000, changes that are in line with neoliberal thinking and the requirements of WTO compatibility. The objective is replace existing one-way trade preferences for the ACP with a series of six Free Trade Areas known as Regional Economic Partnership Arrangements (REPAs). Negotiation of the REPAs is to be preceded by dialog on a framework agreement based on commitment to neoliberal, market-oriented economic policies, and practice of democratic governance and respect for human rights.

Studies commissioned by the EU show that the proposed Free Trade Areas will at best lead to marginal increases in ACP exports to the EU, with more significant increases in EU exports to ACP countries. Many ACP will face severe adjustment problems due to loss customs revenue. Some ACP groups, notably the Pacific and Southern Africa, are also not yet ready for the internal free trade that is a requirement of the REPAs. It may be significant the EU's proposals for REPAs were developed before the commissioning of studies on the likely impact. This suggests that they stemmed from prior commitment to free trade objectives rather than from an empirical analysis of the costs and benefits of the proposed arrangements to the ACP countries.

In the run-up to the ministerial-level negotiations the EU has softened its stance somewhat in terms of the phasing of the implementation of the FTA arrangements. However, the new arrangements seem certain to weaken the cohesiveness of the ACP grouping. The main interest of Caricom countries is in the maintenance of the arrangements relating to sugar, bananas, and rum; and in the possible extension of the terms of the FTAs to include services. They also oppose the inclusion of political conditionalities in the arrangements. Many African countries in the ACP group are LDCs. They rely heavily on EU financial assistance, and have little immediate interest in manufactured exports and services. These countries appear more inclined to accept the proposed EU framework.

From CBI to NAFTA to FTAA

The North American Free Trade Agreement (NAFTA) of 1994 gives Mexican and Canadian producers duty-free access to the US market. It eroded the preferential advantages which Caribbean basin exporters had enjoyed under the Caribbean Basin Initiative (CBI) of 1983 and the 806/807 Customs provisions (Gonzales 1995: 5–10). Caribbean basin governments have been pressing Washington for NAFTA parity—that is, duty-free access to the US market equivalent to that of Mexico and Canada—but the US Congress has been unwilling to give its support for the enabling legislation. The option of NAFTA accession by Caricom or by some of its member states was also contemplated at the time when the US administration had "fast-track" authority to expand NAFTA by means of a series of bilateral negotiations, but this no longer applies. US administration policy now centers on the promotion of the Free Trade Agreement of the Americas (FTAA) by means of hemisphere-wide negotiations (excepting Cuba) which were launched in 1998 with 2005 as the target date for the conclusion. US policy is that the FTAA should be both NAFTA-consistent and WTO-compatible. The agreement will cover liberalization of trade in services and of investment flows, and a whole range of regulatory issues involving government policies and practices.

In the run-up to the FTAA negotiations Caribbean countries had joined forces with Central America in forming the Working Group on Smaller Economies (Report 1997), which grew out of earlier cooperation in lobbying for NAFTA parity. Initially, there were hopes for acceptance of the principle of special treatment for smaller economies as part of the basic negotiating parameters of the FTAA Treaty. Special treatment could mean the granting of one-way nonreciprocal trade liberalization to benefit the small economies of Central America and the Caribbean. Failing this, there could be a longer period of adjustment to full liberalization. The rationale would be their competitive weaknesses due to absence of economies of scale. This principle was not fully accepted by other FTAA participating countries in the preparatory meetings. The Declaration of San Jose includes the principle of "special attention to the needs and conditions" of smaller economies, to be supported by a consultative group on the terms of the negotiations, and the group had to settle for a consultative group rather than a separate negotiating group.

To take advantage of these modest concessions, Caribbean and Central American countries face a formidable task. They will be required to service nine separate negotiating groups with technical and professional personnel whilst using the consultative group to maximum effect. The limitations in bargaining power are shown by the fact that the smaller economies together have less than 1 percent of the aggregate GDP of FTAA-negotiating countries and only 7 percent of the combined population. So far, Caricom has been participating as one unit through the Regional Negotiating Machinery (RNM), while the DR and the Central American (SICA) countries have been coordinating their position. The FTAA negotiations have started in slow gear due to the absence of fast-track authority in the US administration and the effects of the world financial crisis. The devastating effects of Hurricane Mitch in 1998 also led some Central American countries to press for duty-free access to the US market as a special concession.

The bigger picture is that Caribbean and Central American countries could be required within ten years to open up their markets in goods, services, and investment to producers from the US, Canada, and the more industrially advanced Latin American countries; and to compete on an equal footing with them in their traditional US market. Cariforum countries are also bound by the obligations of the current Lome arrangements. Should they participate in a final FTAA Treaty, they will be bound to give free trade privileges to the EU as well. The FTAA is important to Caricom for US market access whilst the EU relationship is important for traditional agricultural exports and for concessional aid. Handling both sets of negotiations simultaneously and the related diplomatic-political relationships (the US, the EU, Central America, and the non-Caricom Caribbean, and the ACP) constitutes a formidable task requiring a high degree of technical preparation and intergovernmental coordination.

The current "banana war" between the US and the EU is a prime example of a number of the issues touched on here. First, it shows how the fate of small economies can be decided by changes in international trading arrangements over which they have virtually no control. Ultimately this dispute, which affects the livelihoods of thousands of small producers in the mini-states of Dominica, St. Vincent and St. Lucia, will be resolved through the negotiation of power relations between the US and the EU. Second, the dispute underscores the new role of the WTO as the institutional mechanism by which the new rules of the open multilateral trading regime are negotiated and enforced. Third, it dramatizes the reduced strategic importance and leverage of the small Caribbean states in the post Cold War era.

Fourth, it shows how the policies of a major power (the US) can be made hostage to corporate interests through the perverse operation of its political system. And fifth, it shows how the short-term interests of different groups of developing countries (in this case the Caribbean and Central/South America) can be pitted against one another as a result of the global thrust towards multilateral free trade driven by transnational corporations (TNCs).

Regional co-operation

One positive effect of globalization-induced trade liberalization has been to stimulate cooperation efforts across traditional linguistic barriers within the Greater Caribbean region. In a sense this was anticipated by the scope of the Caribbean Basin Initiative, which for the first time in history brought together the Caribbean and Central America (Cuba and Nicaragua excepted) within the coverage of a preferential trading arrangement. The 1990s have seen three significant institutional developments in regional cooperation. First, the Lome Convention was expanded to include Haiti and the DR in the ACP group, and these two countries joined with Caricom in forming Cariforum for the purpose of trade and aid negotiations with the EU. Second, the Association of Caribbean States (ACS) was established with membership covering all the independent states of the Greater Caribbean (Caribbean basin). The ACS is a mechanism of cooperation in trade, transport, and tourism. And third, Caricom was expanded to admit its first non-Anglophone members, Suriname and, more recently, Haiti.

To point to the significance of these developments is not to underestimate the obstacles in the way of wider regional cooperation. The membership of the ACS is a highly disparate collection of states in terms of size, per capita income, economic structure, and integration groupings. The ACS will not negotiate as a unit in the FTAA talks; since the majority of members already belong to existing integration arrangements including NAFTA (Mexico), the Central American Integration System, the Andean System (Colombia and Venezuela), and Caricom.

There are also three "non-group" members: Cuba, the DR, and Panama. In the case of Cariforum, the functions are limited to coordinating negotiations with the EU. In the case of Caricom, the procedures to formalize the 1997 decision to admit Haiti have not yet been completed. Moreover, progress in completing the establishment of the Caricom Single Market and Economy has been agonizingly slow.

The difficulties in giving operational effect to new relationships are illustrated in the fate of a recent proposal to forge a strategic alliance between the Caribbean and Central America, with the DR acting as a bridge. This proposal emanated from the new Fernandez administration in Santo Domingo in 1998. It envisaged (a) creation of a free trade area embracing both subregions, (b) functional cooperation in the promotion of investment and tourism and in the liberalization of sea and air transport services, and (c) support of external negotiations over NAFTA parity, the FTAA, and the EU–ACP relationship, and the coordination of WTO negotiations. Step 1, agreement on a DR–Central American Free Area, was completed in April 1998. Step 2, agreement on a DR–Caricom FTA, was completed in outline form in June 1998 but a follow-up meeting on goods to be exempted was aborted due to the

DR's opposition to Caricom's position on the matter. The proposal for a Caribbean-Central American Strategic Alliance was noted at the Cariforum–Cuba summit in August 1998 but no decision was taken.

It is fair to say that there is no strong enthusiasm for the alliance, or for a Caricom–Central American FTA, on either side. Both subregions are preoccupied with the more immediate demands on their attention: Caricom with the EU negotiations and the banana question; Central America with its relations with the US and Mexico and with post Hurricane Mitch reconstruction. In addition as with external trade negotiations, the technical and political requirements of simultaneously servicing a wide range of regional initiatives are a strain on the limited resources of small states. The danger is that government policies will be entirely reactive to short-term pressures as they arise; to the neglect of policies that are guided by long-term strategic planning.

Conclusions: Strategic Responses to Globalization

Responding to globalization evidently requires a "walking on two legs" strategy. The one involves *strengthening the bargaining position and negotiating capacity* of the region's states in their external economic relations. The objective is to maximize the possibilities of outcomes that take account of the interests of small states with the specific production structures of the Caribbean. The other *involves strengthening the productive and competitive capacities of regional producers* to participate successfully in markets that will be increasingly hemispheric and global in scope. This requires technically proficient strategic planning by governments, with industrial policies aimed at diversifying production and strengthening and technological capabilities and promoting innovation. The overall need is to increase the capacity to respond of small economies at the level of governments, firms and the population as a whole. With this in mind, the following suggestions are advanced.

The world financial crisis should be seen as a "window of opportunity" for the South to insert itself into the redesign of the architecture of the international financial and monetary system. It will need to generate technically rigorous reform proposals that are in its own interests of the South as a whole while taking account of the heterogeneous nature of the South. The immediate dangers are those of (1) continuing instability resulting in a global economic depression that impacts further on the lives of hundreds of millions, and (2) negotiation of a new system among the US, the EU, and Japan that fails to take account of the interests of the South, with the latter becoming split into currency zones dominated by the US dollar, the euro, and the yen.

Together with the South, Caribbean countries should challenge the principles of universalistic neoliberalism on which current international trade and economic negotiations are based; seeking recognition of the principles of selectivity, sequence, particularity, pluralism, and learning. Each state should have room to develop its own mix of industrial policy with regard to the role of the state, the private sector, and small-scale and community-based enterprises consistent with the objectives of equitable, participatory and sustainable development.

As an integration grouping, Caricom needs to complete the establishment of the Single Market and Economy in order to strengthen its own bargaining power in regional and international negotiations.

In its external relations, Caricom needs to look beyond the end of Lome and of neocolonial preferential arrangements; defining its strategic long-term interests in common with that of the smaller developing countries, beginning with the nonEnglish-speaking Caribbean and Central America. One option is for Cariforum to be broadened into a cooperation mechanism, as a steppingstone to a Small Country Strategic Alliance between Caricom, the non-Caricom Caribbean (Cuba, the Dominican Republic and Haiti) and Central America. The objective of a Small Country Strategic Alliance would be aim to lobby, bargain and negotiate in favor of the principle of special and differential treatment in trade agreements for small countries and mini-states, on the basis of their size-related environmental, economic, and social vulnerability.

Chapter 7

Chávez, Democracy and Globalization: Business as Unusual

Terry Gibbs

In the context of struggling neoliberal "democracies," many analysts now promote an increased focus on poverty alleviation and the reduction of inequality through carefully managed redistribution. They often fail, however, to question the overall logic of "efficient macroeconomic management" oriented towards market-based reforms. Therefore, these "post-neoliberal" policies should not be seen as an overall structural shift in paradigm but rather as poverty management within the paradigm. The Bolivarian Revolution in Venezuela, on the other hand, represents an all-out assault on neoliberal doctrine and its authoritarian elements, putting into question elite control of the economy. A key aspect of the revolution has been the effort to revitalize citizenship through the construction of mechanisms for public participation in decision-making, particularly aiming at the poor majority. The dramatic transformations taking place in health and education policy in Venezuela are indicative of what can happen when poor communities are invited to participate in decision-making.

What is perhaps lost in the scurry to label and classify the Bolivarian Revolution in Venezuela is the important symbolic value of the social transformation taking place. As analysts and political scientists struggle to define President Hugo Chávez in the populist, neopopulist, socialist, authoritarian, radical democrat camps, etc, they also struggle with the fact that Venezuela's marginalized masses represent unorganized sectors that do not neatly fit into traditional analytic categories. Globalization's lumpenproletariat, that mass that makes up over 50 percent of the "informal economy" in most of the South, and an increasing portion of the "flexible" labor force in the North, makes everyone nervous, theorists and practitioners alike.

Although the marginalized masses are largely irrelevant to the macroeconomic health and stability indicators deemed important by the neoliberal Right, their increasing potential to disrupt economic adjustment measures has made their political relevance clear even in these circles. The Venezuelan Revolution, which captures the aspirations of this sector, has resonance throughout Latin America as it challenges concepts of participation and democracy across the political spectrum. The fact that the values of the Bolivarian Revolution are being disseminated across borders poses a serious threat to the struggling paradigm of neoliberalism. With these issues in mind, this chapter will address a problem that the Venezuelan Revolution brings into focus for democracy globally: the failure of formal democratic institutions to effectively reflect the public will.[1]

In Latin America this issue is reflected in the crisis of legitimacy of traditional political parties and the increase in more direct forms of political activity such as protests, community organizing and creative forms of cross-border solidarity, as well as in developments such as the ever-enlarging informal sector, increasing dependency on remittances and growing criminal networks.

The Venezuelan process points to the possibilities of and challenges to the effort to deepen democracy (improving its quality) and suggests that there are both support and practical channels to build national and transnational democratic processes that can confront the skewed power relationships evident in the processes of neoliberal globalization.[2]

Elites and Problems of Theory

Although elites in Latin America have always attempted to protect their control over their country's wealth, and to insulate political systems against genuine democratic participation, neoliberal elites have had their own variation on this old theme. During their 20-odd years as the dominant decision-makers in the region, neoliberal technocrats, both those within governments and those in the International financial institutions (IFIs), have legitimized a separation of politics and economics. In their view the integrity of "democracy" as a system is not ultimately compromised by the fact that the major elements of decision-making, and thus the tools for national development, are not determined by public will formation but by international institutions collaborating with national elites. Elections, in this sense, have given an air of legitimacy and an illusion of plurality to the democratic process in Latin America, while leaders of all political stripes have felt compelled to implement neoliberal reforms. While many analysts have acknowledged the problem of this technocratic authoritarianism, or "delegative democracy" as Guillermo O'Donnell (1994: 55–69) has more politely called it, the failure of democracy to consolidate is rarely linked to an overall crisis of Western liberal democratic institutions under neoliberal globalization, or to the problem of the "market" in relation to democracy.

Regionalists have tended to focus on the "Latin American problem" rather than on a global problem of a crisis of democratic legitimacy. While many authors now acknowledge the authoritarian nature of neoliberal "democracies" in Latin America, many still assume that market-orientated reform is somehow essential. Michael

---

1   Recent works have emphasized the weakness of traditional definitions of democracy (focusing on elections, rule of law and civil and political liberties) in evaluating prospects in Latin America, turning rather to the notion of the quality of democracy, which allows for the exploration of socioeconomic categories and speaks to a deeper concept of citizenship. See Agüero and Stark (1998), for some excellent contributions opening this debate.

2   Globalization is seen by this author to be in itself a neutral term and process. For this reason I will refer to neoliberal globalization and alternative globalization (versus antiglobalization). Alternative globalization involves elements of redistribution and economic democracy.

Walton and Guillermo Perry reflect the shifting World Bank perspective on balancing elite-driven reforms and popular pressures. In their 2003 report on inequality in Latin America and the Caribbean, Walton and Perry place new emphasis on responsive political institutions and, in particular, participation by marginalized populations— some refer to this shift as the "post-neoliberal" phase. While not questioning the overall logic of "efficient macroeconomic management" orientated towards market-based reforms, they do promote an increased focus on poverty alleviation and the reduction of inequality through carefully managed redistribution.

However, these policies should not be seen as an overall structural shift in paradigm but rather as poverty management within the paradigm. It is not clear how they intend to marry their dual goals of promoting market-oriented reform, including ongoing privatization, with increasing participation by the poor and 'subordinate" groups such as those of African descent and indigenous people. What happens if these more inclusive political institutions come to reflect an agenda that is unpalatable to IFIs and investors? What if the poor, when asked to participate, opt for regressive redistributive policies, or look to halt the process of privatization, or to nationalize key resource sectors, or to increase taxes on corporations, or perhaps even to opt for socialism? It would seem that so-called "post-neoliberals" want to have their cake and eat it too: they see the need for increased participation by the marginalized, the need to decrease inequality and poverty, but they assume that the marginalized will see the wisdom of a primarily pre-packaged agenda.

How large is the gap between what a majority of Latin Americans actually want and what technocrats or analysts feel they need? According to a 2004 United Nations Development Program (UNDP) report on the state of democracy in Latin America, based on extensive polling and interviews throughout the region, a majority of Latin Americans do not believe that the market will resolve their problems and do not automatically associate the market with democracy (UNDP 2005). The report shows that Latin Americans want their leaders to actively intervene in the economy to promote social welfare. In fact, about 70 percent of Latin Americans believe in a strong role for the state in the economy while only 24 percent believe in the market. The fact that elected leaders have been unwilling and/or unable to establish a strong role for the state in the economy has led to the high levels of disenchantment with existing democracy noted in the UNDP report.[3]

This disenchantment is also reflected in the steadily increasing abstention rates in elections in Latin America over the past 15 years. But rather than focusing on the failure of elected leaders in terms of accountability to citizens, many analysts responded to the UNDP report by suggesting that the problem lies with an authoritarian culture in the region that we in the North need to keep an eye on.[4] It is this kind of paternalism that Hugo Chávez has bluntly responded to, earning him the

---

3   The report is based on interviews with 231 leaders from the region—including almost all sitting presidents and living former presidents—and public opinion polls of almost 20,000 Latin Americans, representing all social classes, from 18 countries.

4   See, for example, *Economist* editorials such as "How to protect Latin American democracy," 11 June 2005; and William Ratcliff, "Latin America's flickering democracy," *Christian Science Monitor*, July 27, 2005.

reputation of being a populist with wild and dangerous rhetoric. However, despite US and opposition claims that Chávez governs in an "authoritarian" manner, a 2005 Latinobaro metro poll shows that Venezuelans are an exception to the region's growing disenchantment with democracy. When Latin Americans were asked to rate the level of democracy in their country on a scale of 1 (not democratic) to 10 (totally democratic), more Venezuelans considered their country to be "totally democratic" than the citizens of any other nation. The average Venezuelan gave their country a rating of 7.6, while the regional average was only 5.5. Furthermore, in terms of overall satisfaction with how their democracy functions, Venezuelans were second only to Uruguayans (Latinobaro metro 2005).

Regardless of these conflicting visions of what democracy means in the region and the wishes of a majority of Latin Americans, mainstream analysts, and practitioners concerned with democratic consolidation have continued to argue that "democracy" will only work if elites are on board. Usually this issue is theorized with words such as "pact," "co-optation" or "compromise," and the overrepresentation of elites in decision-making is often conceived, if at times reluctantly, as a given. The concept and import of the elite class as a possible threat to the democratic project as a whole is rarely theorized.[5] In their major regional study of the early 1990s, Rueschmeyer *et al.* attempted to fill this gap by laying bare the class dynamics of democracy in Latin America under capitalist development, noting that "the dominant classes accommodated to democracy only as long as the party system effectively protected their interests." The failed 2002 elite coup in Venezuela certainly bears this out, as do the Cold-War-like interventions of the US in Venezuela's internal politics since 1999 (Rueschemeyer, Stephens and Stephens 1992: 287).

At the root of these problems lies the issue of redistribution. The question for policy-makers becomes how to manage neoliberal reforms against "populist" demands for redistribution. The neoliberal belief that economic growth alone will lead to development and the alleviation of poverty has allowed technocrats to sidestep questions of inequity and justify the dominance of elites in decision-making. Many mainstream theorists have tended to accept that, no matter how small a portion of the population elites represent, an overrepresentation of their interests is a matter of fact in both neoliberal and "post-neoliberal" democracies.

Politics in Venezuela since Chávez are constantly referred to as "polarized" because the role of elites has been challenged. In reality the country is no more polarized than it was under neoliberalism. There was, however, no great emphasis in the media or by mainstream analysts on polarization until the poor became the beneficiaries of policy-making. The polarization that should trouble observers is that of inequitable wealth distribution, which is exactly the problem that the Chávez government is attempting to address.

No amount of persuasion is going to convince those who have enjoyed the privileges of controlling Venezuela's oil wealth for decades that they should share this wealth. They are bound to find the process of wealth redistribution somewhat

---

5   There are important exceptions to this approach, such as Robinson (2003), Cammack (1997), and Agüero and Stark (1998). On the other hand, Diamond, Linz and Lipset (1999) make no connection between the failure of political institutions and capitalist elites.

painful and to view the policies associated with redistribution as "authoritarian." Interestingly, it is not said that this is the bitter medicine that the rich must swallow to see a more just and humane society. The poor, on the other hand, have been asked to swallow the bitter medicine of neoliberal austerity for over two decades in the vain hope that some of the wealth would eventually trickle down.

But in what concrete ways has the Venezuelan process challenged traditional notions of democracy and to what degree does it represent a true alternative to neoliberal orthodoxy? While there are many facets of the Bolivarian Revolution that need to be explored, this paper will focus on the health and education sectors which, it will be argued, represent fundamental arenas of social integration.[6] It will also look at Chávez's alternative vision of globalization.

Building a Counter-project

The Bolivarian Revolution has first and foremost represented an all-out assault on neoliberal doctrine and its authoritarian elements, bringing into question elite control of the economy. While some have tried to characterize the revolution as an expression of "anti-politics," I will argue below that, on the contrary, the Venezuelan project represents a process of repoliticization from the community to the national level, which is why Chávez is seen as dangerous by elites both within and outside Venezuela. Interestingly, the Chávez government is achieving this repoliticization without stepping outside the constitutional framework of democracy in Venezuela.

A key aspect of this process has been the effort to revitalize citizenship through the construction of mechanisms for public participation in decision-making, particularly aiming at the poor majority. Critics of the revolution have charged Chávez with building his own political base by purchasing the support of the poor. While it is true that many of the government's programs have been aimed at the poor—we should bear in mind that this is 70 percent of the population—this argument is less than convincing given the pure self-interest Chávez could pursue by simply doing business as usual in Venezuela.

If there is any incentive—and indeed strong pressure from the international financial institutions (IFIs)—to "buy" political support in the current policy-making climate, it is the support of globally oriented elites, of international investors that is for sale. In fact, purchasing this support is seen as "sound economic policy." There has been little incentive, and hardly any maneuverability, in the neoliberal economic climate to pursue policies of redistribution. Venezuela's revolution, however, has made the concept and practice of redistribution once more fashionable and it is arguably this simple fact that has made Chávez such a controversial figure.

Venezuela's redistributive agenda is largely possible thanks to the country's petroleum reserves—the largest outside the Middle East—which give it both economic flexibility and bargaining power vis-á-vis other international actors. Oil has also provided a channel for Venezuela to influence international politics, leading

---

6 Norbert Lechner (1998: 21–39) has commented on the serious implications of privatization in these sectors, noting how it "tends to weaken the integrative dimension of the public realm."

to a revitalization of OPEC and contributing to the boosting of oil prices to over $50 a barrel by 2005. However, it is important to note that Venezuela's non-oil economy is also healthy by regional standards, showing an impressive growth rate of 17.8 percent in 2004.[7] The Chávez government is attempting to use this wealth to benefit the majority and in this process is coming to be seen by many in and outside the region as offering a real alternative to neoliberalism.

Although protest against neoliberalism has been evident throughout Latin America, the situation in Venezuela is unique in that there is an attempt to institutionalize a counter-project from the constitution down to the every day practices of average citizens. Dissatisfaction with neoliberalism in Venezuela dates back to the 1980s and was most acutely expressed in the demonstrations of February 1989, known as the "Caracazo." Protests erupted across the country as people expressed their discontent with the policies of President Carlos Andres Pérez. Pérez had been elected on a pseudo-left platform and, in an abrupt about-face under IMF supervision, undertook strict austerity measures—including increasing the price of petrol and public transportation—intended to create an attractive investment climate. Pérez responded to the protests by declaring a state of emergency and deploying the army. Confrontations between soldiers and protesters resulted in the deaths of over 250 people.[8] It was a symbolic moment for the Venezuelan political system, ending the stability of the elite "democracy" that had existed since 1958. The poor had decided *en masse* that this system was no longer tolerable.

President Chávez came to power in December 1998 with 57 percent of the vote in an election with 64 percent voter turnout. His campaign promises included the convening of a constituent assembly to draw up a new constitution, the reform of political institutions, an attack on corruption and poverty, and regulating the spending of the state-owned oil company, Petroleos de Venezuela SA (PDVSA). Within this agenda Chávez has placed an emphasis on responding to the demands of Venezuela's poor majority. The Bolivarian Revolution aims to reconnect politics and economics concretely by building participatory, democratic processes from the community level up and building redistributive mechanisms into policy making from the state level down. When speaking of the chief goal of the revolution, "empowering the poor," President Chávez noted:

> This concept entails, among other things, the people's political participation in the control of the state and its decision-making process, a reform of public powers based on the Bolivarian constitution, a fairer distribution of the oil income and the land, the creation of an economic infrastructure and formulation of revolutionary social policies that enable change toward a humanist society based on full respect for citizenship rights: healthcare and education for all, decent employment, land for those who toil it, food security, sports and culture and a genuinely leading role played by the people within the national political dynamics.[9]

---

7   "Venezuela's oil revenue fuels record growth," *Dow Jones Newswire*, February 17, 2005.

8   According to official Venezuelan government sources, 257 people died in the violence. Some NGOs have put the number as high as 2000.

9   Speech by President Hugo Chávez, Meeting of the Heads of State, United Nations, September 2004, emphasis added.

The Bolivarian Revolution effectively began with the revamping of the national constitution. As Gregory Wilpert notes, constitutional change has been an ongoing feature of politics in Venezuela since its founding.[10] There have been 27 constitutions since 1811 with the longest-lasting constitution existing between 1961 and 1999. Following the failed Chávez coup in 1992, there was increasing public support for a new constitution and Chávez captured this sentiment in his Movimiento Quinta Republica (Fifth Republic Movement—MVR), suggesting that only a broad restructuring of the Venezuelan political order could lead to the types of revolutionary changes needed in the country. A significant aspect of the process of constitutional change under Chávez was the public engagement that took place at all stages.

There were three key stages: the approval of Chávez's initial plan for the process; the election of the constituent assembly; and the final approval of the constitution drafted. Eighty-eight percent of voters supported the convoking of a constituent assembly, 82 percent backed the procedures outlined for the process and 70 percent approved the new constitution (Ellner 2001: 5–32). In addition to formal political mechanisms to ensure popular consensus on the constitution, there were also opportunities for public involvement in open sessions. The Minister of Health and Development, Francisco Armada, noted: "When they opened the discussion on the national constitution, this led to an open debate on healthcare, it was a very representative process with public involvement which culminated in three articles of the new national constitution."[11]

While containing much that would be expected in any modern constitution, the Venezuelan constitution contains some elements that are unique, particularly in the areas of education and health. In flagrant opposition to the neoliberal trend away from government guarantees in education and healthcare (or the post-neoliberal focus on targeted programs for vulnerable sectors within an overall framework of state downsizing), access to healthcare and education are seen as fundamental rights with equal standing to civil and political rights. Protections are built into the constitution to safeguard these rights: the constitution forbids the privatization of healthcare and, although privatization of education is not mentioned, state responsibility for education is outlined clearly. And, unlike in other countries where the constitution has little relationship to everyday life, the government has already invested significant resources in the areas of health, education and land reform with programs that have broad popular participation and support. In Venezuela there is a sense that the constitution is a living document; this is epitomized by the cartoon version now being made available to schools and in the individual articles of the constitution found on food packaging in the state-subsidized food stores. During

---

10 For an excellent and detailed analysis on the history and relevance of the new constitution, see Wilpert (2003).

11 Interview with Francisco Armada, Minister of Health and Social Development, Caracas, May 18, 2005.

the 2002 coup, many Chavistas waved the constitution during their protests and emphasized their "constitutional rights" to the media.[12]

Active Citizenship in Healthcare

The attempt to transform the way healthcare is delivered is an important part of the Bolivarian Revolution. Beyond the delivery of services, healthcare is seen as an arena for active citizenship. In fact, it is framed in the constitution as both a right and a responsibility. The rights component deals with questions of accessibility, the responsibility component involves both an emphasis on preventative health strategies and citizen participation in the design and support of healthcare initiatives at the community level. The immediate aim has been to respond to the effects of chronic underfunding during the neoliberal era and to tackle accessibility in the poorest neighborhoods. During the 1980s and 1990s, creeping marketization of healthcare raised public fears about possible privatization, which led to Article 84 of the new constitution expressly prohibiting privatization of the healthcare system. The government's strategy aims to reach those who have been previously excluded, which includes most of the 70 percent of the country's population living in poverty. Reaching this sector has required a creative approach based on Article 84, which calls for a system that is "decentralized and participatory in nature, integrated with the social security system and governed by the principles of gratuity, universality, completeness, fairness, social integration and solidarity."[13]

Social security provision (including support in maternity, paternity, illness, disability, catastrophic illnesses, incapacity, special needs, workplace injury, loss of work, unemployment, old age, widowhood, orphanhood, loss of housing, etc.) is guaranteed and inability to make contributions cannot be a basis for exclusion. In addition, housewives are legally eligible for social security benefits under Article 88. While this particular article may be difficult to implement in the short term, it is indicative of the innovative character of the constitution, as it acknowledges the value of women's work in the home and challenges the traditional public/private dichotomy in terms of the political economy of households.

A key aspect of the government's strategy has been to meet the needs of the most marginalized sectors of the population first, then to build on this effort to develop an integrated, accessible and sustainable system. The Cuban-supported Barrio Adentro Mission—launched in April 2003 with 58 physicians—has been key to achieving the initial objective. By 2005 more than 20,000 Cuban doctors, health workers and physical trainers were working in the program.[14]

---

12 See Kim Bartley and Donnacha O'Braian, *The Revolution Will Not Be Televised*, a 2003 documentary film, for a critical evaluation of the media during the 2002 coup.

13 Constitución de la Republica Bolivariana de Venezuela, *Gaceta Oficial* No. 5.453 Extraordinario, March 24, 2000.

14 As part of the strategy of preventative healthcare, these trainers are concerned with promoting healthy lifestyles and physical activity. For example, there are grandparents' clubs ("clubs de abuelos") focused particularly on improving the quality of life of the elderly.

The mission has required the organization and active participation of poor communities. Neighborhoods form local health committees (Comites de Salud) that manage the clinics. Local families often house and feed the Cuban doctors and other medical staff and some small clinics work directly out of a converted section of a family dwelling. In its first 18 months, the program made services available to 17 million Venezuelans and Chávez was praised by the director of the Pan American Health Organization for his leadership in health (Maybarduk 2004). In addition to being able to access clinics, poor Venezuelans can also purchase drugs at an 85 percent discount in government-subsidized "boticas."[15] For many Venezuelans this has been the first time they have received medical care.

In response to critics who have pointed to possible problems of sustainability in the program, the Minister of Health and Social Development first compared the health situation in Venezuela to a natural disaster: "You can't fail to deal with a disaster because you haven't worked out the specifics of sustainability. The absence of medical assistance for millions of people signals a disaster." He then went on to explain that the government is working to promote sustainability by situating health in the broader process of sustainable economic development that involves, among other things, the massive drive to promote cooperatives and investment in job training. The Ministry of Higher Education is also providing training to about 1,100 Venezuelan doctors currently involved in the program and another 2,500 men and women who will set up their own popular consulting offices. Another aspect of increasing accessibility has been the opening of the well-equipped and well-funded Venezuelan Institute for Social Security (IVSS) hospitals to non-pensioned workers. Previously workers in the informal sector, who make up over 50 percent of the labor force, could not access these hospitals.

While some have argued that investment in other areas of the economy (versus health and education) may better serve economic growth overall and thus sustainability, Health Minister Armado distinguished the Chávez government's approach from this "macroeconomy of health" perspective promoted by a prominent group in the World Health Organization thus: "We believe that the resources that we are putting into health have, even from the point of view of investment, a positive economic effect. We are convinced that more investment in social rights, in areas of fundamental rights like health and education, will give us more possibility for access to an economic development that is sustainable." In a veiled reference to the current approach to health under neoliberalism, Armado stated: "For us health does not mean attention to a specific group, the vulnerable in 'commas' ... it is not a process to repair or remedy the rest of our policies."[16]

An important element of the government's approach to health is that citizens, particularly poor citizens, are not seen as the passive recipients of policy, an

---

15 As part of the government's plan to emphasize improving the health of the poor, Venezuelans can also access basic food products at a 40 percent discount in government-subsidized markets, or "Mercales." The Mercal Mission is having a significant impact on nutrition in poor neighborhoods.

16 Interview with Francisco Armada, Minister of Health and Social Development, Caracas, May 18, 2005.

approach indicative of the poverty alleviation strategies of the IFIs. The process of achieving the stated goals in health requires active participation of communities who are encouraged to examine the health of their communities as part of a larger project of social transformation. This is achieved through local government, various types of neighborhood associations, and health and school committees. These groups are responsible for identifying their community's needs, for contributing to designing programs to solve local problems and for evaluating programs. In this sense community members themselves are required to take responsibility for leadership in health and education so that they themselves are accountable.[17] The government, says Health Minister Armado, does not believe in pre-packaged programs: missions such as Barrio Adentro are only working because of active citizen participation.[18]

Education for the New Citizen

The government's approach to education is intrinsically linked to its healthcare philosophy: that a vibrant democracy requires the active participation of citizens who are well nourished, healthy and educated. In his address to the United Nations in 2004, Chávez noted that his government would give top priority to education in order to address the "neglect" of previous neoliberal governments whose policies were rooted in "privatisation and social exclusion." The public education system, like many in Latin America, was deteriorating, while enrolment in private schools increased steadily. Many poor families could not afford to send their children to school and thousands were excluded from the system. Furthermore, over half a million high school graduates were unable to access a university system that had become increasingly exclusive.[19]

Chávez's government has initiated several missions to tackle these problems. These missions include a countrywide literacy campaign, which uses a Cuban-designed program to teach basic literacy in seven weeks. According to the government, the campaign had resulted in a 90 percent reduction in Venezuela's illiteracy rate by 2005.[20] The education missions also enabled the 1.2 million who had become literate to continue their studies up to Grade Six, integrating English and computer training. Additionally, 770,000 adults completed their secondary education with the possibility of entering university. Finally, the government oversaw a decentralization of higher education to the local level to increase accessibility in various localities. It also enabled the opening of the Bolivarian University of Venezuela (UBV), where students receive a liberal arts education and training for professions such as law and journalism. That UBV lecture halls used to be the luxurious offices of the oil elite is a symbolism not lost on students.

In addition to working through the education missions, the Chávez government is converting primary and secondary schools into "Bolivarian schools." The

---

17 Interview with Professor Lisandro Perez, Jefe Civil, Barrio 23 de Enero, Caracas, April 29, 2005.

18 Interview with Francisco Armada.

19 National Institute of Statistics, Bolivarian Republic of Venezuela.

20 Interview with Francisco Armada.

project was initiated in 1999 with over 500 schools. The goal behind the schools is to improve preschool and basic education with a longer school day that includes cultural activities and sport. Until 1999 the Venezuelan school day was only five hours and the school year only 170 days. By 2000 the school year had been increased to 200 days in Bolivarian schools.

The new curriculum seeks to account for individual differences among students and to recognize Venezuela's cultural diversity. The schools also seek to address nutritional issues by providing students with breakfast, lunch, and an afternoon snack. Cafeterias are run by "madres colaboradores" (mother collaborators) from the community who have attended a government-sponsored intensive course on nutrition. By 2005 over 3,500 schools had benefited from the transformation process, with many undergoing extensive renovations and in some cases obtaining new buildings, while over a million previously excluded Venezuelan children were receiving free education and nutrition. In providing an ongoing space for community activities and participation, and integrating their work into the concrete reality of local populations, the schools have also provided an important source of reflection and pride in local and national culture and history. A director of one Bolivarian school in the Caracas neighbourhood 23 de Enero noted that the schools aim to emphasize 'social values and create a different citizen for the future, a better society overall."[21]

The idea of "integral" education is a key component of the Bolivarian Revolution, meaning that education is not seen as separate from other spheres of life; it is seen to be a critical element in efforts to create direct, participatory democracy. Through thousands of collectives, cooperatives and local associations, the poor are being given unprecedented opportunities to educate and govern themselves. Over two million people are active in "Bolivarian circles" that organize within local communities to discuss, develop and implement a variety of community projects in areas such as education, health and sports. They also provide workshops on the government's reforms and discuss strategies for making the process sustainable.

Direct democracy is also evident in the "land councils," where small groups of representatives from poor communities draw up legislation giving ownership and control of poor areas to local residents. Local governments have been active in creating spaces for community engagement such as local assemblies, neighborhood associations and in sports and social arenas. When asked about his vision of governing, one municipal leader noted: "We think of a popular government where the people are the protagonists of their own destiny ... not like before when we were always in confrontation with the state ... We organize popular participation. For us this is an achievement, because we have pushed for this all our lives."[22]

A Regional Counter-project

The Venezuelan government has sought to implement regionally some of the fundamental concepts of the Bolivarian Revolution. These efforts represent a counter-

---

21 Interview with Arnoldo Sotillo, Director, Escuela Basica Integral Bolivariana Estado Vargas, Caracas, May 17, 2005.

22 Interview with Professor Lisandro Perez.

project to the beleaguered Free Trade Area of the Americas (FTAA) and, ultimately, an alternative vision of globalization. At the conclusion of the 2005 Summit of the Americas in Mar del Plata, Argentina it was evident that the region was divided into two Americas: pro- and anti-FTAA. As a result, the Bush administration failed in its attempt to revive the FTAA. While only five countries –Argentina, Brazil, Paraguay, Uruguay, and Venezuela—at the summit opposed a regional free trade agreement, these nations represent a significant portion of Latin America's population and economic activity. In reference to neoliberalism, Argentina's President Nestor Kirchner noted during the summit that "US policy not only generated misery and poverty but also a great social tragedy that added to institutional instability in the region, provoking the fall of democratically elected governments."[23]

Chávez, meanwhile, spent much of his time in Mar del Plata promoting the Bolivarian Alternative for Latin America and the Caribbean (ALBA), his alternative vision to the FTAA. This alternative globalization project has several components, many of which reflect what the Venezuelan government is attempting to implement at the national level. The first involves a redistribution of wealth to the poorest countries of the region through a "Compensatory Fund for Structural Convergence." The idea is to create a more level playing field for countries attempting to compete in the international economy.

The redistribution idea is also being put into practice through the recent PetroCaribe agreement under which Venezuela supplies poor Caribbean nations with affordable petroleum. The agreement is designed to foster "the development of energy policies and plans for the integration of the nations of the Caribbean through the sovereign use of natural energy resources to directly benefit their peoples."[24] Connected to the notion of sovereignty, ALBA emphasizes "endogenous" development: development that is based on strengthening national productive sectors such as agriculture and industry rather than maquiladora-type industries that are not seen to be solving the underlying causes of poverty or to be building sustainable economies. ALBA also prioritizes food self-sufficiency over short-term profitmaking in the export sector. Additionally, the Bolivarian alternative confronts the intellectual property rights regime currently in place, which is seen to favor the scientific and technical knowledge of Northern countries as opposed to those areas such as biodiversity and indigenous and peasant knowledge systems where the South has obvious advantages. A key aspect of this issue to ALBA proponents is the need for generic medicines. ALBA also emphasizes the right of governments to oppose privatisation and deregulation policies where these conflict with the ability of a government to deliver essential social services. In 2005 the Venezuelan government loaned $500 million to Argentina and $300 million to Ecuador to help those nations diminish their dependence on the Washington-based IFIs (Hoffman 2005).

While these policies are not particularly radical historically speaking, they are designed to conflict with the neoliberal paradigm and, because of this, have been criticized by those who promote and benefit from that paradigm—namely,

---

23 'Skepticism prevails at trade talks," *Washington Post*, November 6, 2005.
24 PetroCaribe agreement signed at the First Energy Summit of Caribbean heads of state and government in Puerto La Cruz, Venezuela, July 2005.

what William Robinson has termed the transnational elite.[25] Just as the Bolivarian Revolution promotes active citizenship at home, it advocates the active participation of states in regional and global decision-making bodies. While the government's redistributive policies, as epitomized in the health and education sectors discussed above, challenge the control that domestic elites have had over the economy, its regional policies could have a similar effect on global elites who have previously relied on open access to Latin America's resources.

Conclusion: Democracy Matters

The continuing tendency of many analysts is to see the rationalization of the state towards efficient and accountable integration into the global capitalist system as a positive, despite the fact that this integration has been managed in highly authoritarian ways and has led across the board to increased inequality. The efficiency of a process and/or institution may be irrelevant if the outcomes consistently favor particular elite interests at the expense of majorities. We have yet to see a convincing counter-example under neoliberal restructuring. Vague references to the need to "maximize economic performance and assure social participation" (Stark 1998) do not answer the question of who these efficient institutions serve and what kind of development they should seek to support.

The Bolivarian Revolution is a concrete attempt to make transparent the kind of development sought by the Venezuelan people. The Venezuelan government has called this project "socialism for the twenty-first century," but the roots of the revolution predate Chávez, who simply became the vehicle for implementing a more just social order that had been called for by average citizens for decades. What the Venezuelan experience highlights is that there are two key components in generating genuine processes of public will formation (i.e. public demands translate concretely into policy outcomes). On the one hand, participatory processes must be put into place, processes that can generate economic, social and cultural projects that are community-designed and community-driven.[26] On the other hand, these processes may mean very little if the national government has little maneuverability on key aspects of economic policy—as is the case in most Southern countries. In this sense the options for many countries may seem bleak, given debt burdens and persistent economic crises. IFI technocrats have penetrated national decision-making structures and accountability to such a degree that reversing this process will be extremely difficult and elements of civil society may simply decide to bypass the traditional political channels, showing a preference for more direct forms of action such as have been witnessed recently in Bolivia.

---

25   Robinson (2003: 39) includes in this class, "the owners of the leading worldwide means of production as embodied principally in the transnational corporations and private financial institutions ... its interests lie in the global over local or national accumulation."

26   This process of decentralization should be distinguished from some current processes that place increasing economic burdens on local/departmental governments or allow for increased "participation" (*à la* World Bank) but without accompanying resources to facilitate translating local control into local development.

In contradistinction to the externally orientated development model, Venezuela's Bolivarian project implies a nationally rooted but regionally integrated approach to development and poverty issues, where development possibilities cannot be solely determined by economic growth. The dramatic transformations taking place in health and education policy in Venezuela are indicative of what can happen when poor communities are invited to participate in decision-making. A majority of Venezuelans have made clear that the pre-packaged neoliberal agenda does not serve their needs and the government's efforts to respond to this citizen input has forced a confrontation with national elites. The qualitative improvements in democratic participation and accountability in Venezuela have not required the overrepresentation of the elite sector—democracy is working quite well without them playing a dominant role. Meanwhile, the US response, which has attempted to undermine the Chávez government, illustrates the unwillingness of international elites to accept a participatory democracy that does not acknowledge the "wisdom" of neoliberal, or post-neoliberal, reforms.

The Venezuelan process suggests that more qualitative forms of democracy and redistribution depend on a certain degree of national sovereignty in economic matters.[27] This in turn points to the need for innovative practical methods of measuring, monitoring, and countering authoritarian practices between states and practices of foreign policy that contribute to and, in some cases cause, the failure of democracy in other countries.[28] During the Cold War interventions were a key feature of the US fight against communism and are now part of the war on terror and the politics of neoliberal globalization.

The fact that these practices have continued during an era of "democratization" has yet to seriously influence the way mainstream practitioners and analysts measure democracy. At its worst, this failure has led to an ongoing paternalism and a sense of the Western burden to civilize the world. It prevents the recognition or acknowledgement of other cultural and political traditions that could have positive impacts in the North, such as indigenous knowledge systems that could contribute to environmental sustainability or ideas that challenge the notion of growth without limits. Finally, it obscures the authoritarian practices of rich democracies in the international arena. An analytical framework that integrates critical analysis of the actions—both positive and negative—of transnational decision-makers, particularly the IFIs, on democracy would result in a more comprehensive analysis of the prospects for democracy in Latin America.

Hopes for an alternative world, however, do not have to be pinned on the success of the Bolivarian Revolution. The point is to recognize what the revolution means

---

27 While some loss of sovereignty is still inevitable and may be desirable even under the Bolivarian model of globalization, the degree and type of external influence on national agenda setting is important.

28 Interventions range on the spectrum from the imposition of austerity measures and unfair trade practices, and active support of violent actors such as armed opposition groups and paramilitaries or coup leaders, to more insidious forms such as funding opposition political parties and groups, control of media/cultural channels, and doing business with human rights violators.

in terms of the particular historical moment we are living and the opportunities that this moment offers for a new politics. The push for redistributive, more radically democratic projects is beginning to take life concretely in communities across Latin America (not to mention pockets in the Northern countries) and not only in the form of survival politics.

Chapter 8

Globalization and Development in Southern Africa: A Contradiction in Terms?

Lisa Thompson

The first public protest against NEPAD occurred at the July 2002 World Economic Forum regional meeting in Durban, where anti-apartheid poet Dennis Brutus, acting secretary of Jubilee South Africa, led more than a hundred demonstrators into horse-charging policemen. Brutus held up a sign for national television viewers: "No Kneepad! ... [t]he document's core premise is that poverty in Africa can be cured, if only the world's elite gives the continent a chance: "[t]he continued marginalization of Africa from the globalization process and the social exclusion of the vast majority of its peoples constitute a serious threat to global stability. (Bond 2002a: 369)

In this chapter "southern Africa" refers to the members of the Southern Africa Development Community (SADC), the regional organization that was founded in 1980 and reformed in 1992. Member states include Angola, Botswana, the Democratic Republic of the Congo (DRC), Lesotho, Madagascar, Malawi, Mauritius, Mozambique, Namibia, South Africa, Swaziland, Tanzania, Zambia, and Zimbabwe. Apart from geographical proximity, many of the 14 members share common colonial experiences and similar societal and political features. While there are some important factors of differentiation (such as recent experiences of warfare and distinctive paths of political transition in countries such as the DRC, Mozambique, or South Africa) membership to the organization in some regards provides cohesiveness to economic and other policy objectives, an aspect that is particularly significant in a discussion of the contours and effects of globalization in the region.

What does globalization mean in the southern African context? The quote above from Patrick Bond's book *Unsustainable South Africa* highlights that negative views of globalization have been absorbed into government rhetoric in southern Africa, as is evident in what the New Economic Partnership for Africa's Development (NEPAD) seeks to achieve. Bond goes on to put the perspective of many left-wing critics by stating that "Africa's continued poverty and degradation ('marginalization') are a direct outcome of globalization, not of a lack of globalization" (Bond 2002a: 369). Marginalization, chronic poverty which manifests itself not only in lack of income but also in terms of access to basic services such as water and sanitation, is the lot of many if not most southern Africans and Africans. Globalization has often been blamed for these problems, both in terms of its marginalization effects, as well as the way in which it widens the gap between rich and poor both within states (especially in Africa) and globally.

But is this because of globalization? Or is this explanation for poverty and lack of development not just a coincidental meeting of the minds between inefficient and/or corrupt government elites and disgruntled left-wing academics? And are they speaking about the same thing when they refer to globalization? Melber (2004: 5) indicates that "globalization" is often taken to mean the current period of capitalist economic expansion that takes a particular form under the so-called neoliberal "Washington Consensus." Within this understanding (which forms perhaps the underlying impetus as well as source of tension within NEPAD) there is an elitist pragmatism which Melber (2004: 5) refers to as "better this capitalism than no capitalism at all."

Scholte (2005a, 2005b) points out that much of what is referred to as globalization in popular academic and media discourse in fact is old wine in new bottles, and clearly this is the case in South and southern Africa. As Scholte (2005a: 54–9) puts it,

> [i]n sum much talk of globalization has been analytically redundant. ... Four main definitions have led into this cul-de-sac: globalization as internationalization; globalization as liberalization; globalization as universalization; and globalization as westernization. ... Deployed on any of these four lines, "globalization" provides no distinct value added ... Critics of "globaloney" are right to assail the historical illiteracy that marks most claims of novelty associated with these conceptions of globalization ... Of course, this is not to suggest that debates about international interdependence, neoliberalism, universalism-versus-cultural diversity, modernity, and imperialism are unimportant. Indeed, a well-fashioned concept of globalization could shed significant light on these issues. However it is not helpful to ... treat [globalization] as equivalent to—internationalization, liberalization, universalization or westernization. Not only do we thereby merely rehash old knowledge, but we also lose a major opportunity to grasp—and act upon—certain key circumstances of our times.

It is worth quoting Scholte at some length, because it helps to clarify in what ways globalization does—and does not—shed light on current historical processes globally, and how such processes shape political and socioeconomic dynamics in different parts of the world. If globalization is not equivalent to international interdependence, for example, as is currently described in the popular media, then what does it mean? And what does it mean to us in southern Africa, where the region's economies have long been structurally dependent on international markets? Do colonialism and neocolonial patterns of trade have any bearing on what we understand as a dynamic, effect, or outcome of globalization? The pronouncements of the South African government and, from another angle, critics like Bond (2002a, 2002b) and the South African antiglobalization movement would both say yes.

Yet the critical aspect of economic globalization is what Scholte has initially termed deterritorialization and later changed to supraterritoriality (Scholte 2005a: 85; Scholte 2005b: 77). "Supraterritorial" refers to the degree to which economic and other activities take place on a global scale that *transcend the territoriality* of the international state system. Examples of this would be e-communications and cyberspace in general; global travel; global factories and global commodity chains; the spread of global products and product names like Nike, Coca-cola and Toyota.[1] Other "transworld" activities and/or evidence of supraterritorialism or globality, as Scholte (2005a: 67) calls them, include global finance, global businesses, global civil society organizations, global military activities, global ecological and health concerns, global laws, and globalized social relations.

Important to the understanding of supraterritoriality and transworld practices is their *decenteredness*. Indeed Scholte argues that understanding globalization requires a shift in methodology, away from our tendency to treat the global arena as composed of distinct territorial spaces of activity (what he calls "methodological territorialism"). Globalization then, refers to activities which call upon us to think about the global arena differently, and to understand globalization in terms of a new language which reflects the simultaneous contraction of time and space with regard to "transworld" and "transborder" connections (Scholte 2005a: 86–7).

Scholte (2005b: 77) also urges us to remember that our current social space "is both territorial and supraterritorial." In other words, he is not arguing that state activity or their geographical significance has no relevance, but he focuses attention on the need to examine what is truly global about how we understand globalization in general and in terms of how it affects lives at different levels in different corners of the globe. As our discussion here emphasizes, while the dynamics of what is new about globalization might refer to supranationality, the fundamental *developmental* impact of globalization is very definitely territorial, if southern Africa is anything to go by. As figures on development (or the lack of it) clearly underline, globalization has had an impact on different geographical areas in different ways and global structural inequalities have been aggravated by globalization (Leysens and Thompson 2006). Recent statistics show that even states in the region with "medium human development" ranking in terms of UNDP indicators, have high levels of poverty. South Africa, the wealthiest state in SADC, has a Human Poverty Index (HPI) of 30.9 percent, and Madagascar (a Low Human Development state and one of the poorest in SADC) has an HPI of 35.3. Mauritius is in fact the only state in the SADC grouping with an HPI below the percentage value of 30. Life expectancy is another indicator that shows the region's poverty dilemma. The probability of not surviving to age 40 is between 43.3 percent (South Africa) and a staggering 74.3 percent (Swaziland). Only Mauritius (5 percent) and Lesotho (27.8) have slightly better statistics (UNDP 2005b). While HIV/AIDs plays a role in the latter statistics, poverty exacerbates the situation.

Sklair (2002: 8) identifies the "unique" aspect of globalization (i.e. that which is different from the internationalization of global capital) is what he terms

---

1   All of these supraterritorial practices are facilitated by what Scholte (2005a: 69) terms global money, "that is some units of account, some means of payment, stores of value and mediums of account that have transplanetary circulation." For example the US dollar, the "Japanese" yen, the "British" pound and other major denominations are much more than national currencies. As supraterritorial monies, they are used anywhere on earth at the same time and move (electronically and via air transport) anywhere on earth effectively in no time.

"transnational practices" (TNPs). The transnational corporation (TNC) "is the major locus of transnational practices ... transnational corporations are the most important and most powerful globalising institutions in the world to day and by virtue of this they make the capitalist global system the dominant global system." Thus TNCs, through transnational practices, make the role of the state less important and bring to the fore issues about global labor organizations and social movements as well as impacts of global economic institutions like the WTO on global economic and social relations, as well as their civil society critics such as the anti-globalization movement. To Sklair (2002: 9) consumerism is very definitely part of globalization as it forms a fundamental part of TNPs. Transnational practices and consumerism— as dynamics of globalization—affect the southern African region very differently. Those countries which are the most marginalized—states like Malawi and Tanzania for example—display very few signs of either: both with a GDP of $580 and HDI indexes of 0,388 and 0,407 respectively, they "fall off the map" as it were in terms of marginalization (UNDP 2004 quoted in McGowan 2006: 310). Is this a cause or an effect of globalization?

The caveat that globalization is both supraterritorial as well as territorial is critical, in my view, to retaining a sense of the way in which globalization processes do not necessarily have a homogenous "globalized impact." If we examine globalization in the context of the development debate trajectory, it is clear to see that globalization has differential impacts on societies and communities. Some may be affected by the sphere of "time–space" shrinkage only partially or in nominal ways in terms of direct impact. After all, in southern Africa there are many people who have never seen a computer, much less sent an email or used the web. In 2005, Lesotho had only 147 host computers (linked to the Internet or web) Malawi had 288, and Tanzania 9, 444. This compared with South Africa which had 451, 500 (CIA 2005 and Internet Consortium online quoted in McGowan 2006: 314).

Cox (1987, 1996b) has discussed at some length how certain economic groups are peripheralized through the globalization of production, trade and financial networks and processes. These marginalized groups occur all over the world but are more prevalent in the South. As the discussion below indicates, southern Africa shows marked characteristics of bifurcated societal relations where organized business and labor form part of globalization dynamics, and marginalized semi-formal labor and semi-subsistence agriculturalists, who do not. Leysens (2005) applies Cox's framework to southern Africa, using Afrobarometer data, demonstrating the ways in which poor communities in the region are marginalized from mainstream political and economic practices.

The Variable Impact of Globalization in Southern Africa

A good illustration of the varied impact of globalization on the region is the changing nature of norms, values and decision-making procedures—what Keohane and Nye (2000) would call the "regime" nature—within the regional organization SADC. SADC can be examined both in terms of its regional institutional dynamics, as well as in terms of the changing nature of the norms, values and decision-making procedures which characterize the nature of the organization. These norms and values form part of the knowledge frame which holds the organization together. This, according to Keohane and Nye (2000) and others is the "glue" that holds international and regional regimes together.

How have the norms and values entrenched in the organization changed since 1992 to reflect the economic, political, cultural, and social aspects of globalization? SADC has gone from being a loose arrangement of states seeking economic independence from South Africa, but committed in many cases to various forms of rather dubious 'socialist" economic practices, to a grouping of rather avid proponents of capitalism seeking foreign assistance to achieve as rapid an absorption into the global capitalist system as possible (Tapscott and Thompson 2001).

The current revamping of the economic aspect of SADC is called the Regional Indicative Strategic Development Plan (RISDP) which draws attention to the need for regional integration European Union (EU) style including goals to have a common currency in the next ten years as well as general macroeconomic convergence (SADC Today, February 2005, Vol. 1; SADC website [please indicate the SADC website here]; Le Pere and Tjonneland 2005: 27). These policies are being pursued with a simultaneous opening up to international (especially EU) markets as the recent SA–EU trade deal illustrates; discussions with the US on the possibility of a free trade area have also taken place (Schoeman 2005). The RISDP is ostensibly also aligned with other continental and international initiatives such as the (NEPAD) and the Millennium Development Goals (MDGs) *(SADC Today*, February 2005, volumes 2–4). Given the level of economic development in the region, the advisability of these regional and global economic strategies remains a moot point, and one that is strongly criticized by the antiglobalization movement in southern Africa (Bond 2002a, 2002b). It is clear though, that the governments of the region, and South Africa in particular, have shifted their policies in response to what they understand as economic globalization, even if they are critical in their pronouncements about its effects. Bond refers to this phenomenon of government behavior as that of "talk left, act right" and points out that antiglobalization pronouncements by the South African government usually follow from social movement activism which shows the government's inability to address the plight of the poor (Bond 2002a: 361–2).

While regional integration in itself does not necessarily indicate globalization, as it prioritizes regional rather than global interconnections (Keohane and Nye 2005; Scholte 2005a) SADC nevertheless shows the impact of globalization in four rather different and multidimensional ways. These connect issues of growing regional and international interdependence to the spread of globalization. These are through a manifestation within the organisation of the following four facets of globalism as outlined by Keohane and Nye (2005: 76–7). According to Keohane and Nye features of economic globalism are "long distance flows of goods, services and capital, as well as the information and perceptions that accompany market exchange." SADC's real (as opposed to policy speak) form of integration into the global political economy occurs increasingly in terms of regional market dependencies on the world trade system—not just individual states, but the global networks of production, finance, and trade. The changing knowledge frame of the organization itself, and its commitment to globalized production and marketing strategies, illustrate the reach of globalized knowledge structures.

- *Military globalism*, according to Keohane and Nye (2005: 76) refers to "long distance networks of interdependence in which force, and the threat or promise of force" are employed. SADC's "two headed" institutional nature in the 1990s, is, as Schoeman 2005: 13) perceptively puts it, a result of the fact that SADC has moved from a "historical-symbolic shared history and a shared security configuration" which is now being replaced by "economic considerations." While Ngoma (2004) has deliberated at length about the potential of the region to become a regional security community, it is more likely that SADC's security concerns reflect globalized security concerns, such as retaining regional peace and stability to ensure the flourishing of a combination of regional and transnational economic practices. Strong evidence of this are the regional moves afoot to establish free trade areas with other stronger economic blocs such as the EU and the United States (Schoeman 2005: 20). The US has also for many years placed pressure on South Africa to play a more prominent peacekeeping role in the region with a clear agenda of keeping the region stable to ensure "economic stability" (read integration into global markets).

- *Environmental globalism*, according to Keohane and Nye (2005: 76) refers to "the long distance transport of materials in the atmosphere or oceans, or of biological substances such as pathogens or genetic materials that affect human health and well-being." There is another aspect to this which Keohane and Nye do not mention, namely global protocols on the environment such as the Kyoto protocol, which attempt to regulate developmental practices in the South, as well as to curb ongoing global environmental degradation (such as the hole in the ozone layer). SADC has a number of environmental treaties regarding various aspects of environmental protection, but is also on the receiving end of toxic waste dumping (Bond 2002a).

- *Social and cultural globalism*, according to Keohane and Nye (2005: 77) involves "the movement of ideas, information, images and people (who of course carry knowledge and information with them)." It is in terms of this aspect of globalization that SADC illustrates the ways in which the region has become more fully a part of globalization practices, at least at the state level. While Scholte (2005a, 2005b) cautions us about equating economic neoliberalism with globalization, we cannot ignore the very obvious fact that currently foreign direct investment (FDI) and transnational practices are integrally part of the spread of international capitalism and the ideology and culture of economic neoliberalism. This of course does not mean that all societies and communities in the region are affected by the social and cultural aspects of globalization in the same way. In this sense the region is characterized by what Held (2004), Keohane and Nye (2005) and others call "thin" globalization.

- *Thin or thick globalization* refers to the relative density of the economic, political, social, and cultural networks, processes, and dynamics that characterize globalized patterns of behavior. Because the spread of these networks, and dynamics are very uneven in southern Africa, the form of globalization we have here is a thin one (although this does also vary from state to state in the region, with South Africa having notably thicker globalization networks at all levels). State level interactions as well as the networks and dynamics that characterize formal economic practices in the region display many of the characteristics of globalization discussed above. The more social and cultural aspects of community integration are harder to estimate, but are discussed in more detail in the following section of this chapter.

In short, there is no doubt that the underlying ethos of SADC as an organization has changed radically in response to the economic imperative of economic globalization. SADC illustrates the power of globally located businesses by drawing attention to the ways in which emergent industries and businesses in the South find it harder and harder to compete with the "lean and mean" economic imperatives of transnational economic practices. Another salient feature of SADC is that its current economic *modus vivendi* is funded by the EU, to the tune of supplying 86 percent of all SADC funding (Schoeman 2005: 17). This funding does not come without strings attached. The spread of international capital and transnational practices occurs in a number of different ways and "spheres of economic influence" are still seen as important by the big (state and regional actors) in the global political system. It is clear at this level that, as Held (2004) and others warn, we should not be tempted to equate economic globalization with a decline in importance of states or state alliances in the global system—not least the ways in powerful states and blocs push their economic agendas through supplying economic assistance.

Yet many people in the region have never heard of SADC, and many communities remain peripherally involved in the type of "supranational" activities that Scholte describes. To make sense of what globalization means to societies in the southern African context requires thinking about state and societal layers of regional realities simultaneously. If we focus at state level on recent changes to national and regional development strategies and relate that to the literature on globalization, there are a number of significant policy changes which have occurred in the last two decades which would seem to give us sufficient proof that economic globalization is having an impact regionally through shifting strategies of regional integration, particularly in terms of the spread of ideas and ideology as well as in terms of communication and "development expertise" (as illustrated through EU support of SADC at this level). This is embodied in the shift in SADC from an economically non-committal sector integration strategy to embracing the principles of economic neoliberalism through its aspiration to become a regional economic bloc based on the EU model.

The entrenchment of neoliberalism regionally and continentally is taken one step further by the establishment of NEPAD and its commitment to the principles of international capitalism, in particular the replacement of former notions of continental economic interdependence with ideas of global integration. At this level we are taking into account state and interstate policies which reflect not only the interests of international capital and the transnational capitalist class but also the interests of state leaders themselves whose future political careers are shaped by the ways in which the international economic system as a whole (particularly trade, finance and production) reacts to national and regional political and economic strategies. Taylor and Nel (2002: 166) state that the driving force behind NEPAD is "the linkage between globalization, export driven trade policies and a nascent transnational elite," and that NEPAD only helps to legitimize the negative aspects of globalization by recognizing that southern Africa and Africa must perforce be integrated rather than face the alternative of further marginalization (see also Melber 2004: 6). As Sklair (2002: 6) puts it, "governments will go along with globalization not because they cannot resist it but because they perceive it to be in their own interests."

If we move on to other levels, particularly the societal and cultural, at which coming to terms with globalization in southern Africa has different impacts and meanings, these are no less demonstrative of the effect that globalization can have, in as much as it has changed the way the world functions, as well as what has been "left out" of the time space shrinkage that is supposed to characterize true "global dynamics." This should perhaps caution us from too-rigid definitions of what globalization means— or does not—in different geographical contexts—because we need to think about how southern Africa is connected to the global system, regionally and nationally *and societally*. There is the actual level of economic activity regionally, excluding the public sector. Statistics released by SADC show that economic integration occurs primarily with richer states in the North. Le Pere and Tjonneland (2005: 29 –30) show that approximately 22 percent of SADC trade is intra-regional, and most of SADC trade is with the EU, the US, Japan, and China. There is also major regional inconsistency with regard to the reduction of trade tariff barriers, which make the process of regional integration very uneven (Le Pere and Tjonneland, 2005: 30). This is old news, as this development trajectory has dogged the old SADCC and is unlikely to go away easily given current levels of economic development as well as regional infrastructural limitations. Yet more importantly, the national economies of SADC remain unevenly integrated into the global system. Indeed there are states like Malawi, Lesotho, and Swaziland for example, who show little sign of being integrated into global transnational economic practices. In this sense thinking about territory is still important, to the extent that some economic, political and social practices are still very much informed by geographical locality.

A related point is that FDI has been largely unforthcoming in the region, showing that in spite of governmental policy commitment to providing a fertile national and regional landing ground for FDI, international capital, and transnational corporations do not necessarily spread their activities and ventures evenly in the global system (Le Pere and Tjonneland 2005). In this context a lot has been said about the marginalization of Africa in the global political economy. Held (2004: 45) points out that the gap between rich and poor globally is shrinking in some regions (Asia for example) and growing in others (sub-Saharan Africa). The gap between rich and poor globally, regionally, and nationally is an often cited argument against economic globalization, arguing that the spread of TNPS amongst other aspects of globalization, is inherently exploitative, as these practices tend to follow cheaper and less organized labor.

A more important inconsistency from the point of view of measuring the impact of globalization, is the degree to which the broader majority of societies in the region are drawn into more formally recognized economic activities, and/or begin to show signs of being drawn in ideologically and culturally into different (consumerist) patterns of consumption and expenditure. These impacts are hard to generalize about, but we can perhaps draw attention to the differential impact of globalization by looking systematically at some of the framing questions regarding the impact of globalization on the region as highlighted in this book as a whole. It is to these that we now turn.

To What Extent is the Current Phase of Globalization New?

Almost all critical analysts of globalization agree that much of what is commonly understood by the term "globalization" is not new. We have discussed above the ostensibly "outstanding" features, which include the notion of the spread of networks and dynamics characterized by time space shrinkage (cyberspace, global telecommunications, international travel) and transnational economic practices. How does this affect the region? If we look at SADC as an example of the regional impact of globalized production, trade, and market strategies, there is evidence at the level of policy of the impact of economic globalization as discussed above.

There is another dimension to the organization, however, where what Schoeman (2005) refers to as the two-headed nature of SADC surfaces, through its twin commitments to deepening market penetration and integration in the region and regional political and military stability. Added to this is SADC's organizational schizophrenia which involves a strong commitment (in policy pronouncements at least) to regional integration with commitments to establishing a common currency and to free trade and the freer movement of people in the region; but at the same time, a distinct lack of regional economic integration and lack of coordinated economic policies aimed in this direction. As Schoeman (2005: 20) points out, while intraregional trade in SADC has increased from 5 percent in 1985 to 25 percent, this is because South African business has moved aggressively into the region and accounts for an increase of intraregional bilateral trade of 248 percent. The economic interdependencies of SADC states remain much the same as they always have, with the exception of the fact that South Africa provides even more of a hegemonic role as the longstanding bastion of Western economic and political ideals in the region. What is depressingly the same, despite the ideological inroads of globalization, is the grinding poverty in the region, particularly in rural areas, and as discussed earlier, even states with better HDI rankings tended to have high HPI indicators. This is a very strong illustration of the degree to which globalization has made the world smaller for some, and larger, even more inexplicable, and impenetrable for others.

What are the Main (Political, Economic, Social) Forces Driving Globalization? Who are the Main Actors?

It should be clear from the preceding discussion that the driving actors of globalization in the region are states and big business. Interestingly, SADC as a regional economic integration organization has played a significant role in grounding the more intangible knowledge dimensions of globalization, such as commitments to transnational practices of multinational companies and foreign direct investment. In its previous incarnation, in the form of the SADCC (and even the early SADC) there was a distinct lack of enthusiasm for these forms of economic "opening up" on the part of states in the region (Thompson 1996). Even while these TNPS have not established themselves evenly in the region, the commitment encouraging FDI through TNPs, as well as a growing tendency to allow this with minimal state regulation, shows a commitment to the principles of economic globalization. Bond (2002a) also discusses the role of the World Bank and IMF in particular in entrenching some of the more negative aspects of globalization in the region. The emphasis on cost recovery for basic services is one very obvious example of how neoliberal thinking can erode principles of environmental and social justice for the poor.

Van der Westhuizen (2006: 1987–8) also highlights how the effects of globalization on developing states leads to "shadow" economies characterized by both licit and illicit forms of trade. The reason for this is

> as globalization reduces the autonomy of the state to determine national development policy, and expands the market, the regulative capacity of (an already weak) state declines as the size and scope of the shadow economy increases. ... [i]n those cases where state weakness has already become highly pronounced—the Democratic Republic of the Congo, Sierra Leone, Somalia—rival social actors emerge, challenging not only the states" monopoly of violence but also even its exclusive licence to tax. In these social spaces unsavoury social forces position themselves: mafias, strongmen and vigilante movements (like Mapogo a Mathamaga in South Africa's northern Province).

Thus while they might not be driving globalization, these social actors have a parasitic relationship with the set of global and governmental actors and dynamics described above which occur as a result of globalization's unequal structural impact on developing economies.

What Are or Should Be the Main Responses to Globalization?

The discussion to this point has tended to refer to civil society somewhat indirectly, and has focused on states response to globalization in the region. On the societal level, in general, manifestations of local citizen action that have global reach, have not been especially significant if we take the region as a whole. South Africa's civil society organizations have tended to have more success in establishing the kinds of local–global linkages and connections which are referred to in the literature on the social and cultural aspects of globalization, while the rest of the region has lagged behind.

The antiglobalization lobby in South Africa, the HIV/AIDS Treatment Action campaign, as well as the environmental movement are examples of this (see Bond 2002a; Robins 2005; Thompson 2005). For the most part, societies in the region remain poorly integrated into participatory democratic practices as it is, let alone into global networks on governance issues (Von Lieres and Robins 2004). "Uncivil" society refers to the bulk of the population in southern Africa who remain unintegrated or marginally integrated into formal economic and political practices and networks. These groups remain largely untouched by the processes that are supposed to characterize globalization. There is another category of uncivil society becoming prevalent in South Africa, which consists of a large number of urban migrants with aspirations to the kind of consumerist lifestyles they observe around them, but without the income or chronic poverty relief they need to do anything about these aspirations, nor the political will to lobby sufficiently hard to get local government representatives to take up their cause for things like better basic services and housing. Many of these communities live in relative, rather than absolute, deprivation, and are affected by economic globalization in terms of the reality of its limited reach, rather than the (neoliberal) imaginary of its all encompassing embrace. This is yet another aspect of economic as well as cultural globalization.

So is globalization a bad thing? Like any either/or question, it invites pronouncements on globalization and its alternatives. Held (2004: 48) asks the crucial question, "how might global market integration hinder or retard the development of the world's poorest countries?" He goes on to discuss the merits of Garrett's (2001) view that "[g]lobal economic integration alone cannot be adequate medicine for low income countries to escape a development trap. While it would be wrong to argue in favor of widespread protectionism, sequencing openness in a set of reforms, and only advocating openness once substantial progress has been made in relation to the development of human capital, physical infrastructure, and independent political institutions is a sensible way to proceed (see also Garrett 2001; Castells 2005). While, as we discussed earlier, the further internationalization of capitalism is not coterminous with globalization, Held (2004) refers to the dominant global *ideology* of globalization which has at its heart a specific set of ideas and practices most tellingly embodied in the neoliberal (Washington) consensus of how development should proceed. It is this ideology which has clearly taken root in SADC's approach to regional development, if not in all the states which belong to it, even while more insidious forms of globalization are manifesting simultaneously, such as Van der Westhuizen's (2006) markets and mafias referred to earlier.

However the troublesome aspects of globalization, as Held (2004: 90–1) states, are that it fundamentally represents the interests of "leading states and vested interests." He goes on to say "despite vociferous dissent of many protest groups in recent years, the promotion of the global market has taken clear priority over many pressing environmental and social issues," and also mentions that developed states ensure which rules of the game are enforced where. Agricultural protectionism continues at the same time as developing states are urged to operate on global free market principles. This accords with the analysis of Bond (2002a) on South Africa's unsustainable development, and how globalization has affected southern Africa negatively, especially in terms of what has become known as "brown" (as opposed to green) environmental issues—that is the appalling urban (and semi-urban) environments in which many poor South (and southern) Africans find themselves in an effort to earn more income.

There is no doubt then that globalization has had a negative effect on southern Africa insofar as it has widened the gaps between the "haves" and the "have-nots," and overall has aggravated rather than alleviated the poverty concerns of the region.

Governments have learned to toe the line or face the consequences. Therein lies the root of "talking left, acting right." This phenomenon is the consequence of the reduced autonomy that globalization brings on governments—especially those with limited resources such as those in southern Africa. The fact that globalization does not serve the interests of the poor is negated by the fact that it does serve the interests of the rich—and the powerful—in the region: business and governments. The prioritization of free markets and economic liberalism also have their negative spin-offs for service delivery and urban poverty relief in general as Bond (2002a) make very clear through his analysis of poor housing, water, and sanitation delivery and the influence of neoliberal economic thinking on water pricing and basic services for the poor.

Held also discusses "the troubling fact that while nearly 3,000 people died on 9/11, almost 30,000 children under the age of five die each day in the developing world of preventable diseases, diseases which have been practically eradicated in the west, and the 'moral gap' defined by ... a world in which, as indicated earlier, over 1.2 billion people live on less than a dollar a day, 46 per cent of the worlds population live on less than 2 dollars a day, and 20 per cent of the world's population earn eighty per cent of its income" (Held 2004: 93). As already mentioned, these disparities manifest themselves in southern Africa as well. Most sub Saharan Africa countries (with the exception of South Africa fall into the "low income" category, and according to World Bank statistics the region receives considerably more aid flows than it does Foreign Direct Investment" (World Bank 2006).

Southern Africa and Africa have taken up some of these challenges through organizations such as the African Union at international fora including World Trade Organization meetings and in terms of lobbying the G8 for debt relief (the Gleneagles conference is a good example of this limited lobbying power). The extent to which government concerns reflect those of social movements is very limited, as the latter are usually very critical of many aspects of government policy as well as how issues of major concern are taken up and resolved at global level. Regionally the extent to which civil society is able to make inroads at the level of global governance structures remains at present somewhat limited. As Bond (2002a: 362) puts it with reference to the environmental movement and activism on brown environmental issues in South Africa "only in exceptional cases do the social and environmental justice movements reach a sufficiently high level of irritation and relevance to worry the ANC" While regional social movements remain relatively weaker than in South Africa, this does not mean that the status quo cannot change over time. South Africa is already showing signs of an increasing groundswell of social movement activity, even among those understood as more marginalized, and it is a matter of time before this begins to manifest more regionally. Ironically, it appears the more globalization processes and networks become thicker, the more sustained the level of civil society participation and resistance becomes. In the long run, this will definitely be a positive, if not *the* positive, consequence of globalization in the South.

PART 3
The Macrodynamics of Antiglobalization

Chapter 9

Power and Globalization in the New World Order[1]

Noam Chomsky

I would like to set the stage for my reflections on the current dynamics of globalization with a few truisms. It is hardly exciting news that we live in a world of conflict and confrontation. There are lots of dimensions of and complexities to this reality, but in recent years, lines have been drawn fairly sharply. To oversimplify, but not too much, one of the participants in the conflict involves concentrated power centers, state and private, closely interlinked. The other is the general or working population, worldwide. In old-fashioned terms, this situation would have been called "class war."

Concentrated power pursues the war relentlessly, and very self-consciously. Government documents and publications of the business world reveal that they are mostly vulgar Marxists, with values reversed of course. They are also frightened— back to seventeenth century England in fact. They realize that the system of domination is fragile and that it relies on disciplining the population by one means or another. There is a desperate search for such means: in recent years, communism, crime, drugs, terrorism, and others. Pretexts change, policies remain rather stable. Sometimes the shift of pretext along with continuity of policy is dramatic and takes real effort to miss: immediately after the collapse of the USSR, for example. They naturally grasp every opportunity to press their agenda forward: 9/11 is a typical case. Crises make it possible to exploit fear and concern to demand that the adversary be submissive, obedient, silent, distracted, while the powerful use the window of opportunity to pursue their own favored programs with even greater intensity. These programs vary, depending on the society: in the more brutal states, escalation of repression and terror; in societies where the population has won more freedom, measures to impose discipline while shifting wealth and power even more to their own hands. It is easy to list examples around the world.

Their victims should certainly resist the predictable exploitation of crisis, and should focus their own efforts, no less relentlessly, on the primary issues that remain much as they were before: among them, increasing militarism, destruction of the environment, and a far-reaching assault against democracy and freedom, the core of "neoliberal" programs.

---

1 The original form of this paper was prepared for and presented at the World Social Summit in Porte Alegre, February 1, 2002.

The Wizards of Davos and the "Other Davos"

The ongoing conflict is symbolized by the World Social Forum (WSF), to date held in Porte Alegre Brazil, and the more established World Economic Forum (WEF), which, until prior to its 2002 meeting in New York had always met in Davos, Switzerland. The WEF—to quote the national US press—is a gathering of "movers and shakers," the "rich and famous," "wizards from around the world," "government leaders and corporate executives, ministers of state and of God, politicians and pundits" disposed to "think deep thoughts" and address "the big problems that confront humankind in the present conjuncture." Press reports give a few examples, such as: "How do you inject moral values into what we do?" Or reference is made to Forum panels with titles such as "Tell Me What you Eat," led by the "reigning prince of the New York gastronomic scene," whose elegant restaurants will undoubtedly be mobbed by forum participants. There is also be mention of an "anti-forum" where 50,000 people are expected. These are "the freaks who assemble to protest the meetings of the World Trade Organization." One can learn more about the freaks from a photo of a scruffy-looking guy, with face concealed, writing "world killers" on a wall.

At their "carnival," as it is described, the freaks are throwing stones, writing graffiti, dancing and singing about a variety of boring topics that are unmentionable or beyond the scope of normal press coverage, at least in the United States: investment, trade, financial architecture, human rights, democracy, sustainable development, Brazil–Africa relations, and other marginal issues. They are not "thinking deep thoughts" about the "big problems" or "critical issues." That is left to the wizards of Davos in New York, the self-appointed guardians of the "New World Order."[2] The infantile rhetoric of the mainstream media pundits is probably a sign of well-deserved insecurity as well as concern for the "new world order."

The "anti-forum" freaks are defined as being "opposed to globalization," a propaganda weapon that readers are advised to reject with scorn. "Globalization" just means international integration and who could be against that? No sane person is "antiglobalization." That should be particularly obvious for the labor movement and the Left. The WSF is one of the most exciting and promising realization of the hopes of the Left and popular movements from their modern origins for a true international, which will pursue an alternative form of globalization concerned with the needs and interests of people rather than of illegitimate concentrations of power. These power-holders, of course, have appropriated as their own the term "globalization"—to restrict it to their peculiar version of international integration, reflecting their own interests. With this ridiculous terminology in place, those who seek a sane and just form of globalization can be labeled "antiglobalization," derided as primitivists who want to return to the Stone Age, to harm the poor, and other terms of abuse with which we are all too familiar.

The wizards of Davos modestly call themselves the "international community," but I personally prefer the term used by the world's leading business journal, the *Financial Times*: "the masters of the universe." Since the masters profess to be

---

2   Editor's note: For an analysis of these self-appointed guardians as a group, and as a class, see Salbuchi (2000).

admirers of Adam Smith, we might expect them to abide by his account of their behavior, though he only called them "the masters of mankind" (this was before the Space Age). Smith was referring to the "principal architects of policy" of his day, the merchants and manufacturers of England, who made sure that their own interests are "most peculiarly attended to however "grievous" the impact on others, including the people of England. At home and abroad, they pursue "the vile maxim of the masters of mankind": "all for ourselves and nothing for other people." It should hardly surprise us that today's masters honor the same "vile maxim" At least they try, though they are sometimes impeded by the freaks—the "great beast," to borrow a term used by the Founding Fathers of American democracy to refer to the unruly population that did not comprehend that the primary goal of government is "to protect the minority of the from the majority," as the leading Framer of the Constitution explained in the Constitutional Convention debates.

A World without War?

I will return to these matters, but first a few words about the theme of the 2001 World Social Forum in Porte Alegre—"a world without war." We cannot say much about human affairs with any confidence, but sometimes it is possible. We can, for example, be fairly confident that either there will be a world without war or there won't be a world—at least, a world inhabited by creatures other than bacteria and beetles, with some scattering of others. The reason is familiar: humans have developed means of destroying themselves, and much else, and have come dangerously close to using them for half a century. Furthermore, the leaders of the civilized world are now dedicated to enhancing these dangers to survival, in full awareness of what they are doing, at least if they read the reports of their own intelligence agencies and respected strategic analysts, including many who strongly favor the race to destruction. Ominously, the plans are developed and implemented on grounds that are rational within the dominant framework of ideology and values, which ranks survival well below "hegemony," the goal pursued by advocates of these programs, as they frankly insist.

Wars over water, energy, and other resources are not unlikely in the future, with consequences that could be devastating. For the most part, however, wars have had to do with the imposition of the system of nation-states, an unnatural social formation that that typically has to be instituted by violence. That is a primary reason why Europe was the most savage and brutal part of the world for many centuries, meanwhile conquering most of the world. European efforts to impose state systems in conquered territories are the source of most conflicts underway right now, after the collapse of the formal colonial system. Europe's own favorite sport of mutual slaughter had to be called off in 1945, when it was realized that the next time the game was played would be the last. Another prediction that we can make with fair confidence is that there won't be a war among great powers; the reason is that if the prediction turns out to be wrong, there will be no one around to care to tell us.

Furthermore, popular activism within the rich and powerful societies has had a civilizing effect. The "movers and shakers" can no longer undertake the kinds of long-term aggression that were options before, as when the United States attacked South Vietnam 40 years ago, smashing much of it to pieces before significant popular protest developed. Among the many civilizing effects of the ferment of the 1960s was broad opposition to large-scale aggression and massacre, reframed in the ideological system as unwillingness to accept casualties among the armed forces ("the Vietnam syndrome"). That is why the Reaganites had to resort to international terrorism instead of invading Central America directly, on the Kennedy-Johnson model, in their war to defeat liberation theology, as the School of the Americas describes the achievement with pride.

The same changes explain the intelligence review of the incoming Bush-I administration in 1989, warning that in conflicts against "much weaker enemies"— the only kind it makes sense to confront—the United States must "defeat them decisively and rapidly," or the campaign will lose "political support," understood to be thin. Wars since have kept to that pattern, and the scale of protest and dissent has steadily increased. So there are changes, of a mixed nature.

When pretexts vanish, new ones have to be concocted to control the great beast while traditional policies are continued, adapted to new circumstances. That was already becoming clear 20 years ago. It was hard not to recognize that the Soviet enemy was facing internal problems and might not be a credible threat much longer. That is part of the reason why the Reagan administration, 20 years ago, declared that the "war on terror" would be the focus of US foreign policy, particularly in Central America and the Middle East, the main source of the plague spread by "depraved opponents of civilization itself" in a "return to barbarism in the modern age," as administration moderate George Shultz explained, also warning that the solution is violence, avoiding "utopian, legalistic means like outside mediation, the World Court, and the United Nations." We need not tarry on how the war was waged in those two regions, and elsewhere, by the extraordinary network of proxy states and mercenaries—an "axis of evil," to borrow George W. Bush's more up-to-date term.

It is of some interest that in the months since the war was re-declared, with much the same rhetoric, after 9/11, all of this has been entirely effaced, even the fact that the United States was condemned for international terrorism by the World Court and Security Council and responded by sharply escalating the terrorist attack it was ordered to terminate; or the fact that the very people who are directing the military and diplomatic components of the re-declared war on terror were leading figures in implementing terrorist atrocities in Central America and the Middle East during the first phase of the war. Silence about these matters is a real tribute to the discipline and obedience of the educated classes in the free and democratic societies.

It is a reasonable guess that the "war on terror" will again serve as a pretext for intervention and atrocities in coming years, not just by the United States; Chechnya is only one of a number of examples. In Latin America, there is no need to linger on what that portends; certainly not in Brazil, the first target of the wave of repression that swept Latin America after the Kennedy administration, in a decision of historic importance, shifted the mission of the Latin American military from "hemispheric defense" to "internal security"—a euphemism for state terror directed against the domestic population. That still continues, on a huge scale, particularly in Colombia, well in the lead for human rights violations in the hemisphere in the 1990s and by far the leading recipient of US arms and military training, in accord with a consistent pattern documented even in mainstream scholarship.

The "war on terror" of course, has been the focus of a huge and growing literature during the first phase in the 1980s and since it was re-declared in the past few months.[3] One interesting feature of the flood of commentary, then and now, is that we are not told what "terror" is. What we hear, rather, is that this is "a vexing and complex question." This is curious, given that there are straightforward definitions in official US documents. A simple one takes terror to be the "calculated use of violence or threat of violence to attain goals that are political, religious, or ideological in nature" This seems appropriate enough, but it cannot be used in official discourse, for two good reasons. One is that it would also define the official policy of "counterinsurgency" or "low-intensity conflict." Another is that it yields all the wrong answers—facts too obvious to review although suppressed with remarkable efficiency.

The problem of finding a definition of "terror" that will exclude the most prominent cases is indeed vexing and complex. But fortunately, there is an easy solution: define "terror" as terror that "they" carry out against "us." A review of the scholarly literature on terror, the media, and intellectual or academic journals will show that this usage is close to exceptionless, and that any departure from it elicits impressive tantrums. Furthermore, the practice is probably universal: the generals in South America were protecting the population from "terror directed from outside," just as the Japanese were in Manchuria and the Nazis in occupied Europe. If there is an exception, I have not found it.

Let us return to "globalization" and the linkage between it and the threat of war, perhaps terminal war.

The version of "globalization" designed by "the masters of the universe" has very broad elite support, as do the so-called "free trade agreements"—what the *Wall Street Journal*, more honestly, has called "free investment agreements." Very little is reported about these issues, and crucial information is simply suppressed; for example, after a decade, the position of the US labor movement on NAFTA, and the conforming conclusions of Congress's own Research Bureau (the Office of Technology Assessment), have yet to be reported outside of dissident sources. And, of course, the issues are off the agenda in electoral politics. There are good reasons for this. The masters know well that the public will be opposed if information becomes available. They are fairly open when addressing one another, however. Thus a few years ago, under enormous public pressure, Congress rejected the "fast track" legislation that grants the president authority to enact international economic arrangements with Congress permitted to vote "Yes" (or, theoretically, "No") with no discussion, and the public uninformed. Like other sectors of elite opinion, the *WSJ* was distraught over the failure to undermine democracy. But it explained the problem: opponents of these Stalinist-style measures have an "ultimate weapon," the general population, which must therefore be kept in the dark. That is very important, particularly in the more democratic society, where dissidents cannot simply be jailed

---

3   This literature is too voluminous to cite but see, in particular, the online and published writings, such as *Global Outlook*, put out by the Montreal Centre for Research on Globalisation (CRG).

or assassinated, as in the leading recipients of US military aid, such as El Salvador, Turkey, and Colombia, to list the recent and current world champions (Israel–Egypt aside).

One might ask why public opposition to "globalization" has been so high for many years. That seems strange, in an era when it has led to unprecedented prosperity, so we are constantly informed, particularly in the United States, with its "fairy tale economy." Through the 1990s, the US enjoyed "the greatest economic boom in America's history—and the world's," Anthony Lewis wrote in the *New York Times* a year ago, repeating the standard refrain from the left end of the admissible spectrum. It is conceded that there are flaws: some have been left behind in the economic miracle, and we good-hearted folk must do something about that. The flaws reflect a profound and troubling dilemma: the rapid growth and prosperity brought by "globalization" has as a concomitant growing inequality, as some lack the skills to enjoy the wondrous gifts and opportunities.

The picture is so conventional that it may be hard to realize how little resemblance it has to reality, facts that have been well known right through the miracle. Until the brief boomlet of the late 1990s (which scarcely compensated for earlier stagnation or decline for most people), per capita growth in the "roaring 90s" was about the same as the rest of the industrial world, much lower than in the first 25 post-war years before so-called "globalization," and vastly lower than the war years, the greatest economic boom in American history, under a semi-command economy. How then can the conventional picture be so radically different from uncontroversial facts? The answer is simplicity itself. For a small sector of the society, the 1990s really were a grand economic boom. That sector happens to include those who tell others the joyous news. And they cannot be accused of dishonesty. They have no reason to doubt what they are saying. They read it all the time in the journals for which they write, and it accords with their personal experience: it is true of the people they meet in editorial offices, faculty clubs, elite conferences like the one the wizards are now attending, and the elegant restaurants where they dine. It is the world that is different.

Let us have a quick look at the record over a longer stretch. International economic integration—one facet of "globalization," in a neutral sense of the term—increased rapidly before World War I, stagnated or declined during the interwar years, and resumed after World War II, now reaching levels of a century ago by gross measures; the fine structure is more complex. By some measures, globalization was greater before World War I: one illustration is "free circulation of labor," the foundation of free trade for Adam Smith, although not his contemporary admirers. By other measures, "globalization" is far greater now: one dramatic example—not the only one—is the flow of short-term speculative capital, far beyond any precedent. The distinction reflects some central features of the version of globalization preferred by the masters of the universe: to an extent even beyond the norm, capital has priority, people are incidental.

The Mexican border is an interesting example. It is artificial, the result of conquest, like most borders, and has been porous in both directions for a variety of socioeconomic reasons. It was militarized after NAFTA by Clinton in order to block the "free circulation of labor." That was necessary because of the anticipated effects of NAFTA in Mexico: an "economic miracle," which would be a disaster for much of the population, who would seek to escape. In the same years, the flow of capital, already very free, was expedited further, along with what is called "trade," about two thirds of which is now centrally managed within private tyrannies, up from half before NAFTA. This is "trade" only by doctrinal decision. The effects of NAFTA on actual trade have not been examined, to my knowledge.

A more technical measure of globalization is convergence to a global market, with a single price and wage. That plainly has not happened. With respect to incomes at least, the opposite is more likely true. Though much depends on exactly how it is measured, there is good reason to believe that inequality has increased within and across countries. That is expected to continue. US intelligence agencies, with the participation of specialists from the academic professions and the private sector, recently released a report on expectations for 2015. They expect "globalization" to proceed on course: "Its evolution will be rocky, marked by chronic financial volatility and a widening economic divide." This means less convergence, less globalization in the technical sense, but more globalization in the doctrinally preferred sense. Financial volatility implies still slower growth and more crises and poverty.

It is at this point that a clear connection is established between "globalization" in the sense of the masters of the universe and the increasing likelihood of war. Military planners adopt the same projections, and have explained, forthrightly, that these expectations lie behind the vast expansion of military power. Even pre-9/11, US military expenditures surpassed those of allies and adversaries combined. The terror attacks have been exploited to increase the funding sharply, delighting key elements of the private economy. The most ominous program involves the militarization of space, also expanded under the pretext of "fighting terror."

The reasoning behind these programs is explained publicly in Clinton-era documents. A prime reason is the growing gap between the "haves" and the "have-nots," which is expected to continue, contrary to economic theory but consistent with reality. The "have-nots"—the "great beast" of the world—may become disruptive, and must be controlled, in the interests of what is called "stability" in technical jargon, meaning subordination to the dictates of the masters. That requires means of violence, and having "assumed, out of self-interest, responsibility for the welfare of the world capitalist system," the United States must be far in the lead—quoting here the diplomatic historian Gerald Haines, also the senior historian of the CIA, in a scholarly study of US strategic planning in the 1940s.

But overwhelming dominance in conventional forces and weapons of mass destruction is not sufficient. It is necessary to move on to the new frontier: the militarization of space, undermining the Outer Space Treaty of 1967, so far observed. Recognizing the intent, the UN General Assembly has reaffirmed the Treaty several times; the United States has refused to join, in virtual isolation. And Washington has blocked negotiations at the UN Conference on Disarmament for the past year over this issue—all scarcely reported, for the usual reasons. It is not wise to allow citizens to know of plans that may bring to an end biology's only experiment with "higher intelligence."

As widely observed, these programs benefit military industry, but we should bear in mind that the term is misleading. Throughout modern history, but with a dramatic increase after World War II, the military system has been used as a device to socialize cost and risk while privatizing profit. The "new economy" is to a substantial extent an outgrowth of the dynamic and innovative state sector of the US economy. The main reason why public spending in biological sciences has been rapidly increasing is that intelligent right-wingers understand that the cutting edge of the economy relies on these public initiatives. A huge increase is scheduled under the pretext of "bioterror," just as the public was deluded into paying for the new economy under the pretext that the Russians are coming—or after they collapsed, by the threat of the "technological sophistication" of Third World countries as the Party Line shifted in 1990, instantly, without missing a beat and with scarcely a word of comment. That's also a reason why national security exemptions have to be part of international economic agreements: it doesn't help Haiti, but it allows the US economy to grow under the traditional principle of harsh market discipline for the poor and a nanny state for the rich—what is called "neoliberalism," although it is not a very good term: the doctrine is centuries old, and would scandalize classical liberals.

One might argue that these public expenditures were often worthwhile. Perhaps, perhaps not. But it is clear that the masters were afraid to allow democratic choice. All of this is concealed from the general public, though the participants understand it very well.

Plans to cross the last frontier of violence by militarization of space are disguised as "missile defense," but anyone who pays attention to history knows that when we hear the word "defense," we should think "offense." The present case is no exception. The goal is quite frankly stated: to ensure "global dominance" or "hegemony." Official documents stress that the goal is "to protect US interests and investments," as well as control the "have-nots." Today that requires domination of space, just as in earlier times the most powerful states created armies and navies "to protect and enhance their commercial interests." It is recognized that these new initiatives, in which the United States is far in the lead, pose a serious threat to survival. And it is also understood that these initiatives could be blocked by international treaties. But as already mentioned, hegemony has a higher value than survival, a moral calculus that has prevailed among the powerful throughout history. What has changed is that the stakes are much higher, awesomely so.

The relevant point here is that the expected success of "globalization" in the doctrinal sense is a primary reason given for the programs of using space for offensive weapons of instant mass destruction. But let us return to "globalization" and "the greatest economic boom in America's history—in the 1990s.

Since World War II, the international economy has passed through two phases: the Bretton Woods phase from the late 1940s to the early 1970s, and the subsequent period based on, among other things, the dismantling of the Bretton Woods system of regulated exchange rates and controls on capital movement. It is the second phase, associated with the neoliberal policies of what Williamson (1990) termed the "Washington consensus," that has been characterized as "globalization." The two phases are quite different. The first is often called the "golden age" of (state) capitalism (Marglin and Schor 1990). The second phase has been accompanied by marked deterioration in standard macroeconomic measures—the growth of the economy productivity, capital investment, and world trade; much higher interest rates; vast accumulation of unproductive reserves to protect the value of diverse national currencies; increased financial volatility; and other harmful economic, social, and environmental consequences have been well documented. There were exceptions, notably the East Asian countries that did not follow the rules: they did not worship at the alter of the "religion" that "markets know best," as Joseph Stiglitz wrote in a World Bank research publication shortly before he was appointed chief economist, later removed (and winning the Nobel prize).

In fact, as acknowledged by, among others, José Antonio Ocampo, director of the Economic Commission for Latin America and the Caribbean (ECLAC), in an address before the American Economic Association in 2001, the "promised land [of bold neoliberal reforms] is a mirage;" growth in the 1990s was far below that of the three decades of 'state-led development" in Phase I. He noted too that the correlation between following the rules and economic outcomes holds worldwide.

Let us return, then, to the profound and troubling dilemma: that the rapid growth and great prosperity brought by globalization has brought inequality because some lack skill. There is no dilemma, because the rapid growth and prosperity are a myth.

Many international economists regard the liberalization of capital as a substantial factor in explaining the poorer outcomes of phase II. But the economy is a complex affair, so poorly understood that one has to be cautious about causal connections. But one consequence of the liberalization of capital is rather clear: it tends to undercut democracy. This was well understood by the framers of the Bretton Woods agreements. One reason why the agreements were founded on the regulation of capital was to allow national governments to carry out social democratic policies that had enormous popular support. Free capital movement creates what has been called a "virtual Senate" with "veto power" over government decisions, sharply restricting policy options. Governments, in this context, face a "dual constituency"—voters, and speculators who "conduct moment-by-moment referenda" on government policies (quoting technical studies of the financial system). Even in the rich countries, the constituency of private interests prevails.

Other components of investor-rights "globalization" have similar consequences. Socioeconomic decisions are increasingly shifted to unaccountable concentrations of power, an essential feature of neoliberal "reforms" (a term of propaganda, not description). An extension of this attack on democracy is presumably being planned, behind closed doors and without public discussion, in the negotiations for a GATS (General Agreement on Trade in Services). Like the ill-fated (defeated, that is) efforts a few years ago to establish the MAI (Multilateral Agreement on Investment), GATS is an attack on the idea of democracy. The term "services" refers to just about anything that might fall within the arena of democratic choice: health, education, welfare, postal and other communications, water and other resources. There is no meaningful sense in which the transfer of such services to private hands could be seen as "trade" but the term has been so deprived of meaning that it might as well be extended to this travesty as well.

The huge public protests in Quebec in April 2001 at the Summit of the Americas, set in motion by the freaks in Porto Alegre a year ago, were in part directed against the attempt to impose the GATS principles in secret within the planned Free Trade Area of the Americas (FTAA). Those protests brought together a very broad constituency, North and South, all strongly opposed to what is apparently being planned by trade ministers and corporate executives behind closed doors.

The protests did receive coverage of the usual kind: the freaks are throwing rocks and disrupting the wizards thinking about the big problems. But the invisibility of their actual concerns is quite remarkable. For example, *New York Times* economics correspondent Anthony De Palma writes that the GATS agreement "has generated none of the public controversy that has swirled about [WTO] attempts to promote merchandise trade"—even after Seattle. In fact, it has been a prime concern for years. As in other cases, this is not deceit. De Palma's knowledge about "the freaks" is surely limited to what passes through the media filter, and it is an iron law of journalism that the serious concerns of activists must be rigidly barred in favor of someone throwing a rock, perhaps a police provocateur.

The importance of protecting the public from information was dramatically revealed at the April summit. Every editorial office in the United States had on its desk two important studies, timed for release just before the Summit. One was from Human Rights Watch, the second from the Economic Policy Institute in Washington—and neither organization is exactly obscure. Both studies investigated in depth the effects of NAFTA, which was hailed at the summit as a grand triumph and a model for the FTAA, with headlines trumpeting its praises by George Bush and other leaders, all accepted as Gospel Truth. Both studies were suppressed with near-total unanimity. It is easy to see why. Human Rights Watch analysed the effects of NAFTA on labor rights, which, it found, were harmed in all three participating countries. Its report was comprehensive: it consisted of detailed analyses of the effects of NAFTA on working people, written by specialists on the three countries. The conclusion is that this is one of the rare agreements that have harmed the majority of the population in all of the participating countries.

The effects on Mexico were particularly severe, and particularly significant for the South. Wages had declined sharply with the imposition of neoliberal programs in the 1980s. This continued after NAFTA, with a 24 percent decline in incomes for salaried workers, and 40 percent for the self-employed—an effect magnified by the rapid increase in unsalaried workers. Although foreign investment grew, total investment declined, as the economy was transferred to the hands of foreign multinationals. The minimum wage lost 50 percent of its purchasing power. Manufacturing declined, and development stagnated or reversed. A small sector became extremely wealthy, and foreign investors prospered.

These studies confirm what had been reported in the business press and academic studies. The *Wall Street Journal* (March 8, 1999) reported that although the Mexican economy was growing rapidly in the late 1990s after a sharp post-NAFTA decline, consumers suffered a 40 percent drop in purchasing power, the number of people living in extreme poverty grew twice as fast as the population, and even those working in foreign-owned assembly plants lost purchasing power. Similar conclusions were drawn in a study of the Latin American section of the Woodrow Wilson Center (Bach 1999), which found that economic power had greatly concentrated as small Mexican companies cannot obtain financing, traditional farming sheds workers, and labor-intensive sectors (agriculture, light industry) cannot compete internationally with what is called "free enterprise" in the doctrinal system. Agriculture suffered for the usual reasons: peasant farmers cannot compete with highly subsidized US agribusiness, with effects familiar throughout the world.

Most of this was predicted by critics of NAFTA, including the suppressed Organic Trade Association and labor movement studies. Critics were wrong in one respect, however. Most anticipated a sharp increase in the urban–rural ratio, as hundreds of thousands of peasants were driven off the land. This did not happen. The reason, it would appear, is that conditions deteriorated so badly in the cities that there was a huge flight from them as well to the United States. Those who survive the crossing—many do not—work for very low wages, with no benefits, under awful conditions. The effect is to destroy lives and communities in Mexico and to improve the US economy, where "consumption of the urban middle class continues to be subsidized by the impoverishment of farm laborers both in the United States and Mexico," the Woodrow Wilson Center study points out (Bach 1999: 22).

These are among the costs of NAFTA, and neoliberal globalization generally, that economists generally choose not to measure. But even by the highly ideological standard measures, the costs have been severe.

None of this was allowed to sully the celebration of NAFTA and the FTAA at the summit. Unless they are connected to activist organizations, most people know about these matters only from their own lives. And carefully protected from reality by the Free Press, many regard themselves as somehow failures, unable to take part in the celebration of the greatest economic boom in history.

Data from the richest country in the world are enlightening, but I will skip the details. The picture generalizes, with some variation of course, and exceptions of the kind already noted. The picture is much worse when we depart from standard economic measures. One cost is the threat to survival implicit in the reasoning of military planners, already described. There are many others. To take one, the International Labor Organization (2001) reported a rising "worldwide epidemic" of serious mental health disorders, often linked to stress in the workplace, with very substantial fiscal costs in the industrial countries. A large factor, it concludes, is "globalization," which brings an "evaporation of job security," pressure on workers, and a higher workload, particularly in the US. Is this a cost of "globalization"? From one point of view, it is one of its most attractive features. When he lauded US economic performance as "extraordinary," Alan Greenspan stressed particularly the heightened sense of job insecurity that leads to reduced costs for employers. The World Bank agrees. It recognizes that "labor market flexibility" has acquired "a bad name ... as a euphemism for pushing wages down and workers out." Nevertheless, "it is essential in all the regions of the world. The most important reforms involve lift ... constraints on labor mobility and wage flexibility, as well as breaking the ties between social services and labor contracts" (World Bank 1995a).

In brief, according to prevailing ideology, pushing workers out, pushing wages down, and undermining benefits are all crucial contributions to economic health.

Unregulated trade has further benefits for corporations. Much—probably most—"trade" is centrally managed through a variety of devices: intra-firm transfers, strategic alliances, outsourcing, and others (UNCTAD, Division of Transnational Corporations 1994). Broad trading areas benefit corporations by making them less answerable to local and national communities. This enhances the effects of neoliberal programs, which regularly have reduced labor's share of national income. In the United States the 1990s was the first postwar period when the division of income shifted strongly towards the owners of capital and investors and away from labor and households. Trade has a wide range of unmeasured costs: subsidizing energy, resource depletion, and other externalities that are not counted. But it also brings advantages, although here too some caution is necessary. The most widely hailed is that trade increases specialization, which reduces the capacity to make choices, including the choice to modify comparative advantage, otherwise known as "development." The capacity for choice and development (and the UNDP, in its notion of *human development*, defines the first in terms of the second) are values in themselves: undermining them is a substantial cost. If the American colonies had been compelled to accept the WTO regime 200 years ago, New England would be pursuing its comparative advantage in exporting fish, surely not producing textiles, which survived only by exorbitant tariffs to bar British products (mirroring Britain's treatment of India). The same was true of steel and other industries, right to the present, particularly in the highly protectionist Reagan years—even putting aside the state sector of the economy. There is a great deal to say about all of this. Much of the story is masked in selective modes of economic measurement, though it is well known to economic historians and historians of technology.

Upon Further Reflection ...

As everyone is aware, at least at the World Social Forum, the rules of the game are likely to enhance deleterious effects for the poor. The rules of the WTO bar the mechanisms used by every rich country to reach its current state of development, while also providing unprecedented levels of protectionism for the rich, including a patent regime that bars innovation and growth in novel ways, and allows corporate entities to amass huge profits by monopolistic pricing of products often developed with substantial public contribution.

Under contemporary versions of traditional mechanisms, half the people in the world are effectively in receivership, their economic policies managed by experts in Washington. But even in the rich countries democracy is under attack by virtue of the shift of decision-making power from governments, which may be partially responsive to the public, to private tyrannies, which have no such defects. Cynical slogans such as "trust the people" or "minimize the state" do not, under current circumstances, call for increasing popular control. They shift decisions from governments to other hands, but not "the people:" rather, the management of collectivist legal entities, largely unaccountable to the public, and effectively totalitarian in internal structure, much as conservatives charged a century ago when opposing "the corporatization of America."

Latin American specialists and polling organizations have observed for some years that extension of formal democracy in Latin America has been accompanied by increasing disillusionment about democracy, "alarming trends," which continue, analysts have observed, noting the link between "declining economic fortunes" and "lack of faith" in democratic institutions. As Atilio Borón (1995), an Argentinian political sociologist, pointed out some years ago, the new wave of democratization in Latin America coincided with neoliberal economic "reforms," which undermine effective democracy, a phenomenon that extends worldwide, in various forms.

It also applies to the United States. There has been much public clamor about the "stolen election" of November 2000, and surprise that the public does not seem to care. Likely reasons are suggested by public opinion studies, which reveal that on the eve of the election, three quarters of the population regarded the process as largely a farce: a game played by financial contributors, party leaders, and the public relations industry, which crafted candidates to say "almost anything to get themselves elected" so that one could believe little they said even when it was intelligible. On most issues, citizens could not identify the stands of the candidates, not because they were stupid or not trying, but because of the conscious efforts of the PR industry. A Harvard University project that monitors political attitudes found that the "feeling of powerlessness has reached an alarming high," with more than one half saying that people like them have little or no influence on what government does, a sharp rise through the neoliberal period.

Issues on which the public differs from elites (economic, political, intellectual) are pretty much off the agenda, notably questions of economic policy. The business world, not surprisingly, is overwhelmingly in favor of corporate-led "globalization," the "free investment agreements" called "free trade agreements," NAFTA and the FTAA, GATS, and other devices that concentrate wealth and power in hands unaccountable to the public. Also not surprisingly, the great beast is generally opposed, almost instinctively, even without knowing crucial facts from which they are carefully shielded. It follows that such issues are not appropriate for political campaigns, and did not arise in the mainstream for the November 2000 elections. One would have been hard-pressed, for example, to find discussion of the upcoming Summit of the Americas and the FTAA, and other topics that involve issues of prime concern for the public. Voters were directed to what the PR industry calls "personal qualities," not "issues." Among the half the population that votes, heavily skewed towards the wealthy, those who recognize their class interests to be at stake vote for those interests: overwhelmingly, for the more reactionary of the two business parties. But the general public splits its vote in other ways, leading to a statistical tie. Among working people, noneconomic issues such as gun ownership and "religiosity" were primary factors, so that people often voted against their own primary interests— apparently assuming that they had little choice.

What remains of democracy is to be construed as the right to choose among commodities. Business leaders have long explained the need to impose on the population a "philosophy of futility" and "lack of purpose in life," to "concentrate human attention on the more superficial things that comprise much of fashionable consumption." Deluged by such propaganda from infancy, people may then accept their meaningless and subordinate lives and forget ridiculous ideas about managing their own affairs. They may abandon their fate to the wizards, and in the political realm, to the self-described "intelligent minorities" who serve and administer power.

From this perspective, conventional in elite opinion, particularly through the last century, the November 2000 elections do not reveal a flaw of US democracy, but rather its triumph. And generalizing, it is fair to hail the triumph of democracy throughout the hemisphere, and elsewhere, even though the populations somehow do not see it that way.

The struggle to impose that regime takes many forms, but never ends, and never will as long as high concentrations of effective decision-making power remain in place. It is only reasonable to expect the masters to exploit any opportunity that comes along—at the moment, the fear and anguish of the population in the face of terrorist attacks, a serious matter for the West now that, with new technologies available, it has lost its virtual monopoly of violence, retaining only a huge preponderance.

But there is no need to accept these rules, and those who are concerned with the fate of the world and its people will surely follow a very different course. The popular struggles against investor-rights "globalization," mostly in the South, have influenced the rhetoric, and to some extent the practices, of the masters of the universe, who are concerned and defensive. These popular movements are unprecedented in scale, in range of constituency, and in international solidarity; the meetings here are a critically important illustration. The future to a large extent lies in their hands. It is hard to overestimate what is at stake.

Chapter 10

Expanding Boundaries of the Political: Globalization Protest Movements and the State

Teivo Teivainen

Movements Politicize the Economic

The separation of the political and the economic is one of the mechanisms through which democratic claims have been contained under capitalism. According to the doctrine of economic neutrality, economic issues and institutions are somehow apolitical, beyond political power struggles, and therefore not subject to democratic claims. With the constant, even if not always lineal, expansion of the social spaces defined as economic over the past decades, the possibilities of democratic politics have been increasingly restricted. If power is increasingly located in the economic sphere, such processes of democratization that only focus on the narrowly defined political sphere become increasingly ineffective.

Many disenchanted people in different parts of the world have come to the conclusion that the existing representative channels through which democracy is supposed to function, such as parliaments of territorial states, are not effective in ensuring democratic control of the key decision-making sites of the capitalist world. Throughout much of the 1990s, it seemed that there was little that could be done to counter that process. The Third Worldism of the 1970s was far behind, and few actors were openly challenging the economists' consensus that accepted the delegation of ever stronger decision-making powers to the central banks, economic ministries, transnational credit-rating agencies, big corporations, and international financial institutions. Whether formally public or private, the doctrine of economic neutrality has been used to shield those institutions defined as "economic" from democratic claims.

One of the ideological contradictions in the expansion of capitalist rule is that once the power of the economic sphere becomes stronger, it may also become more apparent that the economic sphere does have power. The fact that the Zapatista Army for National Liberation (Ejército Zapatista de Liberación Nacional, or EZLN) in Chiapas started its rebellion in 1994 on the very day the North American Free Trade Agreement (NAFTA) became effective was no coincidence. During the second half of the 1990s, there were various protests targeting transnational institutions and instruments defined as "economic." By pointing to the inherently political nature of the "economic" institutions and instruments, the protest movements were expanding the boundaries of the political.

One of the results (and also causes) of the turn-of-the-century intensification of globalization protest movements has been the possibility to radically rethink the economic/political boundary. Even if the boundary is a key element in the reproduction of capitalism, not all these movements are, or consider themselves, anti-capitalist. Some of them aim at creating conditions for a democratic post-capitalist world; others emphasize building democratic organizational forms despite or inside capitalism. Many of the globalization protest movements have aimed at the politicization of global relations of command associated with institutions such as the World Trade Organization, World Economic Forum and transnational corporations. These institutions claim to be purely "economic" and therefore not subject to democratic norms.

The political nature of the economic institutions does not become evident automatically. The contradictions of capitalism create conditions for critical responses, but these responses are not generated without active social forces. The new transnational activism that emerged in the globalization protests of the 1990s has made it more visible that "economy" is a political and historical construction. To the extent the movements can convincingly demonstrate that apparently economic institutions are in reality important sites of power, it becomes more difficult for the latter to be legitimately based on inherently non-democratic principles such as "one dollar, one vote."

Aiming Beyond the State

Redefining the boundaries of the political, especially but not only vis-à-vis the economic, can be considered a necessary condition for any radical democratic transformation of the world. One part of this process is the weakening of the conceptual linkage between the political and the state. In the same spirit that feminist movements pointed to the personal, and not only the state, as a site of the political, globalization protest activists may be pointing to "economic institutions" or "the global" as non-state locations of the political. There are, indeed, many movements that are trying to think of the political beyond the state. Among some movements, especially those identified with autonomist or left-libertarian positions, aiming at conquering state machineries through elections or other means has always been discredited. The anti-state tendencies have, however become prevalent also in wider activist circles.

According to Alejandro Colás, many globalization protest activists reject 'strategic discourses which set medium or long-term political objectives or seek to channel protest into coherent bodies through representative organizations (Colás, 2003: 97–118). The central argument of Colás is worth citing at length:

> because global capitalism relies on mediating political structures for its own reproduction, struggles for the democratization of global governance would do well to focus on "the political" in its various manifestations as a key site of anti-capitalist contestation and transformation; secondly, if such struggles are to be democratic in their practice as well as in their programme, some conception of representation—a clear answer to the question of who or what is the "demos"—is imperative. (Colás 2003: 103)

Even though I agree with much of the criticism that Colás directs against the "flatly unhierarchical anti-politics" of many globalization protest activists, he equates political representation too easily with state structures. We should focus on the political and representation also outside the state. For example, it is important to reflect on what they can mean in transnational non-state contexts such as the articulations and alliances that the movements themselves are constructing.

One of the sites where these articulations take place is the World Social Forum (WSF). Since the first WSF event was held in Porto Alegre, Brazil, in January 2001, it has grown to become perhaps the world's most important space in which social movements and other non-state actors gather. After a period of yearly global forums in which the numbers of participants grew year after year, the process mushroomed into a multiplicity of local, national, regional and thematic forums. The successful fora in Mumbai, India, held in 2004, and in Nairobi, Kenya, in 2007, in particular, gave the WSF process an increasingly global character. At the same time, the expansion of the process has made various controversies of the WSF more visible, one of them being the role of the state.

Among the WSF in particular and the globalization protest movements more generally there are increasing debates about how the existing capitalist world system could be transformed or overcome. One of the various differences among the movements that aim at more democratic futures is between those who emphasize the importance of alliances with the states and those who advocate strategies based on networks that seek autonomy from existing and/or future states. The former have tended to locate the political mainly in the goal of conquering or influencing state or inter-state institutions, often through political parties dedicated to this task. The latter often argue that it is politically important to prefigure principles of the desired democratic futures already in the process of changing the world. Among the latter, it is generally considered that the former overvalue the strategic goal of conquering the state in ways that pay too little attention to the importance of democratic means and modes of internal organization among the movements themselves.

This distinction is by no means absolute, however, and most movements tend to combine both options. Geraldo Fontes, active in one of the major social movements of Latin America, has argued that for the Brazilian Landless Rural Workers' Movement (MST) "there is a tendency towards autonomy but not towards a rejection of the state" (*In Motion Magazine* 2005). There exist, however, clear differences of emphasis about the role of the state and they imply different understandings of the political among the movements. To pick just two examples, organizations that campaign for a reform of the United Nations tend to consider existing states important vehicles in social transformations, whereas groups identified with or inspired by the Zapatista uprising in Mexico hold to a significantly more "autonomist" stance.

States and North–South Inequalities

Some of the recent analyses of global power relations have tended to de-emphasize the division of the world into geographically defined cores and peripheries. For example, Michael Hardt and Toni Negri argue that when capitalism realizes itself in the world market, it "tends toward a smooth space defined by uncoded flows, flexibility, continual modulation, and tendential equalization" (Hardt and Negri 2000: 327). While they insightfully portray some of the novel tendencies of global capitalism that are important in explaining the growing importance of the network form in the organization of power and resistance, they exaggerate its implications for the divisions of core and periphery, or North and South.[1] The world has not become a "smooth space," and a major challenge for any project of global democratization is the lack of power of the poor majority of humankind that lives mostly in the periphery of the capitalist world-system. Even if the core periphery division of the world system should not be seen in entirely territorial terms, this periphery can still be meaningfully defined as the South (taking into account what is sometimes called "the South inside the North").

One of the important aspects of the WSF is its role as an explicitly, even if not exclusively, South-based initiative. To understand how it differs from earlier South-based attempts at global democratization, it is useful to briefly analyze the Third Worldist emancipation projects that prevailed during the anti-colonial struggles for state sovereignty after the Second World War. The history of colonial domination and the attempts to overcome it are, of course, much longer and have not ended with the formal decolonization of Southern countries. Here, however, I will first focus on the series of attempts to democratize North–South relations through concerted action of Third World states and anti-colonial movements that wanted to construct such formally sovereign states. A key moment in these attempts took place in 1955 in Bandung, Indonesia, when delegations from 29 nation-states or nationalist movements met to coordinate anti-colonial activities in the world.[2] The Bandung meeting provided inspiration for various Third Worldist activities of the following years, and even decades (Berger 2004). In the WSF process, the legacy of Bandung has been referred to from different perspectives by Michael Hardt, who has called the WSF a distant offspring of the Bandung Conference (Hardt 2002), and by Indira Ravindran, for whom the forum symbolizes the new, post-Bandung solidarities (Ravindran 2004). During the WSF event of 2006 in Bamako, Samir Amin was once of the key proponents that the globalization protest movements should start building a new Bandung-like front of the South, in which "national democracy" should be considered the key strategic issue.[3]

Anti-colonialism and Third Worldism related to Bandung should not be assumed to form a monolithic unit. In his historical overview of Third Worldism, Mark Berger differentiates between the first-generation and the more radical second-generation "Bandung regimes." The former were closer to what Berger calls nationalist

---

1   For a powerful critique of Hardt and Negri's de-emphasis on core-periphery divisions, see Arrighi (2003: 29–42).

2   The key figures of the Bandung Conference included nationalist political leaders such as Jawaharlal Nehru, Gamal Abdel Nasser, Ho Chi Minh and Kwame Nkrumah. Since Latin American countries were already mostly independent, their participation in the Bandung process was relatively marginal.

3   See *The Bamako Appeal*, available at http://deletetheborder.org/fr/node/698 March 10, 2006.

reformism, whereas the latter, led by governments such as those of Ahmed Ben Bella in Algeria, Samora Moises Machel in Mozambique, Muammar Qaddafi in Libya, and Fidel Castro in Cuba, had more socialist orientations. One of the key events of the second generation was the Tricontinental Conference of Solidarity of the Peoples of Africa, Asia and Latin America that was held in Havana in January 1966 (Berger 2004: 20). If during the first years of the twenty-first century Porto Alegre became at least for a moment the most important symbolic locale of radical transformation initiatives, especially in Latin America but also in the world as a whole, in the last decades of the twentieth century, after the Cuban revolution, Havana played a similar role.

The anti-colonial struggles reaped various victories, and the number of formally sovereign states in the South increased rapidly in the 1950s and 1960s. One of the political consequences of this was the strengthened representation of southern and predominantly poor states in the United Nations. On 1 May 1973 the United Nations General Assembly issued the Declaration on the Establishment of a New International Economic Order (NIEO). The demands for the NIEO included global taxation and redistribution and relied largely on an analogy between the welfare-state programs within some northern nation-states and similar structures between the states in the world as a whole. As the working classes and other previously excluded people had in some parts of the world constructed (partially) democratized state structures through mechanisms of representation, the NIEO strategy assumed that the increased representation of the Southern states in the United Nations could lead to analogous construction of a democratized world.

The attempt to construct the NIEO signaled the emergence of the Third World states as a potentially collective political actor, and Heikki Patomäki even calls it "the beginning of world politics proper" (Patomäki Heikki 2001). The NIEO demands, however, were never met, as the North–South relations were restructured and de-democratized from the late 1970s onward. In this context, "de-democratization" refers to the diminished possibilities to publicly present democratic claims about the North–South relations. The North–South relations had obviously never been particularly democratic, but during the 1980s democratic possibilities were limited as the emerging mechanisms of global representation—based on the principle "one state, one vote" practiced in the UN General Assembly—were marginalized. Blatantly undemocratic international financial institutions, together with transnational corporations, took a leading role in the 1980s as key sites of global decision-making.

In terms of pedagogy of power, the political dead-ends associated with state-centric attempts at global democratization, including the crises of the really-existing "socialism" of Eastern Europe, were a key justification for the claim that radical transformations of the capitalist world would not be possible. Even if there were also non-state actors that supported the goals of the southern leaders, the NIEO campaign and the spirit of Bandung were state-centric, both in their forms of mobilization and aims. As the credibility of state-centric radical politics ebbed during the 1980s and early 1990s, the ideologues of the existing social order were able to disseminate ideas about the end of history, lack of alternatives and inevitability of continuing capitalist globalization. The emergence of the globalization protest movements in the late 1990s challenged not only the existing North–South inequalities but also the state-centric conceptions of global democratic change.

Transnational Networks of Democratic Participation

The disillusionment with the state-centric Third Worldism associated with the NIEO campaign is one of the reasons that explain why non-state movements gradually occupied a more central role in the mobilizations for democratizing North–South relations and why questions of global representation became less important. Instead of changing the world through conquering state power, many social movements started to emphasize the creation of networks with multiple aims in which "participation," as opposed to "representation," was deemed a central issue.

One factor that contributed to the diminished importance of questions of representation among social movements and non-governmental organizations in the 1980s and especially in the 1990s was the pedagogical role of the World Bank. Through its development programs and other mechanisms of co-optation, the World Bank actively promoted "participatory" approaches among the "civil society" organizations of the world. For the decision-making centers of global power, based mostly on the capitalist principle in which one dollar equals one vote, it was important to channel popular demands toward relatively harmless concerns of participation so that questions of global representation would not be politicized.

The strategy of depoliticization and fragmentation of global democratic demands seemed to work relatively well throughout the 1980s and 1990s, epitomized in the claims of an "end of history." It would, however, be misleading to argue that the ideological hegemony of global capitalism was absolute during these golden years of Washington Consensus that lasted until the visible emergence of the massive globalization protest movements on the streets of Seattle in 1999. Opening supposedly neutral spaces of power for democratic claims has formed part of radically democratic projects of social movements well before Seattle. Socialist criticism of the capitalist economy, feminist questioning of patriarchal domination, and many dimensions of the 1968 protests from Paris to Ciudad de México consisted of politicizing claims.[4] Some of these earlier movements were organized transnationally. The struggles against slavery or for women's suffrage had transnational connections. Many of the workers unions since the nineteenth century have been explicitly based on internationalist ideas that aim at creating a counterweight to capitalist power, even if in practice labor internationalism has not always lived up to its ideals (Waterman 2001). Human rights organizing, especially after the coup in Chile in 1973, has become one of the most intensely transnational fields of social activism, although many of its expressions are ambiguous about the attitude toward property rights and therefore often avoid questioning capitalist dimensions of power (Khargram, Riker and Sikkink 2004: 30).

---

4   According to Whitaker (2003: 20–4), many the initiatives that are present in the WSF have descended directly from the May 1968 movements. See also Corrêa Leite (2003: 36) and Arrighi *et al.* (1989) for an insightful analysis of the "1968" as a (failed) world revolution.

Even if during the 1980s and 1990s social activism was generally not focused on radically contesting the key decision-making sites of the capitalist world system, the building of transnational links within and between the movements prepared the ground for concerted action when the ideological contradictions of capitalism became more evident during the last years of the past century. In their pioneering analysis of "transnational advocacy networks," Margaret E. Keck and Kathryn Sikkink have shown how these networks challenge established boundaries, especially the inside/outside boundary of national sovereignty. They locate the emergence of the transnational advocacy networks from 1968 onwards, and they find many commonalities in the emergence of different networks and strategies. They differentiate transnational advocacy networks from other transnational networks because the former are motivated primarily by shared principled ideas or values (Keck and Sikkink 1998). Even if Keck and Sikkink seldom ask questions directly related to global democratization, their analysis highlights mechanisms through which transformative practices are brought into world politics (Reitan 2007). More explicitly related to concerns of global democratization, Ruth Reitan (2007) has made an excellent study of the scale shifts from localized action to transnational coordinated action among various networks that participate in the WSF process.

In the 1990s, there were two transnational political mobilizations that can be considered successful in that they resulted in new institutional (inter-state) arrangements. The Ottawa land mine ban treaty and the International Criminal Court are the results of these mobilizations (Patomäki and Teivainen 2004). One thing that made their success possible is that neither of them created a direct threat to the core institutions of the capitalist world economy, even if the US government soon started an aggressive campaign against the latter. Compared to the spirit of Bandung and the demands for a New International Economic Order, these campaigns of the 1990s were also more focused on changes within countries of the North.

Another transnational initiative that can be deemed successful, even if more defensive, was the transnational campaign against the Multilateral Agreement on Investments (MAI) in 1997–9, which was to a great extent articulated through the Internet. The role of the Internet was important in enabling the groups that were struggling against the MAI to circulate information, share resources, and link their struggles (Kellner 2003: 180–94).

Compared to the land mine ban treaty initiative or activism around the International Criminal Court, the MAI campaign directly politicized a central issue of global capitalism, the attempt to construct legally binding mechanisms though which transnational investors were shielded from the control of national parliaments. The fact that the MAI treaty was at least temporarily halted as a result of transnational activism increased the self-confidence of the movements that participated in the campaign and gave the world an example that social movements were not totally powerless in contesting the de-democratizing tendencies of global capitalism.

The MAI campaign was particularly strong in France where it contributed to the strengthening of the organizations, such as ATTAC, that would soon play a key role in the emergence of the WSF. In North America, networks articulated around the issue of the North American Free Trade Agreement (NAFTA) also played an important role in the MAI campaign. Groups such as the US-based Public Citizen and Council of Canadians were important in mobilizing public opinion around the issues of MAI and NAFTA, but one of the most influential challenges to the power mechanisms of global capitalism emerged south of the Río Grande.

Since before the MAI campaign, the indigenous uprising in Chiapas, Mexico has been one of the most inspiring struggles for transnational social movements. In Latin America, mobilizations and continent-wide articulations between social movements had already taken place during the Continental Campaign of 500 Years of Indigenous, Black and Popular Resistance, waged from October 1989 to October 1992. One of the most significant aspects of the campaign was the attempt, on the one hand, to situate the various forms of popular struggles in a long-term, large-scale context and, on the other hand, to find commonalities between different forms of struggle. The year 1994 is often regarded as a year that "epitomized grass roots resistance," because various mobilizations took place in Mexico, Brazil, Ecuador, Paraguay, Bolivia, and elsewhere (León, Burch and Tamayo 2001: 90). The most important of them was that of the Zapatista Army for National Liberation in Chiapas.[5]

The Zapatistas started a small-scale insurrection on 1 January 1994, the day the NAFTA agreement became effective. Unlike most of the earlier guerrilla groups in Latin America, the EZLN expressed little interest in conquering state power and maintained a distance from political parties, also from the possibility of becoming one (Kovic 2003: 58–79; Rabasa 2001: 191–210). It soon came to symbolize in many parts of the world the possibility to be radically transformative without relying on state-centric representational politics. The *Encuentros* organized by the EZLN and their supporters in Chiapas became landmarks in the emergence of the globalization protest movements in the late 1990s. The Zapatistas have also become an important reference and justification for strategists such as John Holloway who advocate "changing the world without taking power."[6]

One of the first big Zapatista *Encuentros* was the International Meeting for Humanity and against Neoliberalism in July 1996, attended by approximately 5000 people.[7] The issues of North–South solidarity were a key aspect of the claims of the Zapatistas and their supporters. Combining an efficient use of the Internet and a credible appropriation of ancestral indigenous symbols, the EZLN attracted groups from Latin America, Europe, and the United States to participate in solidarity activities. One of the European groups influenced by the EZLN and influential in the globalization protests was the Tute Bianche ("White Overalls"), whose "diplomacy from below" included various journeys to Chiapas to learn from the Zapatistas. The learning process resulted in a project that the Tute Bianche would soon put into practice in protests within Europe and also in Seattle (Hardt and Negri 2004: 266–7), even though their role in the organization of these protests should not be exaggerated. The Zapatistas also inspired many other movements around the world, for example in Argentina where various "autonomist" groups emerged during the outburst of the crisis at the turn of the millennium. *Que se vayan todos* ("let them all go away") was

---

5   On the contradictions within the EZLN, see Nuijten and Van der Haar (2000: 83–90).

6   *Potesta and potencia* XXX.

7   Kovic (2003: 58–79); Rabasa (2001:191–210) pp. 191–192.

one of the main slogans of the Argentine protesters and reflected the atmosphere in which the idea of conquering the state had become discredited.

Even if the Zapatistas and their effort to build a "hegemony of the diverse" (Rabasa 2001: 202) are often regarded as one of the key intellectual influences in the emergence of the WSF, their possibilities to formally participate in the WSF have been limited because the latter's Charter of Principles prohibits the participation of military organizations. This paradox was one of the reasons why some of the globalization protesters that had been closely networking with the EZLN, such as the Peoples' Global Action network, maintained a somewhat distant and critical attitude toward the WSF. While some of the groups connected to the Zapatista process decided not to directly participate in the WSF process, others built "autonomous spaces" such as the Caracol Intergaláctica that repeatedly took place in the margins of the WSF events. The role played by the Zapatista *Encuentros* has been different than that of the WSF, but the two have similarities as Latin-America-based experiences that have contributed to the strengthening and radicalization of the transnational globalization protest movements. Another commonality is that both of them have contributed to the emergence of the non-state-centric conceptions of the political.

Expanding the Boundaries of the Political in Seattle and Davos

An important landmark in the growing awareness about the need to expand the boundaries of the political was the World Trade Organization meeting held between late November and early December 1999 in Seattle. The massive street protests in Seattle boosted the local, transnational, and global organizations and movements opposing undemocratic sites of global power (Sader 2001: 5–8). Even if the novelty of the Seattle protests was partially created by the media (Smith and Hank 2002: 4), they did have many new features. As noted by Rodrigo Nuñez (as discussed by Smith and Hank in the cited page (4)), it was the first time "networked politics" was affirmed loud and clear on such a scale. For Jackie Smith, until the Battle of Seattle the relations between social movements and intergovernmental organizations had been mostly accommodative (Smith and Johnston 2002: 208). The Seattle protests highlighted the key ideological contradiction of the capitalist world system: the process in which formally economic undemocratic institutions become increasingly important political actors and at the same time their political nature becomes increasingly evident and therefore open to the possibility of democratic contestation. In this sense, the attempts to expand the boundaries of the political in Seattle were potentially very problematic for the hegemonic expansion of capitalism.

While the Seattle protests included a great variety of movements and organizations with different aims, according to Smith virtually all sought to "democratize and incorporate values other than profit-making into global economic institutions" (Smith 2002: 209). Even if "virtually all" might be an overstatement, I share her main conclusions and think that democratization is one the key aims and ideals, even if not always explicit, of the globalization protest movements. The concept of democracy and strategies of democratic transformation, of course, vary. In Seattle some groups, such as the Boston Tea Party, whose banners wanted "no globalization without representation" (Smith 2002: 208), operated with the ideals of the early struggles for representative democracy in the United States and Europe, making an explicit analogy between their demands in the global context and earlier demands in national contexts. Others relied on more participatory concepts of democracy and emphasized non-state strategies of transformation.

Even if in Seattle the adversary of the globalization protest movements was symbolically located in an inter-state institution, the World Trade Organization, there has been a growing awareness that global capitalist elites are increasingly organized in less state-centric articulations. For some of the activists, the emphasis on network-based conceptions of radical political agency is considered necessary because the adversary—global capitalism for some, its "neoliberal" or excessive elements for others—has also become more network-based. According to Christophe Aguiton, an active participant in the International Council of the WSF, "two armies cannot fight if they do not have the same arms. That is why we need to organize in networks. To struggle against companies like Nike, there exists a structural necessity to organize in networks."[8]

While the multilateral institutions and transnational corporations have been relatively visible objects of the protests, the meetings of the formally private elite organizations such as the Bilderberg Society, Trilateral Commission, and Mont Pelerin Society have attracted less public attention. Nevertheless, they constitute highly influential networks of transnational coordination in matters of global governance. Even if not formally authorized to make binding political decisions, they articulate powerful social forces oriented toward the reproduction of social and material privileges of capitalism.[9]

One of the most influential and controversial network-based institutions defending the structures and values of global capitalism is the World Economic Forum (WEF). The first informal business gathering in Davos, a Swiss mountain town, took place in January 1971 under the name of European Management Forum. Since 1982 the Davos meeting has focused on bringing world business leaders to its annual meetings, and in 1987 it got its present name: World Economic Forum.[10]

In January 1999, before the protests of Seattle and after years of preparations, various organizations started organizing a counter-event in Switzerland under the banners of "another Davos" and "anti-Davos." Apart from the World Forum of Alternatives, these included the French journal *Le Monde Diplomatique* and ATTAC, founded in France in June 1998 (Amin and Founou-Tchuigoua 2002). In the first major anti-Davos event, organized simultaneously with the WEF 2000, various groups ranging from the World Women's March to the Brazilian Landless Rural Workers' Movement (Movimento de Trabalhadores Rurais Sem Terra, or MST) first had a

---

8   Comments in the Globalization Studies Network Conference in Dakar, Senegal, on 30 August 2005. See also Aguiton and Cardon (2005).

9   See Starr (2000: 13) who has analyzed how the consensus reached in the informal elite meetings can be "transferred into consistent domestic and international policies."

10 For a semi-official historical overview of the WEF, see http://www.weforum.org/site/homepublic.nsf/Content/Our+History (13 April 2002).

seminar in Zurich and then marched to Davos to hold a press conference and, some 150 of them, to face cold weather and Robocop-like police in a demonstration.[11]

Inside the hotel where the WEF 2000 was held, *Time Asia* editor Don Morrison wrote in his diary that the arrival of the protesters meant that "Davos could take its place alongside Seattle as a buzzword for something new and ugly on the global scene" (Morrison 2005). The difficult geographical conditions and heavy police presence contributed to convincing some of the key protest organizers that it would be difficult to organize a huge anti-Davos gathering in Davos itself.[12] The situation also inspired two Brazilians that were visiting Paris who, observing the debates around Davos, came up with the idea for a different kind of anti-Davos event: the World Social Forum.

Exclusion and Presence of Governments in the WSF

Among the various controversies that have emerged in the WSF process since it started in 2001 is its relationship with states. Similar to the exclusion of political parties, the WSF Charter of Principles defines the forum as a "non-governmental context." The wording of the Charter, however, also suggests a slight difference between these exclusions. Whereas it is categorically stated that party representatives shall not participate in the Forum, "government leaders and members of legislatures who accept the commitments of this Charter may be invited to participate." According to the Charter, this participation is to take place in a "personal capacity," even if in practice this clause is mostly nonsense: no president or governor that has appeared in the WSF events has participated, or been perceived to participate, solely in "personal capacity."

Even if it is one thing to value the strategy of conquering the state, and another to argue that governments should have more presence in the WSF, there exists an empirical connection between the two. The left-wing turn in Latin American electoral politics during the first years of the 2000s has revived the debates on the potential importance of progressive governments as allies. These governments have mainly included Fidel Castro's government in Cuba, Hugo Chávez's government in Venezuela, Lula da Silva's government in Brazil, Tabaré Vásquez's government in Uruguay, and also Néstor Kirschner's government in Argentina. The electoral victory of Evo Morales in Bolivia in December 2005 caused particularly great enthusiasm among globalization protest movements in Latin America and elsewhere. In November 2006, the election of Rafael Correa as the new president of Ecuador further increased the number of leftist governments that many of the South American social movements have found worth supporting.

Whereas Evo Morales and one of Correa's predecessors Lucio Gutiérrez participated in the WSF events before they became presidents of Bolivia and Ecuador, Lula da Silva and Hugo Chávez have participated as government leaders in various WSF events. The attitude of the social movements within the WSF toward

---

11 Personal communication with Susan George, 15 April 2002.
12 Personal communication with Bernard Cassen, 16 April 2002.

them has never been that of unanimous support, and especially in the case of Lula there was a significant change of mood after it became clear his government was not going to meet the expectations of radical transformations. In the WSF 2005 in Porto Alegre, among the more radical participants much of the enthusiasm that Lula had received in the earlier editions of the Forum was transferred toward Hugo Chávez. In his speech in Porto Alegre, Chávez called the WSF "the most important political event in the world" and advocated "relaunching the conscience of the South," stating that the conscience had been born in the Bandung meeting of 1955. While many of the WSF participants had become disillusioned with the politics of the PT (Workers' Party: *Partido dos Trabalhadores*) government, for some of them Chávez represented the possibility to support a more outspoken form of state-centric transformation strategy.

The state-centric spirit of Bandung, analyzed above, has been revived in events such as the "Rebuilding the South front, fifty years after Bandung" meeting organized by radical intellectuals such as Samir Amin one day before the polycentric WSF in January 2006 in Bamako, Mali. The concept of a "South front" suggests a more inclusive attitude toward Southern governments than the "civil society" defined by the WSF Charter of Principles. The announcement of the meeting was dubbed "Operation Bandung" by some critical commentators who feared that it might imply an attempt to move the WSF process toward a traditional political agency in which governments play an increasingly dominant role.

The following polycentric WSF in Caracas brought into further debate the linkages between the movements and governments. The government of Hugo Chávez sponsored not only the WSF held in Caracas but also the WSF held in Bamako, Mali, the week before. His government was perceived by groups such as the Brazilian Landless Workers' Movement MST as an ally in the struggles against capitalism and imperialism. While many other WSF participants have considered the Chávez government worth supporting or at least dialoguing with, groups such as the Articulación Feminista Marcosur have been critical of the possibility that the movements may lose their autonomy if linkages with Chávez become too strong. The doubts have highlighted the organizational issue about to what extent is it appropriate for any governments to participate in the Forums, but it is also a question of ideological assessment. For some feminists and others, the problem with Chávez was not only his being a governmental leader but also that some of his policies were considered antidemocratic, militaristic, or reflecting a patriarchal approach.

In the constitution of the boundaries of the WSF, there has existed a (mostly implicit) special role given to the governments of the hosting country, including municipal and state governments. The participation of Lula da Silva in the WSF 2001 and 2002 was technically as representative of an NGO he had founded.[13] Having become the president of Brazil his participation was of a different status in the WSF 2003. As a response to the accusations of using different criteria for different governmental participations, the role of the hosting governments, from the municipal to federal levels, were given a special status in semi-official formulations

---

13 The most common references to Lula in the media were, however, either as presidential candidate or as the honorary president of the PT.

of the WSF procedures.[14] Therefore as representative of a hosting country it was possible to include Lula in the official program, whereas Hugo Chávez, who surprisingly arrived in Porto Alegre during the 2003 forum,[15] was not provided a space within the official venues of the forum.[16]

In the first WSF in 2001, the visible presence of representatives of the Cuban government raised mixed feelings. In the closing ceremony, the Cuban delegation received the strongest applause, comparable only to those of the MST and of the French peasant activist José Bové.[17] Even if open disapproval of the Cuban government's participation came mostly from outside the meeting, particularly from the local press, its visible presence in the official ceremonies of the WSF was annoying to some of the organizers as well.

In the state of Rio Grande do Sul, during the electoral campaign of 2002 the opposition repeatedly claimed that the PT state government wanted to transform the state into "another Cuba." For the electoral strategy of the PT it was important to create an image that would not dissuade potential moderate voters. It was therefore not surprising that the Cuban governmental representatives no longer had a prominent official role in 2002, even though the total Cuban delegation was more numerous than the year before.[18] To explain the diminished presence of the Cuban governmental delegates in the central panels of the WSF after 2001, both the calculations related to the Brazilian political context as well as the boundaries established by the Charter of Principles need to be taken into account. In the following fora the presence of the representatives of the Cuban government was of relatively low profile, but in the Caracas WSF in 2006 their visibility increased, reflecting the close links between the governments of Hugo Chávez and Fidel Castro.

---

14 In a meeting with the International Council during the WSF 2003 Walden Bello asked Lula if he would accept an invitation to take part in the WSF 2004 in India. Lula responded positively, but at the same time expressed his view that the WSF should not be transformed into a "parade of presidents." He added—half-seriously, half-jokingly—that if the organizers in India should have problems in inviting a foreign president, they should remember that his comrades in the Brazilian trade union still consider him a trade union leader and he could always be invited as such. See also "Fórum Social deve evitar chefes de Estado, diz Lula" (*Jornal da Manhã*, 26 January 2003: 3).

15 Chávez had been invited by ATTAC-Venezuela and according to some versions the original invitation had been made by Lula during the inaugural ceremony of the presidency of Lucio Gutiérrez in Ecuador. Lula's advisor Oded Grajew, however, denied this, arguing that Lula would not interfere in such way with the autonomy of the WSF organizers ("Chávez deverá participar de Porto Alegre," *Folha de São Paulo*, 23 January 2003: A10).

16 Nevertheless, in many press reports the visit of Chávez was described as if it had formed part of the official WSF program. For example: "Chávez participa de Fórum Mundial. Presidente chegou ontem a Porto Alegre," *Correio do Triângulo—Uberlandia* (24 January 2003: A3); "Chávez participa do Fórum no Brasil," *Diário Catarinense* (23 January 2003: 13); "Hugo Chávez, presidente da Venezuela, poderá participar do Fórum Social no domingo," *Gazeta do Povo* (23 January 2003: 17).

17 "Bové termina como a estrela do Fórum Social," *O Estado de São Paulo* (31 January 2001: A3).

18 João Domingos, "Guevara é mais lembrao no fórum," *Folha do Estado Cuiabá* (23 January 2003: 4).

Even if it received some criticism, various ministers from the government of France were allowed to participate visibly in the WSF 2002. On the eve of the same forum, the Brazilian Organizing Committee told the Belgian prime minister who had announced a visit that he would not be welcome. The decision on the Belgian prime minister was at partially based on an ideological assessment based on the Charter of Principles; he was considered to represent "neoliberalism" whereas the French ministers formed part of a center-left alliance in their country.[19] Similar mixing of organizational form and ideological orientation in assessing the limits to participation has taken place as regards intergovernmental organizations. For example, United Nations Development Fund for Women (UNIFEM) organized activities in the first WSF events, even if the official line has been that intergovernmental bodies cannot participate. The participation of UNIFEM, considered a relatively progressive intergovernmental agency by many women's movements, never caused visible tensions, whereas any attempt to similar participation by the World Bank would have met major protests.

Many of the globalization protest movements have perceived the world in a less state-centric manner than their predecessors. Instead of asking that a particular Third World state be given more decision-making power in global affairs, today's activists may ask for more power to the non-state groups that confront both governmental and corporate power all over the world. This trend holds many promising aspects. In order to imagine and construct institutional features of alternative futures, however, we need political institutions that "civil society," as it is generally conceived, is unlikely to deliver.

---

19 One factor that helps explain the different treatment of the French and Belgian ministers and was that that Bernard Cassen, one of the key initiators of the WSF process, told the Brazilian Organizing Committee, "do not worry about the French ministers, I can control them."

Chapter 11

From Globalization to Antiglobalization

Henry Veltmeyer

The aim of this concluding chapter is to unmask globalization as imperialism and to point out the limits of the antiglobalization movement. As I see it, this movement is fundamentally flawed in ways that will limit its capacity to bring about fundamental change. For one thing, movement activists fail to recognize that the issue is not globalization in one form or another; it is *imperialism*—the projection of state power under conditions of a renewed form of US-led imperialism. Until this problem is grasped and dealt with in thought and practice the forces of resistance cannot be fully mobilized in the struggle for social change.

The argument is constructed as follows. First, I turn towards the ubiquitous search for an alternative form of development and globalization. I argue that there is both more to and less than meets the eye in the movement on which the political Left has pinned its hopes and expectations. I then turn towards the concept of "imperialism" as a more useful tool for analyzing the dynamics of global developments and of the forces of resistance. In the following section I address, and challenge, the mythical notion of a powerless state, undermined by a process of globalization.

This chapter then moves into a discussion of the form that imperialism is taking in the current world context. To this end I begin by discarding the notion, advanced by Hardt and Negri (2000), of an "Empire without Empire." Then I turn towards various alternative conceptions of the "new" imperialism—neomercantilist and "postmodern." In this intellectual and ideological context, and with reference to argument advanced by James Petras in this volume (Chapter 2), I argue that imperialism is very much on the agenda—that the US state is leading this project.

In the following two sections I examine the question of "democracy" and its meaning for both the agents (and ideologists) of imperialism and its opponents in the popular movement. At issue here is the nature of the state and its relation to "civil society"—and the different forms taken by "democracy" as well as its alternate uses. For the most part, the idea of "democracy" has served as an ideology, to obfuscate and camouflage the interior design (and fascistic fist) of the imperialist project. At the same time, "democracy" has served the popular movement in creating spaces for the accumulation, and mobilization, of the forces of opposition and resistance. In this sense—that is, as development "from below"—democracy can be viewed as a two-edged sword, with a progressive side.

In the last two parts of this argument I turn back towards the antiglobalization movement before reviewing the form that the struggle against neo-imperialism is taking on the Latin American periphery of the system. Here we bring into focus three waves of sociopolitical movements in the mobilization of the popular forces of opposition and resistance. I argue that these movements provide the best opportunity for progressive change and the forces of social transformation in the struggle against capitalism and imperialism. However, the political problems involved in this process are considerable. I conclude that the Left needs to overcome its penchant for sectarian politics and unite in a common struggle.

Neoliberalism and the Dynamics of Antiglobalization

In the wake of the financial crisis which hit Mexico in 1995 and then spread to Asia and elsewhere in 1997, the neoliberal model of capitalist development has been seriously tarnished, abandoned by all except for a few ideological diehards. Even erstwhile ideologues of free market capitalism such as Carlos Salinas de Gortari, the now disgraced ex-president of Mexico but once the darling of the international neoliberal jet set; George Soros, self-appointed guardian of the world capitalist system, President of the Quantum Fund and the Soros Foundation, and "retired" financier, expert manipulator of the free market in speculative capital; Joseph Stiglitz, formerly chief economist at the World Bank; and—most surprisingly perhaps—Michel Camdessus, until a few years ago managing director of the IMF; all have turned against or distanced themselves from neoliberalism (Soros in Bordegaray, Soledad and Toti Flores 2001: 66–7; Stiglitz in Stiglitz 1998). These and other erstwhile advocates of capitalism in its neoliberal form, while wedded to the notion of globalization in its diverse dimensions, have joined critics in the search for an alternative form of organizing and developing the economy.

The shared concern—not to put too fine a point to it and to exaggerate only slightly—is *not* with globalization per se (globalization or antiglobalization) but the form that the alternative to neoliberalism should take. At stake, as George Soros (in Bordegaray *et al.* 2001: 67) notes, is the survival of global capitalism. To prevent its destruction, he further notes, fundamental reforms are required— and not those that have dominated economic and political developments over the past two decades. These neoliberal reforms, designed to take the state out of the process of economic development, to reduce its weight and role (and power), to restore the power of private property and the workings of the free unregulated market, as argued by so many critics in the antiglobalization movement, in fact constitute the "problem"—the source of the crisis that besets the system as a whole. The issue, in other words, is what form the alternative to neoliberalism should take. What changes, for example, are needed in the financial architecture that supports the international flows of productive and speculative capital? What sort of regime should there be put into place to control the ballooning free flow of speculative and volatile short-term capital? What should be the institutional framework of this new regulatory regime and what connections should there be to the broader institutionality of the system? And within this framework what sort of policies should be pursued and implemented vis-à-vis "good governance"—and the neoliberal program of stabilization and structural adjustment and measures? That is, how are we to move beyond and away from the tarnished "Washington Consensus" identified by Williamson (1990)?

The problem behind these questions was first clearly posed, in 1996, by Robert Kapstein, Director, at the time, of the trilateralist US Council on Foreign Relations.[1] As Kapstein saw it, the problem was rooted in a tendency of neoliberal or free market capitalism, freed from all constraints and state regulation, towards excessive social inequalities in the distribution of global resources, and income, leading toward social discontent the forces of which could be mobilized politically in ways that are destabilizing for democratic regimes and the system as a whole. However, on the left of the political spectrum, within the antiglobalization movement the concern is not so much with the (potential) political instability as with the moral issue of unfairness or injustice represented by a system in which, as the UNDP, in its 1996 *Human Development Report*, pointed out, some 385 individuals could receive (or appropriate) as much of the world's wealth and income as 1.4 billion of the world's poorest, and the top 10 percent of income "earners" receives over 40 percent of world income (UNDP 1996b).

Most critics within the antiglobalization movement see this maldistribution of wealth and income not as Kapstein sees it, that is, as a political problem; nor as more radical critics on the Left see it—also as a *political* problem but one of "the North robbing the South" or exploitation (and oppression, to boot)—but as a *moral* issue, that is, as inequitable or unfair, a matter of social justice. In fact, this was by far the dominant theme of the vast majority of 28 conferences, 200 or so seminars and close to 800 workshops that made up the second WSF in 2002. According to Martin Khor, director of the Malaysia-based Third World Network and a keynote speaker at the WSF, among the diverse ways in which countries in the South are "cheated" are through the predatory operations of speculative capital, the siphoning off of profits by transnational corporations and the protectionist trading measures adopted by the industrialized countries. On these issues also see, among many others, Falk (2000) and the Canadian columnist Naomi Klein (2000), who not only provide a moral critique of the corporate agenda but address directly or indirectly the question of "democracy" or "good governance"—holding the corporations accountable, if not to some electorate then at least to a more representative "global civil society" (Corpwatch 2001). The securing of good governance is, in fact, the remedy proposed by both the advocates and opponents of "globalization."

Despite their concerns about "globalization" the guardians of the NWO, who meet annually at the WEF, count on the antiglobalization movement to provide the broad contours and critical elements, if not the actual design, of a solution to the "problem" that has beset the 'system"—a problem (ungovernability, lack of good governance) that in some contexts has reached critical proportions. This is

---

1 The Council on Foreign Relations, and its executive Trilateral Commission, constitutes, it could be argued (Salbuchi 2000), the "brain of the world," "the hidden side of globalization." It is composed of the biggest makers and shakers of US foreign policy. But it also part of a broader network that involves an international "advisory board" that includes Canada's (now Britain's) Conrad Black and Muhammad Yunus, founder of the Graneen Bank. Also part of this network is an "International Crisis Group" that includes Graca Machel, Managing Director of Mozambique's Foundation for Community Development and Carlos Salnas de Gortieri, ex-President of Mexico, as well as George Soros, also a key member of the Davos-based WEF.

one reason why the World Bank and other sponsors of multilateral "aid" and global development finance, as well as the governments in the G8 and, more broadly, the OECD, are prepared to finance the activities of its critics in the antiglobalization movement—up to 80 percent, it has been estimated (Okonski 2001).

Another reason for this funding is that it provides a mechanism of what could be termed "controlled opposition and dissent"—to contain the forces of opposition and resistance, and to direct them towards a system-bound solution, a respect of its fundamental institutionality and seeking alternatives "within," on the basis of acceptable (because necessary) reforms achieved through dialog. A case in point is the World Bank's sponsorship, funding and use of many albeit selected nongovernmental organizations (NGOs) as a "sounding board" of possible opposition to, and changes in, its policies—as a forum for dialog and critical engagement with dissenting opinion and alternative ideas. Another example of such a mechanism of controlled opposition and informed dissent can be found in the WSF. Held for the first time in January 2001 (WSF I) and again in 2002 (WSF II), in Porto Alegre, Brazil, it represents a major advance in the antiglobalization movement—in the tracking, from Seattle to Genoa and Qatar, of policies set and decisions made by the economic and political elite of what Leslie Sklair (1997) among others, define as the "international capitalist class."

The WSF provides an organizational context for the opponents of "globalization" not as such but in its manifest neoliberal form (the world "as it is")—to discuss, and debate, the alternative ("another world is possible"). These opponents and critics represent a broad array of nongovernmental organizations and a spectrum of ideas that is at once broad and narrow—broad in its agreed-upon principles (social justice and equity, popular participation, and democracy, etc.) and diverse proffered solutions (ideas for a new more humane and socially just world) yet narrow in its political scope (liberal, state-led reforms to the existing system impelled by an emerging (and growing) "global civil society").

In this connection, "radical" solutions predicated on systemic transformation, viz. its basic institutionality (private property, wage labor, markets, state, etc.), and "confrontationalist politics" (as opposed to humanizing social reforms and a pacifist politics of nonviolence and dialog) are explicitly ruled out. This is one reason why with few exceptions (the MST, for one) organizations of the "Revolutionary Left" (for example, FARC) that call for and espouse such a path towards change were expressly excluded from the WSF II. In practice, as well as theory, the "other world" sought by the directorate of the antiglobalization movement ("another world is possible") is predicated on the principles of a renovated social democracy—on what, after Anthony Giddens (1995), has been termed "the third way."

In the 1980s, in the context of a widespread restructuring of the state—and its ostensible retreat from the conduct (planning, regulation, etc.) of economic affairs—there was a veritable explosion of NGOs, formed in the concern with not only the provision of basic human needs (shelter, food, health, security, etc.), which is the major concern of the grassroots organizations of civil society, but with diverse issues ranging from human rights, the environment, the exclusion of women, widespread urban poverty and the lack of economic development or "democracy."

The nongovernmental (social or civic) organizations that were formed in this process, and that generally cast themselves into the role of "critical opposition"—to globalization in its neoliberal form as well as associated government policies—were (and are) widely (and alternatively) perceived to represent either a new social movement," "grassroots postmodernism," "democracy without social movements," or, more recently, an emerging "global civil society," and, as such, the latest expression of a popular or grassroots movement against the structures of economic and political power.

In practice, however, many of these NGOs have been pushed into an effective, if (often) undeclared, partnership with the operating institutions and agents of the system, particularly the World Bank and other agents of "overseas development assistance" or international finance. In this partnership, the keystone of a strategy designed by the World Bank but soon adopted by virtually all of the multilateral and bilateral institutions as well as the other operating agencies of the undoubtedly unjust global economic system, the NGOs cast themselves (and were cast) into the role of intermediary between the donor agencies and the target of the international development or donor organizations, the poor and their communities.

In effect, these NGOs were converted into the executing agencies of government policy or the donors' agenda. Although widely (and erroneously) identified with, and seen as part of "the grassroots organizations" of civil society, many of these NGOs could be viewed as "agents of imperialism," unconsciously (for the most part) serving the "interests of capital" just as surely—albeit more obliquely—as the international financial institutions and restructured reformist states in Latin America and elsewhere.

In any case, the NGOs within "civil society" are positioned somewhere in between those agencies seeking to promote development or initiate projects "from above and the outside" and those who do so "from below and within." In this somewhat ambiguous position they are also part of two seemingly contradictory "projects." On the one hand, they are conscious participants in the broad search for an alternative form of "development" (to neoliberal capitalism) and "globalization"—to "improve [the lives] in the world's poorest countries" (Gerry Barr, president of CCIC, *Reality of Aid*, a semi-annual review of ODA, 2002).

In this search they are part of an emerging global network of individuals and organizations that make up "civil society"—a complex configuration that like all structures has an influence vastly greater than the sum of its parts and tends to take on a life of its own. On the other hand, this "global civil society" is also part of something quite different, a more nefarious network of which many of the participant individuals and organizations are not even aware. To understand how this can be, by way of an analogy, consider the parasitic wasp, of the genus *Hymenoepimecis*, which, unknown to the spider that it targets and penetrates, lays its eggs in the spider's abdomen. The spider goes to work oblivious of the growing larvae in its abdomen, which, nourished on the spider's fluids, chemically induces the spider to modify or change its behavior. In fact, the spider is induced to spin a cocoon web that is useless to the spider but necessary to the larvae. As soon as the spider has finished its work, the larvae consume the spider and hang the pupal cocoon in the special web constructed unwittingly by the spider for the wasp. Nourished on the fluids of the unknowing host organism whose behavior it has manipulated, the larvae are transformed into wasps capable of stinging their prey in its global reach for sustenance and—to extend our analogy—profits on their invested capital. To complete this analogy, in the process of "development" or "globalization" the parasite might not consume its host as long as it does not need to do so; that is, as long as the host organization, a global network of antiglobalization forces, continues to serve as means of manipulating the broader apparatus of civic governance into building the web that serves their purpose and as a means of derailing the forces of opposition to its globalization project—to channel these forces into acceptable forms or, even better, to demobilize them.

Development, Globalization or Imperialism?

Few words have gained as much currency in such a short period of time (since around 1986) as "globalization." Although used in different ways it generally denotes a multifaceted process characterized by increased international flows of capital, goods and services, information and cultural values, and ways of doing things—and an associated "interconnectedness of social phenomena" (Therborn 2000) and, at a different level, "economic integration." However, in these terms, the term "globalization" explains little of what is actually going on across the world and, as noted by most contributors to a special theme issue of the *Cambridge Review of International Affairs* (Desai *et al.* 2000), serves better as an *ideology*, a means of masking what is going on or to promote a certain desired form of action or thought, than as *theory*, an explanatory device—or even as a means of describing well the dynamics of a supposed paradigmatic (and historical) shift.

For one thing, the term entirely eludes reference to the structures of political and economic power or the practice (foreign policy) in which these structures are imposed by some states, or peoples, on others. The reality of this institutionalized practice is better described, and explained, by use of a term given to Marxist discourse but abandoned by many: "imperialism." Oddly enough, this point has been grasped well by some supporters and advocates of neoliberal capitalism than by the many critics of "corporate capital" or "neoliberal globalization" in the AGM. In this connection, Martin Wolf (*Financial Times*, 5 February 2002) writes of the "ritualistic concern with unbridled corporate power" expressed by the critics and protesters at this year's meeting in New York of the World Economic Forum (WEF) as "paranoid delusion."

However, in defense of the many critics and opponents of corporate global power it could be said that if it can be demonstrated that these corporations do indeed have command of a large measure of economic, if not political, power, which is used in the (their own) interest (profits), then the concern with corporate global power of critics such as Anderson and Cavanagh, Susan George, Martin Khor, David Korten, and, closer to home (Canada, that is), Maud Barlow and Tony Clarke, among many others, denotes neither paranoia nor delusion. However, Wolf is also correct in pointing out that "corporations are not unchallenged masters of the universe;" nor are they "autonomous" agents of the system or "as powerful as critics claim." Indeed, "[t]he change ... seen over the past twenty years ... is market-driven globalization unleashed, consciously and voluntarily by governments." Wolf makes an important point here. But where the defenders of "market-driven globalization" such as Wolf are remiss (and knowingly so) is in failing to point out that some "governments" indeed do have the will and capacity to unleash such power, and that they do so on the basis of an imperialist agenda. On this point see the discussion in the following two sections.

The Myth of the Powerless State

One of the biggest myths propagated in the double ideological turn towards a discourse on globalization and civil society[2] is that of a powerless state, hollowed out and stripped off its functions vis-à-vis the economic development process, prostrate before unbridled global corporate power (Weiss 1998). But in actual fact, the welfare states in the North and the developmental states in the South, while partially "dismantled," have been neither weakened nor reduced in terms of its various "powers;" rather, they have been restructured to better serve the interests of the transnational capitalist class.

In the post Second World War period, the nation-state was widely regarded, and generally used, as an instrument for advancing the interests of diverse economic groups and incorporating, by degrees, both the middle and working classes into the development process as well as the political system. In the North (the OECD) this resulted in the evolution of what was dubbed the "Keynesian" and "welfare state," characterized by the growth of the public sector both in the economy and the provision of social services (welfare, education, and health); in the South (developing countries in Latin America, Asia and Africa), under different conditions (*inter alia*, nationalization—of industrial enterprises in strategic sectors) it entailed both this "development" and the consolidation of the state as an agency of economic development at the level of ownership, planning and the regulation of private capitalist enterprise.

Nowhere in Latin America was this process as advanced as in Chile, where, under Salvador Allende, the working class managed to reach into the state apparatus, compelling the propertied classes to at least acknowledge and respond to some of its claims and concerns, if not share actually state power. However, with the intrusion of Agusto Pinochet into Chilean politics ("We will teach the world a lesson in democracy") and the institution of a military dictatorship, one of a number fomented by the US in its battle against "international communism," Chile also represents a critical turning point in this non-revolutionary (in the case of Chile) development: a counterrevolution in development thought and practice—and (a U-turn) in the relation of capital to labor (Crouch and Pizzorno 1978; Davis 1984; Toye 1987).

---

2   On the parallel (to globalization) "civil society" discourse, see Howell and Pearce (2001). In the 1990s, both bilateral and multilateral organizations of "overseas development assistance" turned away from a "third sector" discourse towards one based on the "strengthening civil society." As Mitlin (1998) points out, this shift has to do with a new agenda of incorporating the "private sector" into the development process. For a critical perspective on this agenda see Karliner (1999).

In the North, this counterrevolution was part of a series of structural and strategic responses of the capitalist class and the state to a systemic crisis;[3] in the South it involved the arrest, and reversal, of the process of incorporating the working class into the development and political process—and the recapture of the state apparatus by the propertied and capitalist classes. This process would take close to two decades to unfold but by the end of the millennium the state, with diverse permutations North and South, had been duly restructured to serve the imperial agenda and interests of capital.

Not only was the state been restructured to advance the agenda and more clearly reflect the interests of transnational capital but also in the case of the United States, it has been reshaped so as to advance the imperialist design, and foreign policy agenda (to reassert its declining hegemony over the whole system), of the new regime. The formation of what could well be termed the "imperial state" has been years in the making but it took a giant step forward in 2001 after the events of 9/11. As it turns out, these events created conditions not only for the concentration of presidential power over the state apparatus but in the projection of imperial power in various areas of strategic geopolitical interest to the United States.

The 1980s and 1990s saw an erosion of US economic and political power in the Middle East, Europe, Asia and, despite gains in Central America, in Latin America. In the Middle East, in a major area of strategic interest viz. the supply of petroleum, both Iran and Iraq were able to escape the efforts of the US to assert its power and trade directly with the European Community. In Europe itself, a series of unilateral actions by the US state were unable to circumvent the relative ascendancy of the Europeans in the region. Only in the Balkans did US foreign policy and the projection of (naked or well-clothed) political and military power bear fruit. In Latin America most governments had been reduced into submissive client states on the basis, and through the actions, of the functionaries of the World Bank, the IMF, and other international organizations dominated by the United States. However, the policies foisted on Latin American states by these institutions, or adopted by servile client regimes, have not only undermined these regimes but have generated formidable forces of opposition and resistance in the most important countries, particularly as relates to the "strategic triangle" of Colombia, Venezuela, and Ecuador that control the access of US TNCs to strategic resources (petroleum and energy, etc.). And the same applies to Argentina and Brazil, and Bolivia, and, in the immediate backyard of the US, Mexico, and Central America.

9/11 was by no means responsible for the form that US imperialism has taken in this historic conjuncture. However, it did allow President George W. Bush to launch a brutal offensive against Afghanistan and to extend it into a global war without specific location or end in sight—against "international terrorism;" it also provided his regime a considerable supply of political capital for dealing with possible dissent and advancing an imperialist agenda without the encumbrance of democracy. But two

---

3   There are a number of diverse interpretations of this crisis, which, by most accounts was evidenced in a slowdown of system-wide economic activity, a drop in productivity growth, conditions of a "profit crunch" and a systemic tendency towards a fall in for average profits (Marglin and Schor 1990).

of the characteristic features of US imperialism in this conjuncture—unilateralism in decision-making and increased reliance on, and use of, the repressive apparatus—were in response to a general erosion of US economic and political power, especially vis-à-vis the EU, which had been making considerable gains vis-à-vis the United States in regards to Latin America (for example, in the takeover of lucrative state enterprises).

This turn towards unilateralism and militarism—and towards what could be termed "neomercantilism" (the projection of imperial state power in lieu of reliance on the functionaries of the World Bank, the IMF, and other international financial institutions or IFIs)—is also (in part) a response to the onset and conditions of an economic crisis "at home" (in the US), the conditions of which for some time (1995–2000) had been masked by a speculative boomlet. By 9/11, however—certainly by October 7—it was evident that the US economy was in crisis. The signs were serious enough and increasingly evident, exposing cracks that went to the very foundations of the system. In the manufacturing sector, for example, a "recession" (declines in output) had been officially registered for 15 consecutive months and continued for another six, up to a New York meeting of the WEF to seek ways of activating the economy by raising the confidence of investors and consumers.

At the level of the national accounts, a trade deficit of US$430 billion (representing 4 percent of GNP in 2000) reflected a growing weakness in the export sector of industrial production while a huge mass of functioning capital (hundreds of billions of dollars) invested in the high-tech industries of fiberoptics, informatics and biotechnology had evaporated. By 2001, only 4 out of 20 leading informatics firms in the United States had achieved profitability, recovering returns on huge investments. Under such conditions, the US imperial state could hardly afford to provide what was demanded (or rather, timorously requested) of it by its client states and regimes such as Argentina or Colombia—a new Marshall Plan (or, at least, an IMF bailout) that would provide an economic development fund of a sufficient size to activate economies that are everywhere in decline or crisis.

But the US state, under pressure and with the imperative need to activate its own economy, responded instead with a plan to convert the entire region into one free market (LAFTA) and, at a different level, to extend "Plan Colombia" (to the Andean countries of Ecuador, Peru, and Bolivia; Venezuela and the Brazilian Amazon). Deploying some US $40 billion of largely military "aid"—constituting, after Israel, the largest program of US "overseas development assistance"—this imperialist counteroffensive is aimed squarely at the most powerful force of opposition and resistance to US power in the region: the FARC. Officials of the US state, in this geopolitical and strategic context, view the FARC as the largest (and most effective) insurgent force in the region (with an armed force of 20,000 with a projected power in at least 40 percent of the national territory, including in the oil-rich strategic region), to be the major threat to its interests in the region.

Not only does it threaten the stability, even the survival, of the regime in Colombia, an important client state, but, it is calculated, as FARC goes so does the Left (other forces of opposition and resistance in the region, mostly social movements based in the peasantry or indigenous communities). The forces of Leftist opposition to US imperialism in the region would be seriously undermined and demoralized by a victory of the United States and the Colombian state over FARC.

Empire and the State

Building an empire is not a tea party (Lieutenant Colonel US Marine Corp.).

In the debate as to the impact of globalization on the nation-state, a number of theorists such as Antonio Negri (Hardt and Negri 2000) have argued that the state is becoming, or has become, increasingly a less important factor in both the regulation and management of the global economy and in mobilizing the forces of resistance into (in Gramscian terms) a "counter-hegemonic force" or (in Negri's own terms) a "counter-power" based on "the multitude" within "civil society." The state, in this analysis, is no longer a significant actor on the world scene.

To take the case of Argentina: once upon a time the state was a powerful instrument for advancing the national interest; but today state officials, from the president down, are unable to exercise any crucial state powers with regard to the economy—they can execute strategic decisions but do not make them. These are largely made, as it happens, in Washington—by members of the Trilateral Commission or the Council of Foreign Relations, Wall Street, the White House or the Secretary of State, the IMF, the World Bank, etc. This might be somewhat of an exaggeration, but recent (as yet ongoing) events in Argentina related to pressures exerted by the IMF on the government—to have it "face reality" as relates to the requirements of the "international financial community" (financiers, investors, etc.)—suggest that governments such as Dualde's Argentina in the current context have no room to maneuver, or to make any independent decisions, in the setting of macroeconomic policy.

Notwithstanding the erosion of certain powers experienced by many governments and states, the problem in this analysis, and with the conclusions drawn by Negri and others, is at once both a lack of specificity and overgeneralization. The fact is while the power of some states might be reduced or circumscribed that of others, in what could be viewed as the center of the system, has been reinforced. Nothing could be further from the truth than Hardt and Negri's notion of an "empire without imperialism." The US state, in particular, is a powerful instrument for the projection of both economic and political—not to speak of military—power. The facts here are too numerous and obvious to warrant discussion (see our discussion above). However, in this connection we can—and do—note that the state is but one of a complex of institutions that serve the interests of, and are controlled by, the transnational capitalist class—the economic, political, and other members of the elite that represent the interests of this class.

As to whom this elite might be, or the class that it is a part of, the facts are not hard to discern. The US Council on Foreign Relations (CFR), for example, like the WTO, the latest addition to the global power structure of this elite, might make decisions behind closed doors but they do not operate in secret. Nor are the major nodal points of the complicated and broad network of institutions set up and controlled by this class difficult to identify, notwithstanding the fact that many are hidden (and like all structures visible only in their effects). They include various institutional networks and forums that bring together representatives and members of this class that run the TNCs and financial institutions that dominate the world economy. On this point we need but look at and examine the membership of the CFR (Salbuchi 2000) and regular participants in the WEF.

The entire debate as to whether the these TNCs, as argued by Korten (2001) and so many others in the antiglobalization movement, are free to operate globally over and above the nation-state, whose powers they supposedly exceed, is misplaced. The fact is that these TNCs do not roam the world at will, free from state control and regulation; they generally have their home-base and decision-making centers in the industrially advanced or "developed" societies at the centre of the system— the G8—and, to a considerable extent, are still subject to government control and regulation. The vast majority of the top TNCs (*Financial Times'* or *Forbes'* Top 100) are located in the United States (49 percent), the European Community (37 percent), or, to a lesser degree, Japan (9 percent). The leading directors and CEOs of these TNCs are integrated into a network of institutions, including the US imperial state, controlled by the transnational capitalist class, whose members are also largely located in these societies.

In this context, the US state still serves as the major source of imperial power, particularly in its political and military dimensions but also economic. It is the US state that backstops the institutions of economic power, paving the way for the operation of these institutions and creating the facilitating conditions. For example, the IMF might well be the force behind the policies adopted by virtually every government in Latin America but behind the IMF and other such international organizations can be found the power of the imperial state system, particularly the US. It is also this power that lies behind the imposition of tariffs and other free trade barriers that protect US capital in its home market operations from foreign competition.

It is the US state that has levied a 27 percent import duty on Canadian lumber. It is the US state that levies prohibitive duties on the import of steel and other goods and services from Europe, Asia, and Latin America whenever producers in these countries "threaten" the interests of the United States—that is, out-perform uncompetitive US producers on the domestic market. In short, there is no question of an "empire without imperialism." Any such intellectual construction is both misleading and politically dangerous, leading minimally to a failure to understand the forces at play in the so-called globalization process.

The Contradictions of Imperialism: From Neoliberalism to Neomercantilism

In the turn towards what has been termed the "short twentieth century" (1917–89) Lenin identified five structural features of imperialism, regarded not as an adjunct to but as the most advanced phase of capitalist development at the time. One of these features was the exchange of raw materials produced in the non-capitalist world in exchange for goods manufactured in a process of capitalist development— what would become "the old imperialism." In the 1970s, however, history took a new turn in the context of, and response to, a deep systemic crisis. As in Lenin's time, at a critical conjuncture of modernization, we can at this point identify five major structural features of capitalist development arising out of diverse strategic responses made to this crisis. The first is what has been described alternatively as a New International Division of Labor (Fröbel, Heinrichs and Kreye 1980) and a "Second Industrial Divide" (Piore and Sabel 1984), a structure arising out of strategic decisions of the TNCs to relocate their labor-intensive operations closer towards sources of cheaper labor. A second feature of the "new imperialism" is a shift in, or transformation of, the dominant mode of regulating labor at the point of production—from Fordism to Postfordism (Lipietz 1982, 1987; Boyer 1989). A third feature is based on a process of productive transformation and technological conversion, characterized by the evolution of new production technologies as well as the shedding of vast numbers of workers, replenishing thereby what Marx had termed the "industrial reserve army"—a huge and growing reserve of surplus labor. A fourth feature is a major change in the structure formed by the relation of capital to labor. The defining characteristic feature of this new structure is a qualitative shift in labor's participation in the process of economic production—in its share of income and value added to production.

The effects of this shift—the compression and dispersal of wages, a fall in their real value and a decline in the purchasing power and consumption capacity of workers—have been well documented and analyzed, particularly in regards to Latin America. As with the associated restructuring of the labor market they generally relate to conditions of "social exclusion" that can be directly traced back to a process of class struggle—the assault of the capitalist class on labor (Gazier 1996; Paugam 1996). The fifth characteristic feature of the new imperialism, defined as Lenin did, that is, not in strategic or political but in structural terms, is precisely a tendency towards globalization and the integration of country after country into an extended capitalist economy.

Although often defined in "structural" terms imperialism in any form entails a relation of domination between states at the "center" of the system and those on its "periphery." And the structure of this relation is maintained by a projection of political—and military—power, concentrated in the imperial state system, which, in the current context, is made up of the state apparatus of the United States and the major "powers" in the European Community.

Notwithstanding the theorizing of Hardt and Negri about the end of imperialism, on the one hand, and, on the other, the ideology of globalization, the *reality* of this power structure is evident and not just in its effects. However, just as evident is the fact that the system as a whole is in trouble, riven by internal contradictions. First, in the global workings of this system, more and more direct producers are being separated from their means of social production. At the same time, large numbers of workers are subjected to diverse conditions of "exploitation" or "social exclusion"—unemployment, precarious forms of labor and employment, and low income. Under these and other such conditions the process of capital accumulation, although extended on a global scale, is reaching its structural—and political—limits. Although it is sustained by the productive capacity of the leading capitalist enterprises and established markets at the centre of the system as well as a number of "emerging markets," the capital accumulation process is, at the same time, undermined by the growth of large sectors of the world population without any productive capacity or insufficient purchasing power. As we have noted, there are signs that this problem is generating cracks in the very foundation of the system. And, at the political level, it is giving rise to forces of opposition and resistance that are being mobilized against the system and its supports. In all of the leading countries on the Latin American periphery of the US empire both the status quo and the system itself are under attack.

The current US imperial worldwide offensive, launched in the wake of 9/11, faces two types of contradictions with both conjunctural and structural features. First, in regard to the "war against international terrorism" the military build-up and campaign against Afghanistan, the Al-Qaeda network, Iraq (and possibly Iran, the other threat to US interests in the Gulf region); and, in Latin America, against the FARC and other forces of subversion ("narcotrafficking," "terrorism," etc.) and opposition to US interests, each projection of military power has resulted in a "blowback" (Chalmers 2000) and over the medium and long term is very costly; and these costs of necessity will escalate. In this regard, the officials of the US imperial state have not learnt an elemental historical lesson—that the military costs of defending the empire sooner or later will undermine, and irrevocably damage, the imperial economy that it is designed to protect. In this connection, it might be expected that an expansion of the military apparatus would dynamize an important sector of the economy — the industrial enterprises that service this apparatus.

However, this idea is misplaced. The costs of "defending the empire"—military expansion in a time of deepening economic recession, both locally and worldwide. Military Keynianism—increased war spending—has not and will not reverse the current recession, as few sectors of the economy are affected and the industries such as aerospace that could receive some economic stimulus are hard hit by the recession in the civilian airline market. In addition, the military apparatus of the imperial state is not a cost-efficient service provider, far from it. Expenditures on this apparatus far exceed the immediate benefits to the US-based corporations and have not reversed the tendency towards declining rate of profits or opened up new markets, particularly in the regions of maximum military engagement. Military intervention tends to expand the scale and scope of colonization without increasing returns to capital. Imperial wars tend to undermine non-speculative capitalist investment, even as it symbolically assures overseas investors.

As in Central America, the Balkans, and now in Afghanistan and Colombia, the United States is more interested in destroying adversaries and establishing client regimes than in large-scale, long-term investments in "economic reconstruction." After high military spending for conquest, budget priorities have shifted to subsidizing US-based corporations, and lowering taxes for the wealthy: there can be no more "Marshall Plans." The US state can no longer afford this possibly successful resolution of economic problems generated by imperial policies in the subjugated areas of "pre-modern states." Instead, Washington leaves it to its allies in Europe and Japan to "clean up the human wreckage" left in the wake of US military actions. Post-war reconstruction does not intimidate possible adversaries; B-52 carpet-bombing does.

Any military victory in the present conjuncture leaves unsettled the consolidation of a pro-imperial client regime. Just as the United States financed and armed the Islamic fundamentalists in their war against the secular nationalist Afghan regime in the 1980s and then withdrew, leading to the ascendancy of the anti-Western Taliban regime, last year's "victory" and subsequent withdrawal is likely to have similar results within the next decade. The gap between the high war-making capacity of the imperial state and its incapacity to revitalize the economies of the conquered nations is a major contradiction.

Another even more serious contradiction is found in the aggressive effort to impose neoliberal regimes and policies when the export markets that they were designed to service are collapsing and external flows of capital are drying up. In this connection, the recession in the United States, Japan, and the EU has severely damaged the most loyal and subservient neoliberal client-states, particularly in Latin America. The prices of the exports that drive the neoliberal regimes in the region have fallen and in some cases collapsed: exports of coffee, petrol, metals, sugar, as well as textiles, clothes and other goods manufactured in the "free trade zones" have suffered from sharp drops in prices and glutted markets. The US as an imperial power has responded to this by pressing for greater "liberalism" (free markets) in the South while raising protective tariffs at home and increasing subsidies for exports.

In this connection, tariffs in the Northern imperial countries on imports from the South are four times higher than those on imports from other imperial countries (World Bank 2002). At the same time (2000, that is) support for agricultural TNCs in the imperial countries was $245 billion (*Financial Times*, 21 November 2001: 13). In May 2002 the Bush administration announced US $73 billion of subsidies to the agricultural sector. As the World Bank (2002: 7) has pointed out, with regard to these and such protections against the forces of the world market, "the share of subsidized exports has even increased [over the past decade] for many products of export interest to developing countries."

In effect, the neoliberal doctrine of the "old imperialism" is giving way to the neomercantilist practice of the "new imperialism." State policies dictate the structure of economic exchanges and delimit the role of the market—all to the benefit of the imperial economy. However, the highly restrictive nature of neomercantilist policies tends to polarize the economy between local producers and the imperial state-backed monopolies. While the erosion and destruction of domestic markets under neoliberal policies marginalize large sectors of the economically active population, the collapse of overseas markets negatively affects "neoliberal" export sectors and weakens the position of the bourgeoisie in the client states of the empire. In this situation, imperial free market policies have threatened to "kill the goose that lays the golden eggs"—creating conditions that make it difficult, if not impossible, for the imperial economy to generate needed "resource flows"—in the form of interest payments on loans, profit remittances on direct investments, royalty and license fee payments, dividends on portfolio investments, and "unequal exchange" as well as trade imbalances (Petras and Veltmeyer 2001).

In addition to undermining the economies of its client states, the highly visible role of the imperial state in imposing what amounts to a neomercantilist system is politicizing the growing army of unemployed and poorly paid workers, peasants, and public employees. Take, for example, the case of Argentina, one of the most compliant clients of the United States throughout the 1990s. The collapse of both overseas and domestic markets over the past four years has meant less foreign exchange to service foreign debts. In December of 2001, in the throes of the worst economic and political crisis in its history and days after a massive social "upheaval" of the working and middle classes, the newly formed government announced that it could not and would not service its foreign debt obligations. Fewer exports have also meant a lower capacity to import essential foodstuffs and capital goods to sustain production. Thus the entire export and free market strategy upon which the whole imperial edifice in Latin America is built has been undermined. Unable to import, countries like Argentina will be forced to produce locally or do without—and revert to a domestic market that has been opened up to the forces of "globalization."

However, the definitive rupture with the export-oriented strategy of neoliberal capitalist development and subordination to empire will not come about because of internal contradictions: it requires political intervention. What form shall this intervention take? How has the "system" responded to these (structural) contradictions and (political) challenges? Indications are that rather than, as Hardt and Negri (2000) would have it—the disappearance of imperialism—it is leading to what some have termed its "renaissance," a new form, described by some (Robert Cooper, for example) as "postmodern," and by others (the author, as it happens) as "neomercantilism."

On the New Imperialism in the Postmodern Era—Empire without Imperialism?

> in dealing with more old-fashioned kinds of states outside the postmodern continent of Europe [and North America] we need to revert to the rougher methods of an earlier era—force, preemptive attack, deception, whatever is necessary to deal with those who still live in the nineteenth century world of every state for itself [in the pre-modern world of developing countries]. Among ourselves [postmodern states] we keep the law but ... in the jungle we must also use the laws of the jungle (Robert Cooper, foreign policy advisor to Tony Blair, 2000b: 7).

The need for a new form of "liberal" imperialism has been placed on the agenda on both sides of the Atlantic that separates the postmodern states of Europe and North America. While the Left is caught up and lost in the struggle for and against globalization, the Right is advancing its project to redesign and restore imperialism. Very few have stated the problem as forthrightly and clearly as Robert Cooper and, on the other side of the Atlantic, the journalist Martin Wolf (*Financial Times*, 10 October 2001: 13) who also sees the need for a "new" more direct form of "imperialism" that does not hesitate to use force when and where necessary. In Wolf's words, "To tackle the challenge of the failed state [in an impoverished Third World] what is needed is not pious aspirations but an honest and organized coercive force."[4]

---

4   Another exponent of the need for a new imperialism is the *Washington Post* editorial writer and columnist Sebastian Mallaby, who notes that in the past whenever a great power was threatened by some power vacuum in some corner of the world that this power had at its disposal diverse weapons—an "imperial solution." But, he adds, since the Second World War "well-ordered" societies (in the North) out of political weakness have refused to "impose its own institutions." Nevertheless, he further adds, in today's world of increasingly "repulsive and prolonged wars" this attitude of self-restraint is increasingly more difficult to sustain.

For trilateralists and the foreign policy analysts that inhabit policy forums such as the Council of Foreign Relations (CFR) and other Washington-based financial institutions and foundations, the issue is is not imperialism but a better management of the forces of globalization, even if it means a new form of regulating global movements of capital or capital controls (Rodrik 1997; Stiglitz 1998; Soros 2002). This is, in fact, the essence of the globalization project, both in its neoliberal and alternative forms. However, for Cooper and others searching for a new post-Washington Consensus what is required is a new form of imperialism that is not circumscribed by "humanitarian interventionism"—the "theology of aid for countries seeking to insert themselves into the global economy" (Cooper 2002).

This form of "multilateral imperialism," to date led and protagonized by the World Bank and the other members of the "international financial community," according to Cooper (2000b), is predicated on the enlightened ("humanitarian") "interference" of the international organizations and states that make up the world of "postmodern states" (the OECD). Such interference has been standard procedure as of the mid-1980s under the globalization project but the rationale for it has been restated in the clearest possible terms by MIT economists Rudiger Dornbusch and Ricardo Caballero in the context of recent developments in Argentina. However, Cooper argues, it is clear enough that the multi- or trilateral institutions have been unable to manage the forces of "globalization"—to establish the conditions of "good governance" (governability) and thereby prevent the outbreak or to control the forces of resistance and opposition generated by the "cycle of poverty, instability and violence" that characterize the "pre-modern states" (in the developing world of failed and weak states). "If there were other ways of resolving the problem" (the threat presented by these conditions to the citizens and states [members] of the postmodern and modern world," Cooper notes, the "renaissance of imperialism" would not have been necessary.

This is clear enough. But it is also clear that "overseas development assistance" has not "born fruit" and all other efforts to improve conditions for the countries in the pre-modern world of backward states have failed. As a result, Cooper adds, what is needed is a new form of "colonialism" and an imperialism that does not hesitate to use force—to project power in political and economic forms and military if and where needed—but a force that is "acceptable to all, both weak and strong" ("the weak need the strong and the strong need order"); that rests, in other words, on "voluntary acceptance" or a new consensus (the consent of the governed)—or, in Hardt and Negri's (2000) abstracted conception of the search for hegemony, an "empire without imperialism." Cooper, in this context, notes that order or stability generally depends on a balance of power—a balance in the "power of aggression"—but that this balance is rare; states in the pre-modern world are generally weak, having lost legitimacy and/or their "monopoly in the legitimate use of force."

In this situation, the state is unable to contain the forces of opposition among "non-state actors" which threaten not only stability in these countries but in "the postmodern world," which, in this circumstance," have the right, and the need, to react—to "defend" themselves. One example of this is the US invasion of Afghanistan; another, the war against "subversion" in Colombia and elsewhere.

Development, Democracy and the Empire

In the 1980s, the idea of democracy was advanced in the form of (1) the return to power of civilian-elected and constitutional regimes, and the restoration of the electoral mechanism in the transition from one regime to another; (2) the decentralization of government of services and some powers; and (3) the strengthening of civil society within the framework of government-initiated political and social reforms (Reilley 1995). In the 1990s, however, in Latin America, the idea of democracy was assumed by the popular movement, initiating "from below" or within "civil society," on the basis and in the form of social movements and popular or direct (as opposed to liberal and representative) democracy.

At the base of these grassroots social movements are urban communities, citizens groups or neighborhood associations, or, in the rural sector, indigenous communities of peasant farmers. In general these organizations tend to be profoundly detached from what is perceived to be the "old politics"—a phenomenon mistakenly theorized in diverse contexts as an abandonment of the search for political power and the struggle against the holders of political power (see, for example, Benasayag and Sztulwark 2000; Holloway 2001; Negri 2001).

Thus, the EZLN has been conceptualized as "the first postmodern movement in history" (Burbach 1994). And in similar terms Esteva and Prakash (1998), among others (Escobar and Alvarez 1992) write of Latin American "new" social movements in terms of "grassroots postmodernism." There is an element of truth that is misconstrued in these conceptions: the movements that they seek to describe are characterized by an almost fatal distrust of [the old] "politics," politicians" and their "parties."

Democracy versus Authoritarianism—Hegemony, Terror and Intimidation

What defines the new imperialism in its most recent offensives is not only unilateralism in the projection of state power but an increased use of its repressive apparatus with an aggressive reliance on military force in "defense" of the empire. However, naked power is always destabilizing. To secure the conditions of order, which, Cooper pointed out, are needed by the powerful, a degree of consensus or hegemony is also needed, and—in terms analyzed by Noam Chomsky—duly manufactured. Until recently (viz. the War against International Terrorism), such a consensus was generally sought on the basis, and in terms of, a battle of "democracy" against "international communism." At issue in this ideological struggle was the idea of "democracy"—that decision-making power is exercised, directly or indirectly, by "the people;" that the holders of power represent the people and are held accountable to them; and that politics take the form of dialog and negotiation of conflicting interests rather than violent confrontation—channeling of grievances and demands through forms of "peaceful and civil struggle" (UNRISD 2000).[5] Alternatively, Bultman and

---

5   Thus also the notion that democracies do not go to war—that conditions of war and the violent settling of social conflicts—has been banished in democratic regimes.

colleagues (1995) write of the emergence in Latin America of "democracy without a social movement."

In this context, it was even asserted and argued (by ideologues and scholars alike), despite historical evidence to the contrary, that democracy and capitalism in the (neoliberal) form of private enterprise and the free market were intrinsically connected; that the marriage between free markets (capitalism, economic liberalism) and free elections (democracy, political liberalism) was not one of convenience or historic accident but organic (Dominguez and Lowenthal 1996).

Thus, liberal scholars, both political scientists and economists, have theorized that the institutionalization of democracy (political liberalization) would create the necessary or facilitating conditions of capitalist development (political liberalization) or vice versa. Thus, at the level of practice, within the context of Euro-American imperialism after the Second World War, the iron fist of armed force and political repression has often been cloaked with the idea of democracy and a concern for associated "human rights." However, democracy in this (liberal) form has proven to be a two-edged sword. As Samuel Huntington, a well-known but best forgotten conservative yet trilateralist political scientist and author of *The Clash of Civilizations*, recognized as early as 1974, the year to which the capitalist counteroffensive (and the conservative counterrevolution in development theory and practice) can be traced, that democracy provides conditions under which forces of opposition and resistance can expand and prosper—and be mobilized against the system (Huntington, Crozier and Watunuki 1975).

The issue, from Huntington's view, was the generation of pressures and demands for inclusion that exceeded the institutional capacity of the system and that cannot be accommodated or contained. Thus, in the shared context of conditions under which the globalization project was launched and policies of structural adjustment were implemented, a re-democratization process in Latin America and elsewhere in the Third World[6] generated widespread forces of opposition to, and resistance against, the projects of globalization and imperialism.

How have the guardians of economic and political order responded to the threat of organized and mobilized forces of resistance and opposition? The record here is clear, particularly as relates to the current regime headed by George W. Bush. Whenever and wherever the institution of democracy has proven to be dysfunctional for the system—in securing hegemony—it is jettisoned.

Thus, in the 1960s and 1970s the state invaded, otherwise intervened, or sponsored military coups against one democratically elected constitutional regime in Latin America after another. In this projection of political power a democratic façade was nevertheless maintained (for example, President Johnson's congratulation of the Brazilian military in 1964, hours after their coup against the democratically elected nationalist Goulart regime, for "restoring democracy"). However, where and when necessary this façade is dropped, as, for example, it was in recent efforts of the US state to orchestrate a civilian-military coup against the democratically elected Chávez regime in Venezuela.

---

6   This process took the form of the decentralization of government; the return to state power of civilian constitutional regimes; and the strengthening of "civil society."

The coup failed largely as a result of a mass popular uprising in support of Chávez who had been removed from power and held in detention, prior to being forced to leave the country. But a significant feature of the dynamics preceding and surrounding the coup was the behavior and position of the US administration. The coup was without doubt a rupture of the democratic institutionality to which the US state pays rhetorical homage and which the Organization of American States (OAS) is committed to protect. But it is just as clear that the US itself engineered the coup attempt through the agency of a right-wing coalition of groups and organizations, the machinations of its ambassador and other US officials, and a part of Venezuela's armed forces. However, the United States was totally isolated within the OAS in refusing to see the attempted coup as a rupture with democracy, and in viewing Chávez as the author of his own misfortune.

Despite the lies and counter-images projected by both the mass media inside Venezuela, a major source of anti-government agitation, and the US media, generally an instrument of imperial doublespeak, it was transparently clear that the US state sponsored this as so many other antidemocratic actions in the region and was its architect. No one outside the White House, and likely no one inside, believed for a moment in the weak and failed efforts of the US state to put a democratic gloss on the attempted military coup in Venezuela. As with the lukewarm and failed efforts of George W. Bush to manufacture popular or political consent for its imperialist project, viz. the projection of military power in the form of a fight against the "axis of evil," this particular effort to hide the relations of power and to obfuscate the issues involved did not work. No one believes in it.

Atilio Borón, a well-known Argentine political sociologist, among other analysts, has drawn the not surprising but important conclusion from this and other such failures that "US imperialism might be powerful but not omnipotent." The matter is not only of the limits of political and military power but of the capacity of the US imperial state to secure "hegemony" over the system. In this regard, it is clear enough that despite support from the mass media for the its anti-terrorist campaign the US imperial state is moving towards a serious legitimation crisis, which perhaps helps explain the lack of apparent concern, in Bush's administration of the empire, to maintain a democratic façade for his policies.[7] An appeal to respect for human rights and democracy is simply no longer functional or necessary in the new world order called for by Bush the elder and being brought about by Bush junior.

---

7   The attempted coup against the democratically elected Chávez regime in Venezuela is a clear indication of this. Given the alacrity with which the IMF expressed its support for the short-lived government instituted by the coup-makers, and the absence of any condemnation on the part of the Bush administration, it is, according to a number of analysts in the region (Luzani 2002: 2), "the first sign of a change in US doctrine ... [raising the specter of] a return to the nightmare of coups in the region." Bruce Bagley, Director of Graduate Studies at the University of Miami, has expressed a similar concern, noting that the Bush administration has "returned once more to the unacceptable ... tactics [designed to] overthrow foreign governments [without regard to democratic norms and procedures]" (*Clarin* 2002, Suplemento "Zona," 21 April: 2).

Antiglobalization or Anti-imperialism?

Despite its global extension and its ability to mobilize forces of resistance against, and opposition to, the agenda (and neoliberal program) of global corporate capital the antiglobalization movement is very limited in its capacity to derail the system—or to induce the radical reforms that would be needed to implement its agenda of "creating another (that is, better) world—of social justice, greater equity and more democracy." Adam Morton,(2004) interprets this situation metaphorically by questioning whether the antiglobalization movement can best be viewed as a "juggernaut" ("a vehicle on an inexorable path toward consolidating particular social, political, and economic priorities") or as a "jalopy" ("whose direction is openly contested and that may even be subject to breakdown") and, as such, a "presumptuous pebble" (Singer 1999).

However, in realistic rather than metaphorical terms, the antiglobalization movement can better be viewed as a vehicle that is not going anywhere fast and will likely stall or be derailed rather than overpower the globalization project. The major reasons for this include the fact that the theorists and activists of the antiglobalization movement misconstrue the nature or scope of the problem (fail to see it as systemic) and are unwilling to directly confront the formidable forces mobilized in support of the globalization project with the equally (if potential) formidable forces of opposition and resistance at the disposal of this project. It is not recognized that at issue is a class war waged on a global scale in diverse theaters and with a growing concentration of armed force—and all of the instrumentalities of an imperial state in control of the enemy.

The fact is, the globalization project is part of an ideological counteroffensive in a class war that has been waged by capital against labor at different levels and in different forms since the early 1970s. A politics of peaceful resistance, dialog and partnerships, and other forms of "civil" responses will not change the structure of the system or emancipate working people.

The only way to bring about the end and transformation of the capitalist system is to directly confront the structure of political, economic, and military power and to mobilize the forces of resistance and opposition against this structure. What is needed is not an antiglobalization but an anti-imperialist movement—the mobilization of forces of opposition and resistance against capitalism in its current form; to exploit the opportunities made available by the contradictions of this system. The point is that any given structure—and the structure of the new imperialism no less—provides not only challenges and "constraints" but both opportunities and resources for effective action. This is perhaps the one useful insight achieved by Anthony Giddens (1990), the architect of Tony Blair's "third way" towards political change, in his various theoretical constructions—his "restructuration" theory and that of the consequences of "modernity."

Organizing for Change: Opportunities for the Left within the Empire

US imperialism in its recent and current offensives and counteroffensives is far from omnipotent and, as we have noted, is fraught with contradictions that are generating forces of opposition and resistance.

In terms of these "contradictions," what then are the organizational forms of possible or effective opposition and resistance against the US counteroffensive in the current context of neoliberal capitalist development and neoimperialism—in the conjuncture of the general and specific conditions of the situation in which people in Latin America find themselves today? Unfortunately, several decades of sociological and political studies into the dynamics of these social movements have yielded little information and fewer ideas.[8] Nevertheless, a review of these movements suggests that they have been formed in three distinct but overlapping "waves" of organized resistance.

The first wave hit Latin America in the late 1970 and the early to mid 1980s in the context of a region-wide debt crisis, a redemocratization process and the implementation of the "new economic model" of macroeconomic stabilization and structural adjustment measures. It took the form of what appeared to some as a "new social movement" that brought onto the centre stage of resistance and opposition new 'social actors" in the urban areas (Castells 1983; Slater 1985; Calderón and Jelín 1987; Assies *et al.* 1990; Calderón 1995).

The social or civic organizations at the base of these movements were formed around concern over a wide range of specific issues that ranged from day to day survival and the predations of military dictatorship to respect for human rights, the environment and the situation of women, as well as the search for human dignity and social or cultural "identity" (Scott 1990; Escobar and Alvarez 1992; Calderón 1995; Esteva and Prakash 1998). It involved both grassroots, community-based and civic organizations that sought not social transformation but redress of a wide range of specific concerns and the expansion of local spaces within the existing structure—a direct rather than liberal form of democracy.

These so-called "new social movements" dominated the urban landscape in the late 1980s but the social forces that they had mobilized by and large had dissipated at the turn of the next decade. Only recently have some analysts detected their reappearance in the popular assemblies and social movements formed by diverse neighborhood associations and groups of unemployed workers in the poor *barrios* of Buenos Aires and other urban centers in Argentina. According to the theorists of this sociopolitical "development"—a group of sociologists, political scientists, and philosophers with a postmodernist, nonstructuralist or poststructuralist optic—these movements are "new" in that they are totally disenchanted with politics as practiced to date (*¡Que se Vayan Todos!*) and that in their practice they seek a new way of "doing politics," in the pursuit not of power but, on the contrary, of a "counterpower" (Benasayag and Sztulwark 2000; Holloway 2002; Negri 2000).

A second wave of more antisystemic movements was formed by associations of peasant producers and indigenous communities in the late 1980s. In the 1990s,

---

8   There is, in fact, a fairly large literature on the "new" social movements in Latin America's urban and rural landscape (see, *inter alia*, Assies *et al.* 1990; Foweraker 1995;). But as noted by Munck (1997) in this literature there is a dearth of comparative analysis—at best a series of country case studies and theoretical debates that by and large appears to be disconnected from these studies; that is, they tend to be descriptive and not analyzed within the various theoretical frameworks at issue in these debates.

however, these peasant-based—and peasant-led—sociopolitical movements took their struggle to the cities and urban centers, mobilizing, in the process, other forces of opposition and resistance to both government policy and the broader system behind it.

One of the earliest movements established in this process is the Landless Rural Workers Movement (MST) in Brazil. Although currently facing a serious counteroffensive by the government, the MST has managed to maintain one of the most dynamic social movements in Latin America, occupying and settling on the land in the process of 15 years of struggle and direct action, upwards of 400,000 families since 1995; and organizing agricultural production on this land "expropriated" from its owners in the landed oligarchy.

Other such sociopolitical organizations with both their social base and their leadership in the rural peasantry or indigenous communities include the Confederación Nacional Indígena de Ecuador (CONAIE); the EZLN; the Confederación Nacional Campesino de Paraguay; the Cocaleros of Bolivia; and, to some extent, the FARC, which, as noted above, unlike the other "new peasant sociopolitical movements" formed in this second wave, was formed much earlier—in the 1960s.

As of the mid-1990s it has been possible to identify the emergence of a third wave of sociopolitical movements formed in opposition to both government policies and against the "system." In this case, the social base of the movement is found in the urban working class, restructured under conditions of "productive transformation" (technological conversion) and structural adjustments in government policy under the "new economic model." The working class, formed in this process by and large, and increasingly, is located not in factories and plants in diverse centers of industrial production, nor in government offices, but in the streets under conditions of marginality (precarious forms of employment), social exclusion, unemployment, low income, and poverty. Nowhere has this process advanced to the point that it has in Argentina, with an uninterrupted and deepening crisis in production that has already lasted four years, rates of unemployment that exceed 20 percent in official statistics—in many areas from 30 to 60 percent—and over half of the population subsisting on incomes below conservatively defined poverty lines.

In response to the objectively defined and experienced conditions of the failed attempts by the government to insert the national economy into the process of "globalization," to position itself advantageously in the New World Order, a broad array of workers, both unemployed and unemployed, have taken their antigovernment/antisystemic struggle into the streets, with a combination of strikes, plant takeovers, demonstrations, marchs on government buildings, and, most importantly, the tactic of *cortas de ruta*—cutting off, with barricades and pickets (*piquetes*), road and highway access. In 1997, under conditions of an impending production crisis there were on average 11 *cortas de ruta* or *piquetes* a month. By 1999 this number had doubled while in 2002 it climbed to an estimated 70 or so a month.

The *piqueteros* have clearly established themselves as a beachhead at the crest of a new wave of Leftist opposition and sociopolitical movements directed against government policies and against the system (US imperialism), which they see to be behind it. Whether this movement can advance on the rising tide of this wave, or whether the social forces of opposition that it has mobilized, will once more be dissipated in the ebb and flow of struggle remains to be seen. The organizational and political challenges involved are considerable, perhaps unsurmountable. But they certainly will not be surmounted in the new politics of anti-power, dissolving as it does in thought the political dynamics of the existing power structure. At the same time, there is little to no doubt that the new social movements formed in the second and third "wave" of Leftist or antisystemic opposition have greater mobilizing capacity and political potential than the "juggernaut" (or "jalopy") of the antiglobalization movement. The struggle against imperialism needs of necessity take an anti-imperialist form.

Conclusion

Globalization, when presented as an irresistible force, is a scam. For one thing, it is designed as an ideology and as such, does not explain "what is going on"; rather, it serves to direct action towards an end desired by the apologists, and supporters, of the existing system. In this connection, the antiglobalization movement, notwithstanding its considerable capacity to mobilize intellectual and political forces of opposition and resistance, in political terms is very limited. Much more significant in these terms are the sociopolitical movements being formed in the countryside and urban centers of Latin America and elsewhere on the "periphery" of the world capitalist system. Imperial policies, in fact, are undermining and weakening the middle classes in these societies and polarizing them between the propertied and the working classes—what Hardt and Negri (2000) choose to term "the multitude"—and between the forces of reaction and sociopolitical movements for revolutionary change. Some of these movements are community-based or formed by grassroots forms of organization. However, the most significant of these movements have to be understood in class terms: as involved in a class war, a struggle that is waged worldwide, in diverse contexts, between capital and labor —between member organizations and individuals of the capitalist class and the mass of direct producers and workers that make up the bulk of the world's economically active population.

To gauge the weight and dynamism of the forces for evolutionary or revolutionary change, that is, for social or systemic transformation, and to appreciate what these forces are up against, the notion of "globalization" should be abandoned. More useful in this connection is to conceive of world developments in terms of "neoimperialism," a project designed and put into effect by agents of the system. In the projection of imperial power the international capitalist class has at its disposal diverse instruments and institutions, most notably the state apparatus in the United States and the EU, and, to some extent, Japan. The United States is the major power within this system, both in economic and political, as well as military, terms. Notwithstanding evidence of a continuing inter-imperialist rivalry, and of the manifest difficulties experienced by the US in the search for "good governance" and hegemony, US imperialism remains a powerful force.

But US imperialism is by no means omnipotent. Indeed, the entire system is riven by a series of contradictory developments that provide the Left both space and "opportunities" for successful political intervention. The question is whether the Left is positioned to take advantage of these opportunities or what form political organization and action should take? The answer to this question is not clear but this is a major challenge for the Left—to assess, and help mobilize, the available forces for change. To this end, the Left needs to escape "the old politics" of sectarian partisanship in the struggle for political power without, at the same time, succumbing to the virus of postmodernism or otherwise falling in the trap of the "new politics"— the struggle for democracy and the politics of identity. At issue are class power and systemic transformation.

Conclusion

The study of globalization in its current manifestation (since the appearance in the 1980s of the term in academic and official discourse), has generated an enormous body of work, whose complexity and diversity is not easy to sort out or generalize. According to Paul Bowles in this volume the theoretical perspectives embedded in this body of scholarly work can be placed into four categories. As for the ideological standpoint from which necessarily these studies are conceived and written we can identify permutations of two approaches, each of which can be understood in both theoretical and ideological terms: one that seeks to promote globalization as the only way for all countries, regardless of their position in the structure of international relations, to advance—to enter the path towards economic development and prosperity—and another that is highly critical of the corporate capital agenda and the class interests behind it, and the negative effects on the majority of the world's population of this agenda and these interests.

Notwithstanding the scope and complexity of the globalization literature it is possible to identify a number of critical issues, dominant themes and generalizations that seem to have stood the test of time and criticism. With reference to arguments advanced by authors in this volume, as well as reflections by Jose O'Campo, Secretary-General of ECLAC, which is a major producer and depository of development ideas, these generalizations can be summarized as follows.

First, globalization is not a new phenomenon. It is intrinsically connected to the process of capitalist development, the dynamics of which have generated various cycles and forms of "globalization"—the internationalization of commerce, trade and diverse factors of capitalist production and development, particularly capital and labor; and associated population movements, the integration of diverse national economies, and the increasing interconnectedness of societies all over the world. Of course, the dynamics of the process, and the particular forms of globalization, are historically variable and contingent as well as multidimensional—economic, political, social, and cultural. For example, regarding its economic dimension, computerization and an associated technological conversion of production has not only transformed the conditions and diverse national forms of global capitalist development, but it has revolutionalized communications and dramatically shortened the distance in time and space among societies all over the world. Clearly this process has created conditions that are to an extent "new" and different from earlier periods of globalization from the 1980s to the First World War (Desai 2000). The most recent phase of globalization, in its economic dimension, has taken a neoliberal form, propelled as it is by forces released and generated in a process of neoliberal policy reform. These reforms include the privatization of the means of production, reverting the nationalization policies of the 1950s and 1960; deregulation of private economic activity and markets in labor, tradable commodities and capital; the liberalization of trade and the flow of capital, reverting the protectionist and interventionist policies of the development state established in the Bretton Woods order; administrative decentralization and democratization of the state, incorporating and expanding therewith the role of civil society in the development process.

Second, globalization in this neoliberal form—with diverse national and regional permutations—has had a profound impact on the global distribution of wealth and income, resulting in the deepening and extension of a global divide, with a concentration of wealth (and therefore income) at one pole and growing poverty and immizeration on the other.

Third, these social impacts have generated an array of strategic and political responses that can be placed into two basic categories: (1) efforts to manage the forces released in the globalization process—to secure the sustainability of the process via new forms of global governance; (2) mobilization of the forces of resistance and opposition to the world of neoliberal globalization and the policies that have brought it into being.

At issue in the search for new forms of global governance is to rebalance the relation between the market and the state—between "economic power and public action, limiting the capacity of the former to expand its influence beyond markets" due to its preferential audience in the political system or [and] the control it exercises in other spheres of power ... the mass media in particular" (O'Campo, Jomo and Khan 2007: 17). The concern, in other words, is to replace both the regulatory constraints of the sovereign nation-state and the anarchy (and gross inequalities and inequities) of the market, restoring the dominance of "the public" ("broad social objectives") over the economic system, placing ethical and political limits to the free play of private interests and the "private appropriation of public assets" (O'Campo *et al.* 2007: 18). The issue, not to put too fine point on it, is to re-establish the political conditions of social cohesion, an "ethical framework for the formulation of development policies and political order" (p. 27).

As for the antiglobalization movement, the issues are not that different: to restore or create another world to that of neoliberal globalization—the decidedly unethical appropriation by powerful economic interests of society's productive resources and the concentration of wealth in the hands and banks of the powerful few. The issue— exceedingly excessive inequalities and a growing global divide in power, wealth and income—is the subject of a recent report prepared and published by the UK Ministry of Defence: *Global Strategic Trends 2007–2036*. As the report constructs it, the issue is that of restoring political order in the new world economic order. The authors of the report warn that forces of opposition and resistance may bring down the whole system. The report argues that the widening global divide will likely lead to a "resurgence of not only anti-capitalist ideologies ... but also to populism and the revival of Marxism" (2007: 3). The Ministry is particularly concerned that the widening divide will spawn a mass global justice movement, a broad antiglobalization movement that could unite the most diverse forces of resistance and opposition to neoliberal globalization, threatening the entire system. Although the meaning of this movement and the threat that it presents to the guardians of the new world order are subject to debate (see chapters in this volume by Chomsky, Teivainen, Petras, and

Veltmeyer), there is no question that it might very well scuttle the best-laid plans of the new world order architects for imperial rule. From the ruling class perspective of these architects the antiglobalization movement has to manage, if not controlled or manipulated.

One conclusion that can be drawn from this report and several studies in this volume is that all is not well with the world order decreed and created by the forces of "freedom" (economic and political). Efforts of powerful individuals and groups, acting in their self-interest, to create a system in which these interests can be freed from any and all constraint in the public interest, have backfired. The entire process is economically dysfunctional and politically unsustainable. The carefully constructed mask placed over the free play of class interests, greed and the hubris of the rich and the powerful by the idea of "globalization" has been seen through and forcibly removed in a growing antiglobalization movement of a globalized citizenry.

In this context the opposed forces of globalization and antiglobalization are engaged in what amounts to what Geoffrey Faux (2006) terms a "global class war." How this war might end and the struggle between opposing forces might proceed is unclear. It is too early to tell, requiring a much closer look and further study into these forces as they engage each other in diverse theatres of struggle across the world.

However, we have enough information and clear indications about the general form that this struggle will take. On the one side will be found what John Pilger terms the "new rulers of the world," the "transnational capitalist class" as Sklair (2000) and Walden Bello in this volume have it, a broad array of groups and individuals organized within a growing global "middle class," many of whom are clear (and not so clear in some cases) beneficiaries of neoliberal policies and some of whom are in a position to "service" the interests of the dominant class. Ranged in support of globalization in its current or revised form is also a large part of what Hardt and Negri (2004) have termed "the multitude"—workers and producers all over the world who for one or more reasons or another, while not active participants in the struggle or directly supportive of the "forces of freedom," or even "on side," are nevertheless not opposed, willing to accept whatever crumbs or "poverty alleviation funds" might come their way.

On the other side of a deeply entrenched economic and rapidly emerging political divide are what we might term the "popular classes"—workers in numerous and diverse forms, both waged and self-employed; laboring in the factories, offices, the streets and the countryside in countries all over the world, many of them transnationalized, uprooted and on the move; small and medium-sized independent and peasant producers; and the urban poor, a large and growing underclass whose labor is surplus to the requirements of capital and who increasingly inhabit what Mike Davis (2006) aptly terms "planetary slums."

In the context of this class struggle, globalization remains the rallying point for both the forces of "freedom" that would advance and consolidate it, and the forces of resistance that are mounting but as yet with numerous divisions and no concerted strategy for bringing about "another world."

Bibliography

Agacino, R. and R. Gonzalo (1995), "La industria Chilena despues del ajuste: evaluación y perspectives," *Cambio Tecnológico y mercado de Trabajo, Santiago,* ILO, Office for Latin America and the Caribbean.

Aglietta, M. (1979), *Theory of Capitalist Regulation,* London, New Left Books.

Aglietta, M. (1982), "World capitalism in the 1980s," *New Left Review,* 136 (November – December): 5–41.

Agüero, F. and J. Stark (eds) (1998), *Fault Lines of Democracy in Post-Transition Latin America,* Boulder, CO, Lynne Rienner.

Aguiton, C. and D. Cardon (2005), *Le Forum et le Réseau. Une analyse des modes de gouvernement des forums sociaux.* Communication pour le colloque Cultures et pratiques participatives: une perspective comparative, Paris, LAIOS/AFSP.

Alexander, N. (2002), "The US on the world stage: reshaping development, finance, and trade initiatives," Citizens' Network on Essential Services, Washington, October.

Alimir, O. (1994), "Distribución del ingreso e incidencia de la pobreza a lo largo del ajuste," *Revista de CEPAL,* 52 (Abril): 7–32.

Amin, S. (1994), *Re-Reading the Postwar Period,* New York, Monthly Review Press.

Amin, S. (1997), *Capitalism in the Age of Globalization,* London, Zed Books.

Amin, S. and B. Founou-Tchuigoua (2002), *Integrated Programmes of Third World Forum for Calendar Years 2002, 2003, and 2004,* Dakar, Document of Third World Forum.

Anand, S. and A. Sen (2000), "The income component of the human development index," *Journal of Human Development,* 1 (1): 17–23.

Anderson, P. (2000), "Renewals," *New Left Review* (II), 1 (January – February): 5–24.

Anderson, P. (2001), "Testing formula two," *New Left Review* (II), 8 (March – April): 5–22.

Angell, M. (2000), "Pockets of poverty," in J. Cohen and J. Rogers (eds), *Is Inequality Bad for Our Health?* Boston, MA, Beacon Press.

AP—Japan finance official (1999), "Global economy 'inherently unstable,'" *The Ottawa Citizen,* 20 March.

Arellano, S. and J. Petras (1997), "Non-governmental organizations in Bolivia," in H. Veltmeyer and J. Petras (eds), *Neoliberalism and Class Conflict in Latin America,* London, Macmillan.

Arrida P.J. (1995), "Economía y sindicalismo. Significado económico del marco de relaciones laborales Salvadoreño," *ECA,* 551.

Arrighi, G. (1994), *The Long 20th Century: Money, Power and the Origins of Our Times*, London, Verso.

Arrighi, G. (2003), "Lineages of empire," in G. Balakrishnan (ed.), *Debating Empire*, London, Verso.

Arrighi, G., T. Hopkins and I. Wallerstein (1989), *Antisystemic Movements*, London, Verso.

Arrighi, G. and B. Silver (2001), *Caos e governabilidade*, Rio de Janeiro, Contraponto.

Assies, W. *et al.* (eds) (1990), *Structures of Power, Movements of Resistance: An Introduction to the Theories of Urban Movements in Latin America*, Amsterdam, Centre for Latin American Research and Documentation.

Aulakh, P. and M. Schecter (2000), *Rethinking Globalizations: From Corporate Transnationalism to Local Interventions*, New York, St. Martin's Press.

Bach, R. (1999), *Campaigning for Change: Reinventing NAFTA to Serve Migrant Communities*, Latin American Program Working Paper series, No. 248. Woodrow Wilson Center.

Bairoch, P. (1996), "Globalization myths and realities: One century of external trade and foreign investment," in R. Boyer and D. Drache (eds), *States Against Markets: The Limits of Globalization*, London, Routledge.

Bardhan, P. (1997), *The Role of Governance in Economic Development*, Paris, OECD, Development Centre.

Batra, G., D. Kaufmann and A.H.W. Stone (2003), *Investment Climate Around the World: Voices of the Firms from the World Business Environment Survey*, Washington DC, World Bank.

Bauer, P.T. (1971), *Dissent on Development: Studies and Debates in Development Economics*, London, Weidenfeld and Nicolson.

Bebbington, A. *et al.* (2006), *The Search for Empowerment: Social Capital as Idea and Practice at the World Bank*, Bloomfield CJ, Kumarian Press.

Bello, W. (2002), *Deglobalization: Ideas for a New World Economy*, London, Zed Books.

Bello, W. (2005), *Dilemmas of Domination: The Unmaking of the American Empire*, New York, Metropolitan Books.

Benasayag, M. and D. Sztulwark (2000), *Política y situación: de la potencia al contrapoder*, Buenos Aires: Ediciones Mano en Mano.

Bengoa, J. (2000), *La emergencia indígena en América Latina*, México/Santiago, Fondo de Cultura Económico.

Berenson, A. (2006), "The other legacy of Enron," *New York Times*, Week in Review (29 May), section 4: 1, 4.

Berger, Mark T. (2004), "After the Third World? History, destiny and the fate of Third Worldism," *Third World Quarterly*, 24 (1): 9–39.

Bergsten, F. (2000), "Towards a tripartite world," *The Economist*, 15–21 July: 20–22.

Bieler, A. and A.D. Morton (eds) (2001), *Social Forces in the Making of the New Europe: The Restructuring of European Social Relations in the Global Political Economy*, New York, Palgrave.

Bienefeld, M. (1995), "Assessing current development trends: Reflections on Keith Griffin's 'Global Prospects for Development and Human Security,'" *Canadian Journal of Development Studies*, XVI (3): 371–84.

Bienefeld, M. (1996), "Is a strong national economy a utopian goal at the end of the twentieth century?" in R. Boyer and D. Drache (eds), *States Against Markets: The Limits of Globalization*, London, Routledge.

Blair, H. (1995), "Assessing democratic decentralization," A CDIE Concept Paper, Washington DC, USAID.

Blair, H. (1997), "Democratic local governance in Bolivia," CDIE Impact Evaluation, No. 3, Washington DC, USAID.

Blair, T. (2001), "Travel ban to block 'anarchists,'" *Guardian* (London), 18 June.

Boisier, S. *et al.* (1992), *La descentralización: el eslabón perdido de la cadena transformación productiva con equidad y sustentabilidad*, Santiago, Cuadernos de CEPAL.

Bond, P. (2002a), *Unsustainable South Africa*, London, Merlin Press.

Bond, P. (2002b), *Fanon's Warning: A Civil Society Reader on the New Partnership for Africa's Development*, Trenton NJ, Africa World Press.

Booker, S. and W. Minter (2001), "Global Apartheid," *The Nation*, 9 July.

Boom, G. and A. Mercado (eds) (1990), *Automatización flexible en la industria*, Mexico, Editorial Limusa Noriega.

Booth, K. (1991), "Security in anarchy: Utopian realism in theory and practice," *International Affairs*, 67 (3).

Bordegaray, S. and T. Flores (eds) (2001), *El Foro Social Mundial desde los desocupados*, Buenos Aires, MTD Editora (de la Matanza).

Borón, A. (1995), *State, Capitalism, and Democracy in Latin America*, Boulder and London, Lynne Rienner Publishers.

Borón, A. (2001), "El nuevo orden imperial y como desmontarlo," in J. Seoane and E. Taddei (eds), *Resistencias Mundiales. De Seattle a Porto Alegre*, Buenos Aires, CLACSO.

Bounds, A. (2001), "Costly lessons of Central America bank reform," *Financial Times*, 11 July.

Bowles, P. and B. MacLean (1996), "Regional blocs: Will East Asia be next?" *Cambridge Journal of Economics*, 20: 433–55.

Bowles, P. (2000), "Regionalism and development after (?) the global financial crisis," *New Political Economy*, 5 (3).

Bowles, P. (2007), *Capitalism*, London, Pearson Books.

Boyer, R. (1989), *La teoría de la regulación: un análisis crítico*, Buenos Aires, Ed. Humanitas.

Boyer, R. and D. Drache (eds) (1996), *States Against Markets: The Limits of Globalization*, London, Routledge.

Brennan, T. (2001), "Cosmopolitanism and internationalism," *New Left Review*, II (7), January – February: 75–84.

Brenner, R. (2000a), "The boom and the bubble," *New Left Review*, II (6): 5 –44.

Brenner, R. (2000b), *The Economics of Global Turbulence*, London, Verso.

Brenner, R. (2002), *The Boom and the Bubble*, New York, Verso.

Brenner, R. (2003), "Towards the precipice," *London Review of Books*, 6 February.

Brown, F. and L. Dominguez (1989), "Nuevas tecnologias en la industria maquiladora de exportación," *Comercio Exterior* (Mexico), 39 (3), Marzo.

Bryan, D. (1995), *The Chase Across the Globe: International Accumulation and the Contradictions for Nation States*, Boulder CO, Westview Press.

Bullard, N. (2002), "The puppet master shows his hand," *Focus on Trade*, April 2002 (http://focusweb.prg/popups/articleswindow.php?id=41).

Bulmer-Thomas, V. (1996), *The Economic Model in Latin America and its Impact on Income Distribution and Poverty*, New York, St. Martin's Press.

Bultman, I. *et al.* (eds) (1995), *¿Democracia sin movimiento social?* Caracas, Editorial Nueva Sociedad.

Burbach, R. (1994), "Roots of the postmodern rebellion in Chiapas," *New Left Review*, 205: 113–25.

Burbach, R. and W. Robinson (1999), "Globalization as Epochal Shift," *Science & Society*, 63 (1).

Business Week (2004), "Japan's joyride on China's coattails," 1 March.

Calderón, F. (1995), *Movimientos sociales y política*, Mexico, Siglo XXI.

Calderón, F. and E. Jelín (1987), *Clases y movimientos sociales en América Latina. Perspectivas y realidades*, Buenos Aires, Cuadernos CEDES.

Cammack, P. (1997), *Capitalism and Democracy in the Third World*, Leicester, Leicester University Press.

Carriles, L. (2001), "Contratos sin riesgo y territorio a transnacionales," *Milenio*, 222 (17 December).

Castañeda, J. (1993), *Utopia Unarmed*, New York, Vintage Books.

Castells, M. (1983), *The City and the Grassroots: A Cross-Cultural Theory of Urban Social Movements*, Berkeley CA, University of California Press.

Castells, M. (2001), *The Internet Galaxy*, Oxford, Oxford University Press.

Castells, M. (2005), "The rise of the Fourth World," in D. Held and A. McGrew (eds), *The Global Transformations Reader* (2nd edition), Cambridge, Polity Press.

CEPAL (1994), *Panorama Social*, Santiago, CEPAL.

CEPAL (1998), "Progresos realizados en la privatización de los servicios públicos relacionados con el agua: reseña por países de México, América Central y el Caribe" (LC/R. 1697; restricted document).

CEPAL—Comisión Ecónomica de America Latina y el Caribe (1991), *Internacionalización y regionalización de la economia mundial: sus consequencias para Latina America*, LC/L 640, September 3.

Chalmers, J. (2000), *Blowback: The Costs and Consequences of American Empire*, New York, Metropolitan Books.

Chan, Y.P. (2001), "Democracy or bust? The development dilemma," *Harvard International Review*, Fall, XXIII (3).

Chomsky, N. (1998), *Neoliberalism and Global Order: Doctrine and Reality*, New York, Seven Stories Press.

Chomthongdi, J. Chai (2000), "The IMF's Asian legacy," in *Prague 2000: Why We Need to Decommission the IMF and the World Bank*, Bangkok, Focus on the Global South.

Chortareas, G. and T. Pelagides (2004), "Trade flows: a facet of regionalism or globalization?" *Cambridge Journal of Economics*, 28 (2), March: 253–72.

Chossudovsky, M. (1997), *The Globalization of Poverty: Impacts of IMF and World Bank Reforms*, Zed Books and Third World Network.

Clark, M. (1977), *Antonio Gramsci and the Revolution that Failed*, Harvard, CT, Yale University Press.

Clary, I. (1998), "US Treasury Chief proposes global financial reforms," *Reuters*, 1 October.

Cockburn, A. and J. St. Clair (2000), *Five Days That Shook the World: Seattle and Beyond*, London, Verso.

Cohen, J. and J. Rogers (2000), *Is Inequality Bad for Our Health?* Boston MA, Beacon Press.

Colás, A. (2003), "The power of representation: democratic politics and global governance," in D. Armstrong, T. Farrell and B. Maiguashca (eds), *Governance and Resistance in World Politics*, Cambridge, Cambridge University Press.

Colectivo Situaciones (2001a), "Conversaciones con el MTD en Solano," *Situaciones 4*, Deciembre.

Colectivo Situaciones (2001b), *Contrapoder: una introducción*, Buenos Aires, Ediciones de Mano en Mano.

Conable Jr, B.B., R.S. Belous, S.D. Stern, and N.C. Kent, (eds) (1995), *Foreign Assistance in a Time of Constraints*, Washington DC, National Planning Association.

Cooper, R. (2000a), "The Post-modern State, Reordering the World; the Long Term Implications of September 11," Hoxton, London,The Foreign Policy Centre.

Cooper, R. (2000b), "The new liberal imperialism," *Guardian*, 7 April.

Cornia, A., R. Jolly and F. Stewart (eds) (1987) *Adjustment with a Human Face*, Oxford, Oxford University Press.

Coronil, F. and J. Skurski (1991), "Dismembering and remembering the nation: The wemantics of political violence in Venezuela," *Comparative Studies in Society and History*, 33 (2), April: 288–337.

Corpwatch (2001), *Holding Corporations Accountable*, 5 November, http://www.corpwatch.org (accessed 2 June 2006).

Cox, A. and J. Healey (2000), *European Development Cooperation and the Poor*, London, Macmillan.

Cox, R.W. (1981), "Social forces, states and world orders: Beyond international relations theory," *Millennium: Journal of International Studies*, 10 (2): 126–55.

Cox, R.W. (1987), *Production, Power and World Order: Social Forces in the Making of History*, New York, Columbia University Press.

Cox, R. W. (1992), "Global perestroika," in R. Miliband and L. Panitch (eds), *The Socialist Register: New World Order?* Merlin Press.

Cox, R.W. (1996a), "The global political economy and social choice," in Cox, with T.J. Sinclair, *Approaches to World Order*, Cambridge, Cambridge University Press.

Cox, R.W. (1996b), "Production, power and world order" in Cox with Sinclair, *Approaches to World Order*, Cambridge, Cambridge University Press.

Cox, R.W. (ed.) (1997), *The New Realism: Perspectives on Multilateralism and World Order*, London, Macmillan.

Cox, R.W. (1999), "Civil society at the turn of the Millennium. Prospects for an alternative world order," *Review of International Studies*, 25: 3–28.

Cox, R.W. with T.J. Sinclair (1996), *Approaches to World Order*, Cambridge, Cambridge University Press.

Crotty, J. (2002), "Why there is chronic excess capacity," *Challenge*, November – December: 24.

Crouch, C. and A. Pizzorno (1978), *Resurgence of Class Conflict in Western Europe Since 1968*, London, Holmes & Meier.

Crozier, M, S.P. Huntington and J. Watanuki (1975), *The Crisis of Democracy: Report on the Governability of Democracies to the Trilateral Commission*, New York, New York University Press.

Cumings, B. (1993), "Rimspeak; or the discourse of the 'Pacific Rim'," in A. Dirlik (ed.), *What's In a Rim? Critical Perspectives on the Pacific Region Idea*, Boulder CO, Westview Press.

Dasgupta, B. (1998), *Structural Adjustment, Global Trade, and the New Political Economy of Development*, London, Zed Books.

Davis, M. (1984), "The political economy of late-imperial America," *New Left Review*, 143, January – February: 6–38.

Davis, M. (2006), *Planet of Slums*, London, Verso.

De Ferranti, D., G. Perry, F. Ferreira, and M. Walton, (2003), *Inequality in Latin America and the Caribbean: Breaking with History?* Washington DC, World Bank.

De Long, J. B. (2001), "Globalization" and "Neoliberalism," www.j-bradford-delong.net/ (accessed 31 May).

De Palma, A. (1999), "NAFTA: An interim report on partial progress and some problems," *Wall Street Journal*, 8 March.

De Tray, D. (2006), "Comments at Luncheon sponsored by the Carnegie Endowment for International Peace," Washington DC, 21 April.

Deffeyes, K.S. (2001), *Hubbert's Peak: the Impeding World Oil Shortage*, Princeton NJ, Princeton University Press.

Desai, M. (2004), *Marx's Revenge: The Resurgence of Capitalism and the Death of Statist Socialism*, London, Verso.

Desai, M., J. Petras and H. Veltmeyer, R. Scrire, L. Sklair, G. Sen, and D. Lal (2000), Essays in *Cambridge Review of International Affairs*, XIV (1), Autumn – Winter.

Diamond, L., J. Linz, and S.M. Lipset (eds) (1999), *Democracy in Developing Countries: Latin America*, Boulder CO, Lynne Rienner.

Díaz-Polanco, H. (2002), "Renovación de la crítica en la era de la globalización," *Memoria*, 156.

Dicken, P. (1992), *Global Shift: The Internationalization of Economic Activity*, New York, Guilford Press.

Dominguez, J. and A. Lowenthal, (eds) (1996), *Constructing Democratic Governance*, Baltimore MD: John Hopkins University Press.

Dominguez, J. and A. Lowenthal (1996), *Constructing Democratic Governance in Latin America and the Caribbean in the 90s*, Baltimore MD, John Hopkins University Press.

Doremus, P. *et al.* (1998), *The Myth of the Global Corporation*, Princeton NJ, Princeton University Press.

Drake, P. W. (1994), "Introduction. The political rconomy of foreign advisors and lenders in Latin America," in Paul W. Drake (ed.), *Money Doctors, Foreign*

Debts, and Economic Reforms in Latin America from the 1890s to the Present, Wilmington DE, Scholarly Resources.

Drucker, P. (1993). *Post-Capitalist Society*, New York, HarperCollins.

Du Boff, R. and E. Herman (1997), "A critique of Tabb on globalization," *Monthly Review*, 49 (6): 27–35.

Durbin, A. (1997), *Joint NGO Statement On The Multilateral Agreement On Investment (MAI)*, Revised: 7 November 1997, http://www.hartford-hwp.com/archives/25/037.html.

Eckstein, S. (2000), "Resistance and reform: power to the people?" *DRCLAS News*, Winter.

ECLAC (1990), *Productive Transformation with Equity*, Santiago, Chile.

ECLAC (1996), *Economic Survey of Latin America and the Caribbean 1994–1995*, Santiago, ECLAC.

ECLAC (1998), *Social Dimensions of Economic Development and Productivity: Inequality and Social Performance*, Santiago, ECLAC.

ECLAC—United Nations Economic Commission for Latin America and the Caribbean (2001), *Preliminary Overview of the Economies of Latin America and the Caribbean*, Santiago, ECLAC.

Economist (2005), "How to protect Latin American democracy", editorial, 11 June.

Ekins, P. and M. Max-Neef (eds) (1992), *Real-Life Economics: Understanding Wealth Creation*, London, Routledge.

Ellner, S. (2001), "The radical potential of Chavismo in Venezuela: The first year and a half in power," *Latin American Perspectives*, 28 (5): 5–32.

Escobar, A. (1995), *Encountering Development: The Making and the Unmaking of the Third World*, Princeton NJ, Princeton University Press.

Escobar, A. and S. Alvarez (eds) (1992), *The Making of Social Movements in Latin America: Identity, Strategy, and Democracy*, Boulder CO, Westview Press.

Esteva, G. and M. Suri Prakash (1998), *Grassroots Post-Modernism*, London, Zed Books.

Eurostep (1998), "Commission free trade area arrangement studies are not Positive on FTAs with the ACP," 20 November.

Fajnzylber F. (1983), "Growth and equity via austerity and competitiveness," *The Annals*, 505 (1): 80–91.

Falk, R. (2000), "The quest for human governance in an era of globalization," in D. Kalb, *et al.* (ed.), *The End of Globalization, Bringing Society back In*, Lanhan, Rowland & Littlefield.

Faux, G. (2006), *The Global Class War*, Hoboken NJ, Wiley.

Feldstein, M. and C. Horioka (1980), "Domestic savings and international capital flows," *Economic Journal*, June: 314–29.

Ferguson, N. (2001), "Globalization in historical perspective: The political dimension," contribution to panel discussion, 5 May, mimeograph, in M.D. Bordo, A.M. Taylor and J.G. Williamson (eds), *Globalization in Historical Perspective*, Chicago IL, The University of Chicago Press, 2003.

Ferriol Muruaga, A. (2000), "External opening, labor market and inequality of labor incomes," *Working Paper*, Series 1, New York: New School University, Center for Economic Policy Analysis (CEPA), February.

Ferriol, A. (1998), "La reforma económica en Cuba en los 90 [Economic Reform in Cuba in the 1990s]," *Pensamiento Propio*, 7: 5–24.

Filgueira, F. and J. Papadópulos (1997), "Putting conservatism to good use? Long crisis and vetoed alternatives in Uruguay," in D. A. Chalmers *et al.* (eds), *The New Politics of Inequality in Latin America*, New York, Oxford University Press.

Fischer, S. (1999), "On the need for an international lender of last resort," Paper delivered at IEA, 3 January, IMF website, http://www.imf.org/external/np/speeches/1999/010399.htm (accessed 4 March 2007).

Fligstein, N. (2001), *The Architecture of Markets: An Economic Sociology of Twenty-first Century Capitalist Societies*, Princeton NJ, Princeton University Press.

Foster, J. B. (2002), "Monopoly capital and the new globalization," *Monthly Review*, 53: 1–16.

Foweraker, J. (1995), *Theorising Social Movements*, Boulder CO, Pluto Press.

Freire, P. (1970), *Pedagogy of the Oppressed*, Harmondsworth, Penguin Books.

Friedman, M. (1982), *Capitalism and Freedom*, Chicago IL, University of Chicago Press.

Fröbel, F., J. Heinrichs and O. Kreye (1980), *The New International Division of Labour. Structural Unemployment in Industrialised Countries and Industrialisation in Developing Countries*, Cambridge, Cambridge University Press.

FTAA (1998), *Summit Of The Americas: Fourth Trade Ministerial, San Jose, Costa Rica. March 19th, 1998: Joint Declaration,* http://www.ftaa-alca.org/EnglishVersion/costa_e.htm (accesed 5 January 2007).

Fukuyama, F. (2001), "The West has won," *The Guardian*, 11 October 2001.

G-24 (1999), Communique, 26 April.

Gachúz M., Juan C. (2000), *La Globalización de las Empresas Petroleras Multinacionales: Alternativas para Pemex*, Mexico, FCPS, UNAM.

Ganuza, E. and L. Taylor (1998), "Macroeconomic policy, poverty and equality in Latin America and the Caribbean," Working Papers on Globalization, Labor Markets and Social Policy, *Working Paper*, No. 6, New York, Center for Economic Policy Analysis, New School University, March.

Gasper, D. (2002), *Is Sen's Capability Approach an Adequate Basis for Considering Human Development?* The Hague, Institute of Social Studies, February.

Gazier, B. (1996), "Implicites et incompletes: les théories économiques de l'exclusion," in Serge Paugam, (ed.), *L'exclusion. L'Etat des savoirs*, Paris, Ed. La Découverte.

George, S. (1994), *Faith and Credit: the World Bank's Secular Empire*, Boulder CO, Westview Press.

George, S. (1999), *The Lugano Report: On Preserving Capitalism in the 21st Century*, London, Pluto Press.

Germain, R. (1997), *The International Organisation of Credit: States and Global Finance in the World Economy*, Cambridge, Cambridge University Press.

Germain, R. (ed.) (2000), *Globalisation and Its Critics: Perspectives from Political Economy*, London, Macmillan.

Giddens, A. (1990), *The Consequences of Modernity*, Cambridge, Polity Press.

Giddens, A. (1995), *Beyond Left and Right: The Future of Radical Politics*, Cambridge, Polity Press.

Gill, H.S. (1991), *The NAFTA Problematique and the Challenges for the Caribbean Community*, Miami, North-South Center.

Gill, S. (1990), *American Hegemony and the Trilateral Commission*, Cambridge, Cambridge University Press.

Gill, S. (2000), "Toward a postmodern prince? The battle in Seattle as a moment in the New Politics of Resistance," *Millennium: Journal of International Studies*, 29 (1): 131–40.

Gill, S. (2003), *Power and Resistance in the New World* Order, Basingstoke, Palgrave Macmillan.

Gill, S. (ed.) (1993), *Gramsci, Historical Materialism and International Relations*, Cambridge, Cambridge University Press.

Gill, S. and D. Law (1989), "Global hegemony and the structural power of capital," *International Studies Quarterly*, 33 (4): 475–99.

Gills, B.K., J. Rocamora and R. Wilson (eds) (1993), *Low Intensity Democracy: Political Power in the New World Order*, Pluto Press.

Gills, B.K. (ed.) (2000), *Globalisation and the Politics of Resistance*, London, Macmillan.

Gilpin, R. (1987), *The Political Economy of International Relations*, Princeton NJ, Princeton University Press.

Girvan, N. (1998) "Cuba: structural adjustment with a human face?" *Pensamiento Propio*, 7: 25–30.

Glynn, A., A. Hughes, A. Lipietz and A. Singh (1990), "The rise and fall of the Golden Age," in S. Marglin and J. Schor (eds), *The Golden Age of Capitalism: Re-interpreting the Post-War Experience*, Oxford, Clarendon Press.

Goldsmith, E. (1999), "Is free trade working for everyone?" *Prospect Magazine*, 47, December.

Golinger, G. (2004), *The Adaptable US Intervention Machine in Venezuela*, Communication and Information Ministry, Bolivarian Government, November.

Gonzales, A. (1995), *The Impact of NAFTA on Caribbean Industry: Trade and Investment Effects*. Unpublished study prepared for UNIDO, 21 October.

González Casanova, P. (1999), *La Explotación Global*, Mexico, CEIICH, UNAM.

Goodwin, N. (2001), "Civil economy and civilized economics: Essentials for sustainable development," *Working Paper*, No. 01-01, Boston MA: Tufts University, Global Development and Environment Institute.

Gordon, R. (1999a), "Has the new economy rendered the productivity slowdown obsolete," http://faculty-web.at.nwu.edu/education/gordon/researchhome.htm.

Gordon, R. (1999b), "U.S. economic growth since 1870: One big wave?" *The American Economic Review*, 123–8.

Gramsci, A. (1971), *Selections from the Prison Notebooks*, Quintin Hoare (ed.), London, Lawrence and Wishart.

Gramsci, A. (1977), *Selections from Political Writings, 1910–1920*, Quintin Hoare (ed.), London, Lawrence and Wishart.

Gramsci, A. (1994), "Letter to Tatiana Schucht" (25 April 1927), in Frank Rosengarten (ed.), *Letters from Prison*, Vol. 1, New York, Columbia University Press.

Greenspan, A. (2004), Remarks on *"Globalization and Innovation"* at the Conference on Bank Structure and Competition, sponsored by the Federal Reserve Bank of Chicago, Chicago, Illinois, 6 May.

Griffin, K. (1995), "Global prospects for development and human security," *Canadian Journal of Development Studies*, XVI (3): 359–70.

Grootaert, C. (1998), "Social capital: The missing link?" *Social Capital Initiative Working Paper*, No. 3. Washington, DC: The World Bank Social Development Family Environmentally and Socially Sustainable Development Network.

Gunnell, B. and D. Timms (eds) (2000), *After Seattle: Globalisation and Its Discontents*, Catalyst.

Halimi, S. (1998), "Liberal dogma shipwrecked," *Guardian Weekly*, 159 (17); 25 October.

Haq, M. (1994), "New imperatives of human security: Barbara Ward Lecture," *Development*, 2.

Hardt, M. (2002), "Porto Alegre: Today's Bandung?" *New Left Review*, 14, March – April: 114.

Hardt, R. and A. Negri (2000), *Empire*, Cambridge MA, Harvard University Press.

Hardt, M. and A. Negri (2004), *Multitude: War and Democracy in the Age of Empire*, New York, The Penguin Press.

Harriss, J. (2001), *Depoliticising Development. The World Bank and Social Capital*, New Delhi, Left Word Books.

Harrod, J. (1987), *Power, Production and the Unprotected Worker*, New York, Columbia University Press.

Harvey, D. (2003), "The new imperialism: Accumulation by dispossession," in L. Panitch and C. Leys (eds), *The New Imperial Challenge* (Socialist Register, 2003), New York, Monthly Review.

Harvey, D. (2004), "Neoliberalism as creative destruction," mimeograph.

Hawkins, J. J. (1991), "Understanding the failure of IMF reform: The Zambian case," *World Development*, 19 (7): 839–49.

Hayden, R. (2002), "Dictatorships of virtue? States, NGOs and the Imposition of Democratic Values," *Harvard International Review*, 24 (2): 56–61.

Hayter, T. (1971), *Aid as Imperialism*, Harmondsworth, Penguin Books.

Held, D. (1995), *Democracy and Global Order: From the Modern State to Cosmopolitan Governance*, Stanford, Stanford University Press.

Held, D. (2004), *Global Covenant: the Social Democratic Alternative to the Washington Consensus*, Cambridge, Polity Press.

Held, D. and A. McGrew (2002), *Globalization and Anti-Globalization*, Cambridge, Polity Press.

Held, D. *et al.* (eds) (1999), *Global Transformations: Politics, Economics and Culture*, Stanford, Stanford University Press.

Helleiner, E. (1994), *States and the Re-emergence of Global Finance: From Bretton Woods to the 1990s*, Ithaca NY, Cornell University Press.

Helleiner, G.K. (1992), "The IMF, the World Bank and Africa's adjustment and external debt problems: An unofficial view," *World Development*, 20 (6): 779–92.

Hellinger, D. (1991), *Venezuela: Tarnished Democracy*, Boulder CO, Westview Press.

Helliwell, J. (1998), *How Much Do National Borders Matter?* Washington DC, Brookings Institution.

Hellman, J.H. (1995), "The riddle of new social movements: Who they are and what they do," in S. Halebsky and R. L. Harris (eds), *Capital, Power and Inequality in Latin America*, Boulder CO, Westview Press.

Herrera, G. (1995), "Tendencias del cambio tecnológico en la industria Chilena," *Economía y Trabajo en Chile, No. 5 Inf, 1994–1995*, Santiago, ILO—Programa de Economía del Trabajo (PET): 77–94.

Higgott, R. (1998), "The Asian economic crisis: A study in the politics of resentment," *New Political Economy*, 3 (3), November: 333–55.

Higgott, R. and R. Stubbs (1994), "Competing conceptions of economic regionalism: APEC versus EAEC in the Asia Pacific," *Review of International Political Economy*, 2 (2), Summer: 523.

Hirst, P. and G. Thompson (1996), *Globalization in Question*, Cambridge, Polity Press.

Ho-fung, H. (2006), "Rise of China and the global overaccumulation crisis," paper presented at the Global Division of the Annual Meeting of the Society for the Study of Social Problems, August 10–12, Montreal, Canada.

Hobson, J. and M. Ramesh (2002), "Globalization makes of states what states make of it: Between agency and structure in the state/globalization debate," New *Political Economy*, 7 (1): 5–22.

Hoffman, S. (2005), "Venezuela loans money to Ecuador," *Emerging Markets*, 2 August, http://www.emergingmarkets.org/article.asp?ArticleID=1016294&Cate goryID=198&PageMove=28.=.

Holloway, J. (2001), *Contrapoder: una introducción*, Buenos Aires, Ediciones de Mano en Mano.

Holm, H.-H. and G. Sorensen (eds) (1995), *Whose World Order? Uneven Globalization and the End of the Cold War*, Boulder CO, Westview Press.

Howard, M. and J. King (eds) (1976), *The Economics of Marx: Selected Readings*, Harmondsworth, Penguin Books.

Howell, J. and J. Pearce (2001), *Civil Society and Development: A Critical Exploration*, Boulder CO, Lynne Rienner.

Human Rights Watch, (2001), *Trading Away Rights*, April.

Huntington, S. (1996), *The Clash of Civilizations and the Remaking of the World Order*, New York, Simon & Schuster.

IDB (1991), *Economic and Social Progress in Latin America. 1991 Report*, Washington DC, IDB.

IDB—Interamerican Development Bank (1996), *Modernización del estado y fortalecimiento de la sociedad civil*, Washington DC, IDB.

ILO—International Labor Organization (1996), *World Employment 1996*, Geneva, ILO.

ILO—International Labor Organization (2001), *World Employment Report 2001: Life at Work in the Information Economy*, Geneva, ILO.

In Motion Magazine (2005), "Interview with Geraldo Fontes of the MST," 26 May, available at http://www.inmotionmagazine.com/global/gf_mst_int.html (accessed 12 March 2006).

Informe Latinobarómetro 2005 (2005), Santiago, Chile, Corporación Latinobarómetro, October.

International Forum on Globalization (2001), "Does globalization help the poor," San Francisco CA, August.

Jacques, M. (2004), "Face it: No one cares," *The Guardian*, 29 July.

Jameson, F. (2000), "Globalisation and political strategy," *New Left Review* II (4), July – August: 49–68.

Johnson, C. (2000), *Blowback*, New York, Metropolitan Books.

Jorgenson, D. and K. Stiroh (1999), "Information technology and growth," *American Economic Review*, 89 (2), May: 109–115.

Juhasz, A. (2006), *The Bush Agenda: Invading the World, One Economy at a Time*, New York, HarperCollins Publishers.

Kamat, S. (2003), "NGOs and the New Democracy: The False Saviours of International Development," *Harvard International Review*, 25 (1): 22 March: 65–9.

Kapstein, E. (1996), "Workers and the world economy: Breaking the postwar bargain," *Foreign Affairs*, 75 (3), May – June: 11.

Karliner, J. (1999), *A Perilous Partnership: The UNDP's Flirtation With Corporate Collaboration*, Oakland, CA, TRAC-Transnational Resource and Action Center.

Kawachi, I., B.P. Kennedy and R.G. Wilkinson (eds) (1999), *The Society and Population Health Reader*, Vol. I, New York, The New Press.

Keck, M.E. and K. Sikkink (1998), *Activists Beyond Frontiers*, Ithaca NY: Cornell University Press.

Kellner, D. (2003). "Globalization, technopolitics and revolution," in J. Foran (ed.), *The Future of Revolutions. Rethinking Radical Change in the Age of Globalization*, London and New York, Zed Books.

Kenen, P. (1994), *Managing the World Economy*, Washington DC, Institute for International Economics.

Keohane, R.O. and J.S. Nye (1989), *Power and Independence*, New York, HarperCollins.

Keohane, R. and J. Nye (2000), "Globalization: What's new? What's not? (And so what?)," *Foreign Policy*, 118, Spring: 104–19.

Khagram, S., J.V. Riker and K. Sikkink (2004), "From Santiago to Seattle: Transnational advocacy groups restructuring world politics," in Khagram *et al.* (eds), *Restructuring World Politics. Transnational Social Movements, Networks and Norms*, Minneapolis MN, University of Minnesota Press.

Khor, M. (1995), *States of Disarray: The Social Effects of Globalization*, Geneva, United Nations Research Institute for Social Development.

Kiely, R. (2000), "Review of global transformations: Politics, economics and culture," *The Journal of Development Studies*, 36 (4), April: 182–98.

Klare, M. (2001), *Resource Wars*, New York, Metopolitan Books.

Klein, N. (2000), *No Logo. Taking Aim at the Brand Bullies*, Flamingo.

Klein, N. (2001), "May Day's lessons for the rootless," *Guardian*, 3 May, http://www.guardian.co.uk/world/2001/may/03/mayday.politics.

Kolko, G. (1974), *Políticas de Guerra*, Barcelona, Ediciones Grijalbo.

Kolko, G. and J. Kolko (1972), *The Limits of Power: The World and United States Foreign Policy, 1945–1954*, New York, Harper & Row.

Korten, D. (1995), *When Corporations Rule the World*, West Hartford CT, Kumarian Press.

Korten, D. (2001), *When Corporations Rule the World*, 2nd Ed., Bloomfield, Conn., Kumarian Press.

Kovic, C. (2003), "The struggle for liberation and reconciliation in Chiapas, Mexico. Las Abejas and the path of nonviolent resistance," *Latin American Perspectives*, 30 (3), May: 58–79.

Krueger, A., C. Michalopoulos, and V. Ruttan (1989), *Aid and Development*, Baltimore MD, Johns Hopkins University Press.

Krugman, P. (1998) "What happened to Asia?" Conference presentation, http://web.mit.edu/krugman/www/DISINTER. html.

Laibman, D. (1997), *Capitalist Macrodynamics*, London, Macmillan.

Langley, P. and M. Mellor (2002), "Economy, sustainability and sites of transformative space," *New Political Economy*, 7 (1): 49–65.

Latinobaro metro (2005), *Corporación Latinobarómetro*, Santiago, Chile, www.latinobarometro.org.

Laxer, G. (2001), "The movement that dare not speak its name: The return of left nationalism/internationalism," *Alternatives*, 26 (1): 1–32.

Laxer, G. (2003), "The defeat of the multilateral agreement on investment: National movements confront globalism," in G. Laxer and S. Halperin (eds), *Global Civil Society and Its Limits*, London, Palgrave Macmillan.

Laxer, G. (2004), *US Empire and Popular Sovereignty*, mimeograph.

Le Pere, G. and Tjonneland, E. (2005), "Which way SADC? Advancing co-operation and integration in Southern Africa," Occasional Paper No. 50, Midrand, Institute for Global Dialogue.

Lechner, N. (1988), Los patios interiores de la democracia: Subjetividad y política, Santiago, FLACSO.

Lechner, N. (1998), "The transformation of politics," in F. A. Felipe and J. Stark (eds) (1998), *Fault Lines of Democracy in Post-Transition Latin America*, Boulder, CO, Lynne Rienner.

Leite, J.C. (2003), "Internacional: O processo Fórum Social Mundial," *Teoria y Debate*, 15, 53, Mai.

León, O., S. Burch and E. Tamayo (2001), *Social Movements on the Net*, Quito, Agencia Latinoamericana de Información.

Levins, R. (2000), "Is capitalism a disease?" *Monthly Review*, 52 (4), September: 8–33.

Levitt, K. (2001), "Development in question," Keynote Address, Canadian Association for International Development Studies, Toronto, 31 May.

Lewis, P. (1999), "Beyond bananas: Globalization, size and viability in the Windwards Islands," paper presented at Department of Government Seminar on Globalisation and Small States, UWI, 13 January.

Leysens, A. and L. Thompson (2006), "The evolution of the global political economy," in P. J. McGowan, S. Cornelissen and P. Nel (eds), *Power, Wealth and*

Global Equity: an International Relations Textbook for Africa, Cape Town: UCT Press.

Lipietz, A. (1982), "Towards global Fordism," *New Left Review*, 132, March – April: 33–47.

Lipietz, A. (1986), "Behind the crisis: The tendency of the profit rate to fall. Considerations about some empirical French works," *Review of Radical Political Economics*, 18 (1–2): 13–32.

Lipietz, A. (1987), *Mirages and Miracles: The Crisis in Global Fordism*, London, Verso.

Lipsey, R., M. Blomstrom and E. Ramstetter (1995), *International Production in World Output*, NBER Working Paper No. 5385, Cambridge MA, NBER.

Lodoño, J. L. and M. Székely (2000), "Persistent poverty and excess inequality: Latin America, 1970–1995," *Journal of Applied Economics*, III (1), May: 93–134.

Lucas, K. (2002), "Ecuador: IMF wants future oil revenues to service debt, not health," *Inter Press Service*, May 29.

Lucas, R.E. (2000), "Some macroeconomics for the 21st century," *Journal of Economic Perspectives*, Winter, 14 (1): 159–68.

Lustig, N. (ed.) (1995), *Coping with Austerity: Poverty and Inequality in Latin America*, Washington DC, The Brookings Institution.

Luzzani, T. (2002), "El Viejo fantasma que agito a Latinoamerica: la democracia en guardia," Suplemento Zona, *Clarin*, April 21, http://www.clarin.com/suplementos/ zona/2002/04/21/z-00215.htm.

MacEwan, A. (1999), *Neo-Liberalism or Democracy? Economic Strategy, Markets, and Alternatives for the 21st Century*, London, Zed Books.

MacLean, B. (1999), "The transformation of international economic policy debate 1997–98," in B. MacLean (ed.), *Out Of Control*, Toronto, James Lorimer.

Maddison A. (2002), "Why there is chronic excess capacity," *Challenge*, November – December.

Magdoff, H. (1969), *The Age of Imperialism*, New York, Monthly Review Press.

Magdoff, H. (1978), *Imperialism: From the Colonial Age to the Present*, New York, Monthly Review Press.

Magdoff, H. (1992), *Globalization: To What End?* New York, Monthly Review Press.

Maier, C. (1977), "The politics of productivity: Foundations of American international economic policy after World War II," *International Organisation*, 31 (4): 607–33.

Mallaby, S. (2007), "Why globalization has stalled," *Washington Post*, 24 April: A17,http://www.washingtonpost.com/wp-dyn/content/article/2006/04/23/AR200 6042301016.html.

Mander J. and E. Goldsmith (eds) (1996), *The Case Against The Global Economy and for A Turn to the Local*, San Francisco CA, Sierra Club.

Manzo, J.L. (1996), *¿Qué Hacer con Pemex?* México, Grijalbo.

Marglin, S. and J. Schor (eds) (1990), *The Golden Age of Capitalism: Reinterpreting the Postwar Experience*, Oxford, Clarendon Press.

Márquez M.G. and C. Alvarez (1996), "Poverty and the labor market in Venezuela 1982–1985," in *Inter-American Development Bank*, 96–101, December, http:// www.iadb.org/sds/doc/pov96-101e.rtf.

Márquez, G. (1995), "Venezuela: Poverty and social policies in the 1980s," in N. Lustig (ed.), *Coping with Austerity: Poverty and Inequality in Latin America*, Washington DC, Brookings Institute.

Márquez, P. (1999), *The Street is My Home: Youth and Violence in Caracas*, Stanford University Press.

Martin, A. and G. Ross (1999), "In the line of fire: The Europeanisation of labour representation," in Andrew Martin and George Ross *et al.* (eds), *The Brave New World of European Labour: European Trade Unions at the Millennium*, Berghahn.

Marx, K. (1998), *Capital*, Vol. III, in K. Marx and F. Engels, *Collected Works*, Vol. 37, London, Lawrence and Wishart.

Maybarduk, P. (2004), "A people's health system: Venezuela works to bring healthcare to the excluded," *Multinational Monitor*, 25 (10), http://www.multinationalmonitor.org/mm2004/102004/maybarduk.html.

McGowan, P. (2006), "The southern African regional sub-system," in P.J. McGowan, S. Cornelissen and P. Nel (eds), *Power, Wealth and Global Equity: An International Relations Textbook for Africa*, Cape Town, UCT Press.

McGrew, T. (2001), "Review of 'globalization: A critical introduction' by Jan Aart Scholte," *New Political Economy*, 6 (2): 293–301.

McQuaig, L. (1998), *The Cult of Impotence: Selling the Myth of Powerlessness in the Global Economy*, Toronto, Viking.

McQueen, H. (2001), *The Essence of Capitalism: The Origins of Our Future*. Sydney, Hodder Headline.

McWhirter, C. and M. Gallagher (1998), "Contributions buy influence," *The Cincinnati Enquirer*, Sunday May 3, http://enquirer.com. contributions_buy. html.

Meiksins Wood, E. (1995), *Democracy Against Capitalism: Renewing Historical Materialism*, Cambridge, Cambridge University Press.

Meiksins Wood, E. (2003), *The Empire of Capital*, New Delhi, LeftWord Books.

Mekay, E. (2002), "Jeffrey Sachs to poor nations: Forget debt, spend on AIDS," *Inter Press Service*, August 2, http://www.commondreams.org/headlines02/0802-02.htm.

Melber, H. (2004), *South Africa and NEPAD – Quo Vadis?* Southern African Regional Poverty Network (SARPN), http://www.commondreams.org/headlines02/0802-02.htm.

Meltzer, A.H. (2000), "International financial institutions reform: report of the international financial institutions advisory commission," report to US Congress, Washington DC, March, http://www.eldis.org/go/display/?id=28196&type=Document.

Mitlin, D. (1998), "The NGO sector and its role in strengthening civil society and securing good governance," in A. Bernard, H. Helmich and P. Lehning, (eds), *Civil Society and International Development*, Paris, OECD Development Centre.

Mittelman, J. (2000), *The Globalization Syndrome: Transformation and Resistance*, Princeton NJ, Princeton University Press.

Mittelman, J. and N. Othman (eds) (2000), "Special issue: Capturing globalisation," *Third World Quarterly*, 21 (6), http://www.informaworld.com/smpp/title~content=g713448867~db=all.

Montero, A.P. (2005), "From democracy to development: The political economy of post-neoliberal reform in Latin America," *American Research Review*, 40 (2): 253–67.

Montesinos, M. and R. Góchez (1995), "Salarios y productividad," *ECA* 564, Octubre.

Moore, M. (2001), "Liberalisation? Don't reject it just yet," *The Guardian*, 26 February, http://icdasecretariat.tripod.com/article3.htm.

Morales, J. (1992), "La reestructuración industrial," in J. Morales (ed.), *La Reestructuración industrial en México*, Mexico, IIE, UNAM, Editorial Nuestro Tiempo.

Morales-Gómez, D. (ed.) (1999), *Transnational Social Policies: The New Development Challenges of Globalization*, London, Earthscan Publications.

Morley, S. (2000), "Efectos del crecimiento y las reformas ecónomicas sobre la distribución del ingreso en América Latina," *Revista de la CEPAL*, No. 71, Agosto: 23–41.

Morrison, D. (2005), "Hail the new economy," *Time Europe*, 29 January, available at http://www.time.com/time/europe/davos2000/davos3.html (22.12.2005).

Morton, A.D. (2001), 'La Resurrección del Maíz: Some aspects of globalisation, resistance and the Zapatista question," paper presented at the 42nd Annual Convention of the International Studies Association, Chicago, 20–24 February.

Morton, A.D. (2004), "The antiglobalization movement: Juggernaut or jalopy?" in Henry Veltmeyer (ed.) *Globalization and Antiglobalization*, Aldershot, Ashgate.

Mosley, P., J. Harrigan and J. Toye (1991), *Aid and Power: The World Bank and Policy-Based Lending*, London and New York, Routledge.

Munck, G. (1997), "Social movements and Latin America: Conceptual Issues and empirical applications," paper presented to the Latin American Studies Association, Guadalajara, 17–19 April.

Murphy, C. (1998), "Globalisation and governance: A historical perspective," in Roland Axtmann (ed.), *Globalisation and Europe: Theoretical and Empirical Investigations*, London, Pinter.

Naim, M. (1993), *Paper Tigers and Minotaurs: The Politics of Venezuela's Economic Reforms*, Washington DC, The Carnegie Endowment for International Peace.

Narayan, D. and P. Patesch (eds) (2002), *Voices of the Poor, Vol. 3*, Washington DC, World Bank.

Naughton, B. (ed.) (1997), *The China Circle: Economics and Technology in the PRC, Taiwan and Hong Kong*, Washington DC, Brookings Institution Press.

Navarro, V., J. Schmitt and J. Astudillo, (2004), "Is globalization undermining the welfare state?" *Cambridge Journal of Economics*, 28 (1): 133–52.

Negri, T. (2001), "Contrapoder," in *Colectivo Situaciones de Buenos Aires, Contrapoder: una introducción*, Buenos Aires, Ediciones de Mano en Mano. Also available at: http://contraelpoder.blogspot.com/2004/11/contrapoder-por-negri.html.

New York Times (2006), "Chief named for troubled GM unit," 31 May, http://www. nytimes.com/2006/05/31/automobiles/31auto.html?ex=1306728000&en=c9077 66a98eb821b&ei=5090&partner=rssuserland&emc=rss.

Ngomas, N. (2004), "SADC's mutual defence pact: A final move to a security community? *The Round Table*, 93 (375), July: 411–23.

Nudler, J. (2002), "Imperialismo para poner orden," *Página 12*, April 13, http://www.pagina12.com.ar/diario/economia/2-3956-2002-04-13.html.

Nuijten, M. and G. van der Haar (2000), "The Zapatistas of Chiapas: challenges and contradictions," *Revista Europea de Estudios Latinoamericanos y del Caribe*, 68, April 83–90, http://www.cedla.uva.nl/60_publications/PDF_files_publications/68RevistaEuropea/68Nuijten_VDHaar.pdf.

O'Brien, R., A-M. Goertz, J.A. Scholte, J., and M. Williams (2000), *Contesting Global Governance: Multilateral Economic Institutions and Global Social Movements*, New York, Cambridge University Press.

O'Brien, R. (2000). "Workers and world order: The tentative transformation of the international union movement," *Review of International Studies*, 26 (4): 533–55.

O'Donnell, G. (1994), "'Delegative democracy," *Journal of Democracy*, 5 (1): 55–69.

O'Hara, Philip A. (2006), "The contradictory dynamics of globalization," in B.N. Ghosh and H.M. Guven (eds), *Globalization and the Third World*, Basingstoke: Palgrave Macmillan.

O'Hara, P.A. (2003), "Recent changes to the IMF, WTO, and SPD: Emerging global mode of regulation in social structures of accumulation for long wave upswing?" *Review of International Political Economy* 10 (3), August: 481–519.

Ocampo, J.A. (2002), Presentation to the XIII Congress of the International Economic History Association, Buenos Aires, 22 July.

Ocampo, J.A. (2006), "Latin America and the world economy in the long twentieth century," in Jomo K.S. (ed.), *The Great Divergence: Hegemony, Uneven Development, and Global* Inequality, New York, Oxford University Press.

Ocampo, J., J.S. Jomo and S. Khan (eds) (2007), *Policy Matters: Economic and Social Policies to Sustain Equitable Development*, London UK, Orient Longman; New York, Zed; Penang Malaysia, Third World Network.

OECD (1997), *Final Report of the DAC Ad Hoc Working Group on Participatory Development and Good Governance*, Paris, OECD.

Ohmae, K. (1990), *The Borderless World*, London, Collins.

Ohmae, K. (1996), *The End of the Nation State: The Rise of Regional Economies*, Free Press.

Okonski, K. (2001), "Riots Inc. The business of protesting globalization," *The Wall Street Journal*, editorial page, August 14, http://www.nettime.org/Lists-Archives/nettime-l-0108/msg00143.html.

Ominami, C. (ed.) (1986), *La tercera revolución industrial, impactos internacionales el actual viraje tecnológico*, Mexico, RIAL-Anuario-Grupo Editorial Latinoamericano.

Ostry, S. (1990), *Government and Corporations in a Shrinking World: Trade and Innovation Policies in the US, Europe and Japan*, New York, Council on Foreign Relations.

Ottaway, M. (2003), *Democracy Challenged: The Rise of Semi-Authoritarianism*, Washington DC, Carnegie Endowment for International Peace.

Oxfam (1998), "A future for Caribbean bananas?" An Oxfam briefing paper, February, London.

Panitch, L. (1994), "Globalisation and the state," in R. Miliband and L. Panitch (eds), *The Socialist Register: Between Globalism and Nationalism*, Merlin Press.

Panitch, L. (1996), "Rethinking the role of the state in an era of globalization," in J. Mittleman (ed.), *Globalization: Critical Reflections. Yearbook of International Political Economy*, Vol. 9, Boulder CO, Lynne Rienner.

Panitch, L. (2000a), "Reflections on strategy for labour," in L. Panitch and C.Leys, with G.Albo and D. Coates (eds), *The Socialist Register: Working Classes, Global Realities*, Monmouth, Wales, Merlin Press.

Panitch, L. (2000b), "The new imperial state," *New Left Review,* (II), 2 (March – April): 5–20.

Panitch, L. and S. Gindin (2004), "Global capitalism and American empire," in L. Panitch and C. Leys (eds) *The New Imperial Challenge. The Socialist Register*, New York, Monthly Review Press.

Patomäki, H. (2001) *After International Relations: Critical Realism and the (Re)Construction of World Politics*, London, Routledge.

Patomäki, H. and T. Teivainen (2004), *A Possible World, Democratic Transformation of Global Institutions*, London, Zed Books.

Paugam, S. (ed.) (1996), *L'exclusion. L'Etat des savoirs*, Paris, Ed. La Découverte.

Petras, J. (1987), *Latin America: Bankers, Generals and the Struggle for Social Justice*, New York, Rowman & Littlefield.

Petras, J. (1997), "Latin America: The resurgence of the left," *New Left Review*, 223: 17–47.

Petras, J. (1998), "The political and social basis of regional variation in land occupations in Brazil," *The Journal of Peasant Studies*, 25 (4): 124–33.

Petras, J. (2001), "Globalización: un análisis crítico," in Saxe-Fernández *et.al.*, *Globalización, imperialismo y clase social*, Buenos Aires/México, Lúmen-Humanitas.

Petras, J. and H. Veltmeyer (1999), "Latin America at the end of the millennium," *Monthly Review*, 51 (3), July – August: 31–53.

Petras, J. and H. Veltmeyer (2000), *Ascensão da Hegemonia dos Estados Unidos no Nova Milênio*, Petrópolis,VOZES.

Petras, James and H. Veltmeyer (2001), *Globalization Unmasked: Imperialism in the 21st Century*, London, ZED Press; Halifax, Fernwood Books.

Petras, J. and H. Veltmeyer (2002), *Brasil de Cardoso: Expropriação de un pais*, Petropólis, VOZES.

Petras, J. and H. Veltmeyer (2005), *Empire with Imperialism*, London, Zed Books; Halifax, Fernwood Books.

Phillips, M.M. (1998), "US plans punitive tariffs in dispute with EU," *The Wall Street Journal*, Tuesday, 22 December: A2.

Pilger, J. (2003), *The New Rulers of the World*, London, Verso.

Piore, M. and C. Sabel (1984), *The Second Industrial Divide*, New York, Basic Books.

Piper, N. and A. Uhlin (eds) (2003), *Transnational Activism in Asia: Problems of Power and Democracy*, New York, Routledge.

Polanyi, K. (1968), *Primitive, Archaic and Modern Economies*, G. Dalton (ed.), New York, Anchor Books.

Poon J.P.H., E.R. Thompson and P.F. Kelly (2000), "Myth of the triad? The geography of trade and investment 'blocs'," *Transactions of the Institute of British Geographers*, 25 (4): 427–44.

Price, J. (2000), "Economic turmoil in Asia: A crisis of globalization," in S. McBride and J. Wiseman (eds), *Globalization and Its Discontents*, London, Macmillan.

Pronk, J. (2000), "Development for peace," in K. Sharma (ed.), *Imagining. Tomorrow. Rethinking the Global Challenge*, New York.

Przeworski, A. (2003), *States and Markets; A Primer in Political Economy*, New York, Cambridge University Press.

Rabasa, J. (2001), "Beyond representation? The impossibility of the local. (Notes on Subaltern Studies in light of a rebellion in Tepoztlán, Morelos)," in I. Rodríguez (ed.), *The Latin American Subaltern Studies Reader*, Durham NC, Duke University Press.

Radice, H. (2000), "Globalisation and national capitalisms: Theorising convergence and differentiation," *Review of International Political Economy*, 7 (4): 719–42.

Rajan, R. (2005), "Global imbalances: An assessment,'" Washington DC, International Monetary Fund, October, http://www.imf.org/external/np/speeches/2005/102505.

Ramonet, I. (2002), "The other axis of evil," *Le Monde Diplomatique*, March, http://mondediplo.com/2002/03/01axis.

Rao, V. (2002), *Community Driven Development: A Brief Review of the Research*, Washington DC, World Bank.

Ratliff, W. (2005), "Latin America's flickering democracy," Christian Science Monitor, 27 July, http://www.csmonitor.com/2005/0727/p09s02-coop.html.

Ravindran, I. (2004), "From back office to center stage: India hosts the World Social Forum at a crucial stage in its postcolonial history," *Colorlines Magazine: Race, Action, Culture*, Spring, available at http://www.looksmarthiphop.com/p/articles/mi_m0KAY/is_1_7/ai_n6137062.

Reilley, C. (1995), *New Paths to Democratic Development in Latin America: The Rise of NGO-Municipal Collaboration*, Boulder CO, Lynne Rienner.

Reitan, R. (2007), *Global Activism*, London and New York, Routledge.

Report (1997), *Overcoming Obstacles and Maximizing Opportunities: A Report by The Independent Group of Experts on Smaller Economies and Western Hemispheric Integration*, August.

Reuss, A. (2000), "Cause of death: Inequality," *Dollars & Sense*, May/June, http://www.thirdworldtraveler.com/Health/Cause_Death_Inequality.html.

Robinson, W. (1996), *Promoting Polyarchy: Globalisation, US Intervention and Hegemony*, Cambridge, Cambridge University Press.

Robinson, W. (2003), *Transnational Conflicts: Central America, Social Change and Globalization*, London, Verso.

Rocha, A. (2002), "Silencioso Proceso para Privatizar Pemex: Trabajadores," *Excelsior* (Mexico), May 7, sections A(1) and P(1).

Romero Gómez, A.F. (2001), "Crisis, economic restructuring and international reinsertion," in C. Brundenius and J. Weeks (eds), *Globalization and Third World Socialism: Cuba and Vietnam*, New York, Palgrave.

Rondinelli, D.A., J. McCullough and W. Johnson (1989), "Analyzing decentralization policies in developing countries: A political economy framework," *Development and Change*, 20 (1): 57–87.

Rondinelli, D.A., J.R. Nellis and G.S. Cheema (1983), "Decentralization in developing countries: A review of recent experience," World Bank Staff Paper No. 581, Washington DC: World Bank.

Rose-Ackerman, S. (1998), "Corruption and development," in B. Pleskovic and J. Stiglitz (eds), *Annual Conference on Development Economics*, Washington DC, The World Bank.

Rosen, F. and J.-M. Burt (2000), "Hugo Chavez: Venezuela's redeemer?" *NACLA*, 33 (6), May/June, http://www.nacla.org/iss_theme.php?iss=33|6.

Rosenau, J. (1990), *Turbulence in World Politics*, Princeton NJ, Princeton University Press.

Rosenbluth, G. (1994), "Informalidad y pobreza en America Latina," *Revista de CEPAL*, 52, Abril: 157–77.

Rubin, B. and J. Weisberg, *In an Uncertain World*, New York, Random House.

Rueschemeyer, D., E. Huber Stephens and J.D. Stephens (1992), *Capitalist Development and Democracy*, Chicago IL, University of Chicago Press.

Ruggie, J.G. (1982), "International regimes, transactions and change: Embedded liberalism in the postwar economic order," *International Organisation*, 36.(2): 379–415, http://www.wto.org/english/forums_e/public_forum_e/ruggie_embedded_liberalism.pdf.

Rupert, M. (1995), "(Re-)politicising the global economy: Liberal common sense and ideological struggle in the US NAFTA debate," *Review of International Political Economy*, 2 (4): 658–92.

Rupert, M. (2000), *Ideologies of Globalisation: Contending Visions of a New World Order*, London, Routledge.

Rycroft, R. (2002), "Technology-based globalization indicators: The centrality of innovation network data," Occasional Paper CSGOP-02-09, GW Center for the Study of Globalization, October.

SADC (2005a), *SADC Today*, 7 (6), February.

SADC (2005b), *SADC Today*, 8 (1), April.

SADC (2005c), *SADC Today*, 8 (2), June.

SADC (2005d), *SADC Today*, 8 (4), February.

Sader, E. (2001), "Antes e depois de Seattle," *Observatorio Social de América Latina*, Enero: 5–8. Also available at: http://alainet.org/active/1313&lang=es.

Salbuchi, A. (2000), *El cerebro del mundo: la cara oculta de la globalización*, Córdoba, Ediciones del Copista.

Salop, J. (1992), "Reducing poverty: spreading the word," *Finance & Development*, 29 (4), December: 2–4.

SAPRIN—Structural Adjustment Participatory Review International Network (2002), "Executive review, multi-country participatory assessment of Structural Adjustment."

Sassoon, A. S. (2001), "Globalisation, hegemony and passive revolution," *New Political Economy*, 6 (1): 5–17.

Saxe-Fernández, J. (1989), "Carta de Intención: convergencia subordinada," *Excelsior*, April 18.

Saxe-Fernández, J. (1994), "The Chiapas insurrection: Consequences for Mexico and the United States," *International Journal of Politics, Culture and Society*, 8 (2): 325–42.

Saxe-Fernández, J. (1998a), "Ciclos Industrializadores y desindustrializadores," *Nueva Sociedad*, 158, noviembre – diciembre: 120–38, http://www.nuso.org/upload/articulos/2729_1.pdf.

Saxe-Fernández, J. (1998b), "Neoliberalismo y TLC: ¿Hacia ciclos de guerra civil?" Paper presented for the Asociación Latinoamericana de Sociología Rural, Conference on "Globalización, Crisis y Desarrollo Rural en América Latina," Universidad Autónoma de Chapingo.

Saxe-Fernández, J. (1999), "Globalización e imperialismo," in Saxe-Fernández (ed.), *Globalización: crítica a un Paradigma*, México, Plaza & Janés.

Saxe-Fernández, J. (2002), *La Compra Venta de México*, México, Plaza James.

Saxe-Fernández, J. and O. Núñez (2001), "Globalización e imperialismo: la transferencia de Excedentes de América Latina," in Saxe-Fernández *et al.* *Globalización, Imperialismo y Clase Social*, Buenos Aires/México, Editorial Lúmen.

Saxe Fernández, J., J. Petras, H. Veltmeyer and O. Nuñez (2001), *Globalización, imperialismo y clase social*, Buenos Aires/Mexico City, Editorial Lumen.

Schaefer, B.D. (2001), *Priorities for the President: Reforming International Financial Institutions*, New York, Heritage Foundation.

Schecter, D. (1991), *Gramsci and the Theory of Industrial Democracy*, Aldershot, Hants, UK, Avebury.

Schiff, M. and A.L. Winters (2003), *Regional Integration and Development*, Washington DC, World Bank.

Schoeman, M. (2005), "SADC at 25: An overview of selected issues," *Strategic Review for Southern Africa*, XXVII (2), November: 12–27.

Scholte, J.A. (2005a), *Globalization: A Critical Introduction*, 2nd edition, Basingstoke, Palgrave Macmillan.

Scholte, J.A. (2005b), "What is global about globalization?" in D. Held and A. McGrew (eds) (2002), *The Global Transformations Reader*, 2nd edition, Cambridge, Polity Press.

Scholte, J.A. (2000), *Globalization: A Critical Introduction*, New York, St. Martin's Press.

Scott, J.C. (1985), *Weapons of the Weak: Everyday Forms of Peasant Resistance*, New Haven CT, Yale University Press.

Scott, J. C. (1990), *Domination and the Arts of Resistance: Hidden Transcripts*, New Haven CT, Yale University Press.

Sen, A. (1999a), *Development as Freedom*, New York, Alfred A. Knopf.

Sen, A. (1999b), "Democracy as a universal value," *Journal of Democracy*, 10 (3): 3–17.

Shepard, S. (1997), "The new economy: What it really means?" *Business Week*, November 17, http://www.businessweek.com/ 1997/46/b3553084.htm.

Shields, D. (1996), "Sobreexplotación de yacimientos de petróleo; pérdida de reservas," *El Financiero*, 24 de junio.

Shilling, G. (1998), *Deflation*, Short Hills NJ, Lakeview.

Short, C. (2001). "Globalisation, trade and development in the least developed countries," speech delivered to the Ministerial Roundtable on Trade and the Least Developed Countries (London, 19 March), http://www.globalisation.gov.uk/.

Singer, D. (1999), *Whose Millennium? Theirs or Ours?* New York, Monthly Review Press.

Sivanandan, A. and E. Meiksins Wood (1997), "Globalization and epochal shifts: An exchange," *Monthly Review*, 48 (9): 19–32.

Skirbekk, G. and A. St. Clair (2001), "A philosophical analysis of the World Bank's conception of poverty," in *A Critical View of the World Bank Report: World Development Report 2000/2001. Attacking Poverty*, Bergen, Norway, Comparative Research Programme on Poverty, http://www.crop.org/publications/files/report/Comments_to_WDR2001_2002_ny.pdf.

Sklair, L. (1997), "Social movements for global capitalism: the transnational capitalist class in action," *Review of International Political Economy*, 4 (3): 514 –38.

Sklair, L. (2002), *Globalization, Capitalism and its Alternatives*, New York, Oxford University Press.

Slater, D. (1985), *New Social Movements and the State in Latin America*, Amsterdam, CEDLA.

Smith, J. (2002), "Globalizing resistance: The Battle of Seattle and the future of social movements," in J. Smith and H. Johnston (eds), *Globalization and Resistance. Transnational Dimensions of Social Movements*, Lanham, Rowman & Littlefield.

Smith, J. and H. Johnston (2002), "Globalization and resistance: An introduction," in J. Smith and H. Johnston (eds) *Globalization and Resistance. Transnational Dimensions of Social Movements*, Lanham, Rowman & Littlefield.

Soederberg, S. (2004), "American empire and 'excluded states': The Millennium Challenge Account and the shift to preemptive development," *Third World Quarterly*, 25 (2): 279–302.

Solow, R. (2000), "Notes on social capital and economic performance," in P. Dasgupta and I. Serageldin (eds), *Social Capital: A Multi-Faceted Perspective*, Washington DC, World Bank.

St. Clair, J. (1999), "Seattle diary: It's a gas, gas, gas," *New Left Review* I (238), November – December: 81–96.

Stalker, P. (2000), *Workers Without Frontiers*, Boulder CO, Lynne Rienner.

Stark, J. (1998), "Globalization and democracy in Latin America," in F.A. Felipe and J. Stark (eds) (1998), *Fault Lines of Democracy in Post-Transition Latin America*, Boulder, CO, Lynne Rienner.

Starr, A. (2000), *Naming the Enemy: Anti-Corporate Movements Confront Globalization*, London and New York, Zed Books.

Ste. Croix, G.E.M. (1981), *The Class Struggle in the Ancient Greek World from the Archaic Age to the Arab Conquests*, London, Duckworth.

Stiglitz, J. (1998), "More instruments and broader goals: Moving toward the post-Washington consensus," The 1998 WIDER Annual Lecture, Helsinki, Finland, January 7, http://www.globalpolicy.org/socecon/bwi-wto/stig.htm.

Stiglitz, J. (2002), *Globalization and Its Discontents*, New York, W.W. Norton.

Stillwagon, E. (1998), *Stunted Lives, Stagnant Economies: Poverty, Disease and Underdevelopment*, New Brunswick NJ, Rutgers University Press.

Straits Times (2004), "China the locomotive," 23 February.

Strange, S. (1995), *The Retreat of the State: The Diffusion of Power in the World Economy*, Cambridge, Cambridge University Press.

Stubbs, R. (1995), "Asia-Pacific regionalization and the global economy: A third form of capitalism?" *Asian Survey*, XXXV (9), September, 785–97.

Sunkel, O. (1991), "Del desarrollo hacia adentro al desarrollo dede adentro," *Revista Mexicana de Sociologia*, (1): 3–42.

Sweezy, P. (1997), "More (or less) on globalization," *Monthly Review*, 49 (4): 1–4.

Tabb, W. (1997), "Contextualizing globalization: comments on Du Boff and Herman," *Monthly Review*, 49 (6): 35–9.

Tanzer, M. (1993), "Facing the oil giants: Labor bargaining in the 1990s" *Monthly Review*, April 1993.

Tapscott, C. and Thompson, L. (1998), "Deconstructing development in South Africa," *Southern African Perspectives*, 73, Centre for Southern African Studies, University of the Western Cape, Bellville.

Taylor, I. and P. Nel (2002), "New Africa, globalization and the confines of elite reformism: Getting the rhetoric right, getting the strategy wrong," *Third World Quarterly*, 23 (1): 163–80.

Teeple, G. (2000), "What is globalization?" in S. McBride and J. Wiseman (eds), *Globalization and its Discontents*, Basingstoke, Macmillan.

The Economist (1995), "The Myth of the Powerless State," October, 7:15

Therborn, G. (2000), "Globalizations: dimensions, historical waves, regional effects, normative governance," *International Sociology*, 15 (2), June: 151–79.

Thompson, E.P. (1968/1991), *The Making of the English Working Class*, New York, New Press.

Thompson, E.P. (1978), "Eighteenth century English society: Class struggle without class?" *Journal of Social History*, 3 (2): 133–65.

Thompson, L. (1996), "States and security: emancipatory versus orthodox approaches in governance in Southern Africa," Occasional Paper Series No. 3, University of the Western Cape: School of Government.

Thompson, L. (2005), "Managing mobilisation? Participatory processes and dam building in South Africa, the Berg River Project," Institute of Development Studies (IDS) Working Paper 254, IDS, University of Sussex.

Toye, J. (1987), *Dilemmas of Development: Reflections on the Counter-Revolution in Development Theory and Policy*, Oxford, Basil Blackwell.

Tulchin, J. and Allison Garland (eds) (2000), *Social Development in Latin America*, Boulder CO, Lynne Rienner.

UK Ministry of Defence, DCDC (2007), *Global Strategic Trends 2007–2036*. Shrivenham, Swindon, http://www.dcdc-strategictrends.org.uk.

UNCTAD (1998), "UNCTAD advocates financial safeguard mechanism," TAD/INF/2759, 25 August.

UNCTAD, Division of Transnational Corporations (1994), *World Investment Report: Transnational Corporations, Employment and the Workplace*, New York and Geneva, UN.

UNCTC (1991), *The Triad in Foreign Investment*, New York, United Nations.

UNDP (1990), *Human Development Report*, New York, Oxford University Press.

UNDP (1992), *Human Development Report*, New York, Oxford University Press.

UNDP (1993), *Human Development Report*, New York, Oxford University Press.

UNDP (1996a), *Good Governance and Sustainable Human Development*, governance policy paper, http://magnet.undp. org/policy.

UNDP (1996b), *Human Development Report*, New York, Oxford University Press.

UNDP (1997a), *Governance and Democratic Development in Latin America and the Caribbean*, New York, UNDP.

UNDP (1997b), *Governance for Sustainable Human Development*, policy document, New York, UNDP.

UNDP (1997c), *Participatory Local Governance*, policy document, New York, UNDP.

UNDP (1997d), *Reconceptualizing Governance*, Discussion Paper 2, New York, UNDP.

UNDP (1997e), *Local Governance*, policy document, New York, UNDP.

UNDP (1997f), "Report on the Third International Conference of the New and Restored Democracies on Democracy and Development, Bucharest, Romania, September 2–4 1997," New York, UNDP, http://www.undp.org.

UNDP (1997g), *The Shrinking State: Governance and Sustainable Human Development*, policy document, New York, UNDP.

UNDP (1997h), *Human Development Report*. New York, Oxford University Press.

UNDP (1998). *Overcoming Human Poverty: UNDP Poverty Report 2000*, New York, UNDP.

UNDP (1999), *Human Development Report*, New York, Oxford University Press.

UNDP (2000a), *The UNDP Role in Decentralisation and Local Governance*, New York, UNDP Evaluation Office, February.

UNDP (2000b), *Investigación sobre desarrollo humano y equidad en Cuba 1999*, Havana, UNDP.

UNDP (2000c), *Human Development Report*, New York, Oxford University Press.

UNDP (2001), *Human Development Report*, New York, Oxford University Press.

UNDP (2002), *Human Development Programmes at the Local Level*, report, January, Edinfodec Project, http://www.knledgeplant.undp.org.

UNDP (2005a), *Democracy In Latin America: Towards a Citizen's Democracy*, New York, United Nations.

UNDP (2005b), *Human Development Report*, New York, Oxford University Press.

UNICEF (1989), *Participación de los sectores pobres en programas de desarrollo local*, Santiago, UNICEF.

United Kingdom, Government (2000), "Eliminating world poverty: Making globalisation work for the poor," White Paper on International Development, at http://www.Globalisation.gov.uk/ (accessed 11 December).

United Nations (2003), *World Investment Report 2003*, New York, United Nations.

United Nations (1998), *The UN and Business: A Global Partnership*, http://www.globalpolicy.org/reform/un-bus.htm.

UNRISD (1994), *States of Disarray: The Social Effects of Globalization*, Geneva, UNRISD.

UNRISD—United Nations Research Institute for Social Development (2000), "Civil society strategies and movements for rural asset redistribution and improved livelihoods," Civil Society and Social Movements

Programme, Geneva, UNRISD, http://www.unrisd.org/unrisd/website/ p r o j e c t s . n s f / (h t t p P r o j e c t s F o r P r o g r a m m e A r e a - e n) / 5C8DC3DE789EDE4C80256B5200551D3D?OpenDocument.

US Mission to the European Union (2002), "OECD nations pledge reduction in global steel capacity," 8 February http://www.useu.be/Categories/Trade/Feb0802 Steel Reductions OECD.html.

USIS (1999), "Bananas: US to seek WTO approval for trade sanctions Jan. 25," *Washington File*, 12 January.

Utting, P. (2000), "UN–business partnerships: Whose agenda counts?" *UNRISD News* 23 (Autumn–Winter): 5–6.

Valdés Paz, J. (1997), "Voices on the left," *NACLA Report on the Americas*, XXXI (1), July – August.

Van der Pijl, K. (1984), *The Making of an Atlantic Ruling Class*, London, Verso.

Van der Westhuizen, J. (2006), "Globalization and the south: Markets, mafias and movements," in P. McGowan, S. Cornelissen and P. Nel (eds), *Power, Wealth and Global Equity: An International Relations Textbook for Africa*, Cape Town, UCT Press.

Van Ham, P. (2001), "The rise of the brand state," *Foreign Affairs*, 80 (5), September – October: 2–6.

Veltmeyer, H. (2001), "The politics of language: Deconstructing postdevelopment discourse," *Canadian Journal of Development Studies*, XXII (3): 597–620.

Veltmeyer, H. and J. Petras (1997), *Economic Liberalism and Class Conflict in Latin America*, London, Macmillan Press.

Verdezoto, M. E. (2002), "Dow Jones newswires" (August 2), 50 Years Is Enough Network, http://50years.org.

Veseth, M. (1998), *Selling Globalization, The Myth of the Global Economy*, Boulder CO, Lynne Rienner Publishers.

Wade, R. (1996), "Japan, the World Bank, and the art of paradigm maintenance: The East Asian miracle in political perspective," *New Left Review*, 217 (May–June).

Wallace, T. (2003), "NGO dilemmas: Trojan horses for global neoliberalism?" *Socialist Register 2004*, London, Merlin Press.

Wallerstein, I. (1996), *After Liberalism*, New York, New Press.

Wallerstein, I. (1998), *Utopistics, Or Historical Choices of the Twenty-First Century*, New York, The New Press.

Wallerstein, I. (1999), *The End of the World As We Know It: Social Science for the Twenty-First Century*, Minneapolis MN, University of Minnesota Press.

Waterman, P. (2001), *Globalization, Social Movements and the New Internationalisms*, London, Continuum.

Watkins, K. (2002), "Making globalization work for the poor," *Finance & Development*, 39 (1), March, http://www.imf.org/external/pubs/ft/fandd/2002/03/ watkins.htm.

Weber, H. (2002), "Global governance and poverty reduction: The case of microcredit," in R. Wilkinson and S. Hughes (eds), *Global Governance: Critical Perspectives*, London and New York, Routledge.

Weeks, J. (2001), "A tale of two transitions: Cuba and Vietnam," in C. Brundenius and J. Week (eds), *Globalization and Third World Socialism: Cuba and Vietnam*, New York, Palgrave.

Weisbrot, M. (2002), "The mirage of progress," *The American Prospect*, 13 (1), January: 1–14.

Weiss, L. (1998), *The Myth of the Powerless State*, Ithaca NY, Cornell University Press.

Welder, M. and D. Rigby (1996), *The Golden Age Illusion: Postwar Capitalism*, New York, Guilford.

Whitaker, F. (2003), "O que o Fórum Social Mundial traz de novo como modo de atuação política?" *Democracia Viva*, 14, Janeiro.

Williamson, J. (ed.) (1990), *Latin American Adjustment. How Much Has Happened?* Washington DC, Institute for International Economics.

Wilpert, G. (2003), "Venezuela's new constitution," *Venezuelanalysis*, 27 August, http://www.venezuelanalysis.com/analysis/70.

Wolf, M. (1999), "Not so new economy," *Financial Times*, 1 August.

Wolf, M. (2002), "Countries still rule the world," *Financial Times*, 5 February.

Wolfe, M. (1996), *Elusive Development*, London, Zed Press.

Woods, A. (2000), *Facts about European NGOs Active in International Development*, Paris, OECD.

Woods, N. (2006), "The globalizers in search of a future: Four reasons why the IMF and World Bank must change and four ways they can," CGD (Center for Global Development) Brief, April.

Woolcock, M. (1988), "Social capital and economic development: Towards a theoretical synthesis and policy framework," *Theory and Society*, 27: 151–208.

World Bank (1989a), *Report of the Trade, Finance and Industry Division*, Washington DC, World Bank.

World Bank (1989b), *Report and Recommendation to the Executive Directors*, Washington DC, World Bank.

World Bank (1992), *Governance and Development*, Washington DC, World Bank.

World Bank (1994a), *Adjustment in Africa: Reforms, Results, and the Road Ahead*, Washington DC, The World Bank.

World Bank (1994b), *Governance. The World Bank Experience*, Washington DC, World Bank.

World Bank (1995a), *World Development Report. Workers in an Integrating World*, New York, Oxford University Press.

World Bank (1995b), *Country Strategy Paper—Mexico, Mexican Division*, Washington DC, World Bank Country Department II, Mexico and Central America.

World Bank (1995c), "Hydrocarbon strategy paper," *World Bank Group Energy Program*. Washington DC, World Bank, www.worldbank.org/energy/.

World Bank (2000), *World Development Report 2000/2001: Attacking Poverty*, New York, Oxford University Press.

World Bank (2002), *Global Economic Prospects and the Developing Countries*, www.worldbank.org.

World Bank (2004a), *Partnerships in Development: Progress in the Fight Against Poverty*, Washington DC, World Bank.

World Bank (2004b), *World Bank Indicators*, New York, Oxford University Press.

World Bank (2005), *World Development Report: Equity and Development*, New
    York, Oxford University Press.

World Bank (2006), *Development Indicators*, http://devdata.worldbank.org/wdi2006.

World Bank (n.d.), *Mexico-PCR PERL (First Draft) and Hybrid Loans*, Washington
    DC, World Bank.

World Commission on the Social Dimensions of Globalisation (2004), *A Fair
    Globalization?* February, available at: http://www.ilo.org/public/english/fair
    globalization\report/index.htm.

Zevin, R. (1992), "Are world financial markets more open? If so, why and with what
    effects?" in Tariq Banuri and Juliet Schor (eds), *Financial Openness and National
    Autonomy: Opportunities and Constraint*, Oxford, Clarendon Press.

Index

North American Free Trade Agreement (NAFTA) 123
PetroCaribe agreement 140
policy convergence 121–2
regional cooperation 125–6
World Trade Organization (WTO) 122
Caribbean Basin Initiative (CBI) 122, 123, 125
Caribbean-Central American Strategic Alliance 125–6
Caribbean Community (Caricom) 121, 125–6
Caricom *see* Caribbean Community
Cariforum 121, 125
casino capitalism 98
CBI (Caribbean Basin Initiative) 122, 123, 125
CBOs *see* community-based organizations
Central America Free Trade Agreement (CAFTA) 108
CFR (Council on Foreign Relations) 189, 196–7
Chávez, Hugo 131–3, 134–5, 140, 183–5, 204–5
Chile 61–2, 193 *see also* Latin America
China 63, 100
    overaccumulation 102–4
    overinvestment 102–5
    transnational corporations (TNCs) 103
    United States, economic relationship 105
civil society 49–51, 191
    democracy 4, 49–51
    development 49–51
    discourse 193
    global 30–31, 32, 191
    states 51–3
civil society organizations (CSOs) 52
class and globalization 45
class struggle 198
class war 159
Clinton, Bill 96
Colombia 162–3, 195 *see also* Latin America
colonialism 202 *see also* anti-colonialism
commission on loans 75
commodification 20
community-based organizations (CBOs) 54–6
    evolution of 56–7

Non-Governmental Organizations (NGOs) 55–7
    politicization 60
computers and productivity 37–8
consumer credit 97–8
consumption-driven growth 105
Continental Campaign of 500 Years of Indigenous, Black and Popular Resistance 180
corruption and World Bank 80–81
Council on Foreign Relations (CFR) 189, 196–7
counter-globalization 115–18
crisis, exploitation of 159
CSOs (civil society organizations) 52
Cuba 125, 185 *see also* Caribbean

da Silva, Lula 183–5
Davos
    protests 182–3
    World Economic Forum (WEF) 160–61
decentralization of government 57–60, 65
Declaration on the Establishment of a New International Economic Order (NIEO) 177–8
democracy 203
    antiglobalization 204
    authoritarianism 203–5
    capital liberalization 167
    capitalism 61, 204
    civil society 4, 49–51
    decision-making 170
    development 61–4
    economics 173–4
    globalization 4, 167
    international solidarity 32
    Latin America 130–32, 170–71, 203
    neoliberalism 14
    Non-Governmental Organizations (NGOs) 50–51
    transnational networks 178–81
    United States 171–2
    Venezuela 132
denationalization 70, 73–4
devaluation 99
development 2–3
    civil society 49–51
    decentralization of government 57–60
    democracy 61–4

THE INTERNATIONAL POLITICAL ECONOMY OF NEW REGIONALISMS SERIES

Full series list